MANAGING THE SMALL COLLEGE LIBRARY

Rachel Applegate

LIBRARIES UNLIMITED LIBRARY MANAGEMENT COLLECTION

Gerard B. McCabe, Series Editor

LIBRARIES UNLIMITED

AN IMPRINT OF ABC-CLIO, LLC
Santa Barbara, California • Denver, Colorado • Oxford, England

Library of Congress Cataloging-in-Publication Data

Applegate, Rachel.
   Managing the small college library / Rachel Applegate.
      p. cm. — (Libraries Unlimited library management collection, ISSN 1557-0320)
   Includes bibliographical references and index.
      ISBN 978-1-59158-917-4 (acid-free paper) — ISBN 978-1-59158-918-1 (ebook)
1. Academic libraries—United States—Administration. 2. Academic libraries—
Administration. I. Title.
   Z675.U5A5944   2010
   025.1′977—dc22   2010019617

ISBN: 978-1-59158-917-4
EISBN: 978-1-59158-918-1

14   13   12   11   10   1   2   3   4   5

This book is also available on the World Wide Web as an eBook.
Visit www.abc-clio.com for details.

Libraries Unlimited
An Imprint of ABC-CLIO, LLC

ABC-CLIO, LLC
130 Cremona Drive, P.O. Box 1911
Santa Barbara, California 93116-1911

This book is printed on acid-free paper ∞

Manufactured in the United States of America

For my mom, for Sarah, and for MOST:
you all were there for me

CONTENTS

I. Thinking About Managing

IV. Supporting Teaching, Research, and Service

I
THINKING ABOUT MANAGING

1 INTRODUCTION AND OVERVIEW

INTRODUCTION

The purpose of this book is to give men and women who direct libraries at small colleges the tools and ideas they need to be effective managers. On a daily basis, in yearly cycles and looking at the longer view, there are responsibilities and opportunities. This book reviews the most important core functions of a director—managing people, processes, and ideas—and does so in the context of a small library, one that has one or two or five but no more than 10 master's-level librarians.

WHO SHOULD READ THIS BOOK?

The narrowest audience for this book is new directors of small academic libraries; the broadest, academic librarians; and library school students. The experienced director should be able to read this and say, "Yes, that's what I know and have experienced," "Hummm . . . that's an interesting perspective," and "I should give that some more thought." The more experienced the reader, the less the book will be novel; it should be like having coffee with a peer.

People who are not library directors but who want to be can use this book as a springboard and background briefing. Rather than having to pester mentors about all sorts of basics, they can use this to get the big picture and general insights before seeking specific advice. The book fills in holes and provides information and reminders about aspects of the job for which the director needs to be prepared.

What about the librarian who is just a librarian with no immediate prospects for directorship, and perhaps, at least currently, no desire? The goal for that person is to understand better how the library functions, in itself and on campus. Everyone should wish success for their libraries. Especially in the small library, everyone inevitably bears a large part of the responsibility for that success. Management means making things happen, and the more people know how things can happen, the more successful the library as a whole will be.

For librarians at larger institutions with many more than five to 10 professionals and who make up the majority of academic librarians, their situations may be more similar to the small library than they realize. Half of all librarians in research libraries who are members of the Association for Research Libraries (ARL) have some sort of administrative title. Moreover, library systems on large university campuses have smaller specialized and departmental libraries. If librarians at large institutions desire leadership or even just greater independence, they too should learn to understand those managerial qualities that make one stand out in the crowd.

The definition of a small library in this book is one that has a small staff. When a school of fish is very small, no fish can hide in the middle. In a small library, no librarian really can hide within the library's walls and not think about the campus as a whole. Everyone who wants to know more about how libraries can be successful can get insights from this book.

PERSPECTIVES

The topics covered herein are the same as in any library or management text: selecting, developing, and evaluating people; planning and budgeting; and attending to the core functions of academic life—teaching, research, and service. Basic descriptions of essential elements are provided. However, all of this is

4

conditioned by the small college situation. Both large and small libraries serve their mission and patrons, but there are significant differences in how they are structured, how they interact with other groups on campus, and how individuals relate to each other.

Structure, alignment, and relationships are reflected in what is termed in this book, "perspective" or "organizational theory." Since the turn of the nineteenth century, theorists have attempted to describe organizational features and development in various ways. No one single management theory has universal application, and no one institution can really be understood with one single theory. That is, some theories are more suited to some industries than others, and each theory is inadequate in itself for any specific real case.

This book focuses on three main organizational perspectives:

- Bureaucratic: The legacy of Weber, "scientific management," and Taylorism, which stress rational, impersonal structures and rules
- Political: a recognition that people form alliances and interest groups that work within and alongside rational structures to promote agendas
- Human resources: the idea that men and women have their own personal goals, motivations, and hence reasons for doing or not doing things

These should not be seen as singular and separate theories, but are used here as convenient ways of grouping the wide array of approaches organizational sociologists have used. In brief, they provide three different ways of explaining why things happen.

An initial chapter reviews the concepts in more detail. Then, throughout the content chapters, different perspectives will be brought to bear on all of the issues. The ultimate effect will be to see that all of them provide insight into what happens and why and that they collectively provide the manager with tools for both understanding and influencing what happens in the library and on campus.

Professor Y calls the director:

I need statistics on the elderly in China

Because that's the rule: bureaucratic	Every phone inquiry is worked on in turn.
	or
	All calls from faculty are worked on first.
Because a group wants it to happen: political	Calls from faculty are worked on first because the faculty needs to see that the librarians are useful.
Because individuals want it to happen: human resources	Librarian Z has a good relationship with Professor Y, who always remembers to give Z sufficient time to work on her requests.
	Requests from Professor X, who always delays to the last minute and never acknowledges assistance, are referred to the "first come first served" rule.

TERMINOLOGY

Director. "Influencing what happens." The word "director" rather than "manager" is used throughout. There are overlapping definitions for supervisor, manager, director, and leader. In particular, many have argued that "management" is too weak a word and concept and what organizations and individuals really need is leadership. This author does not disagree, nor does the book specifically tackle leadership. Leadership is crucial, yet whether it can be taught or even adequately described is arguable. Is "vision" something that one can develop by effort?

This book takes both a lower and a higher perspective on this. Extraordinary vision is by definition extra- and non-ordinary. It is creative and exciting and unique. Leaps of imagination are key to the advancement of society, organizations, and the library profession. On the other hand, are "leaders"

6

the only ones with vision? This book takes the position that professional-level librarians, those with graduate degrees or the equivalent, always should be open to imagination and forward thinking. Everyone can "lead" in terms of ideas, even if relatively few "supervise" in terms of personnel. Not only that, but every professional librarian *should* lead. Fifty years ago, it could be argued that the technical demands of librarianship, such as cataloging, indexing, and computing, were so mechanically complex that a professional degree was needed to practice them adequately. In the subsequent decades, both computers and support have taken over virtually everything that can be done routinely, leaving, by definition, professional-level activity to be defined as non-routine. This is non-ordinary; it is extraordinary, in fact, visionary on a real, day-to-day basis.

This book focuses neither on technical skills such as how to catalog an item, how to negotiate a database contract, how to teach a class, nor on leadership or how to initiate something new. It focuses on the essential middle management. Management is the way that ideas become reality; management provides the essential conditions for new ideas to be born and old ideas to honorably retire.

Small (college) library. For this book, "small" is defined as a library that has at least one, perhaps three or four, and up to a maximum of 10 full-time MLS-degreed librarians. Why one? This book presumes a level of library-specific preparation and skills equivalent to the master's level in librarianship. Certainly, sometimes people with degrees in other fields are found in smaller "learning centers" and such, but that is taken as the starting place here. Why is 10 the maximum? Two reasons: hierarchy and responsibilities.

A library with fewer than 10 librarians is likely to have a relatively flat hierarchy, generally with two or at most three levels (staff→director, staff→department heads→director). This derives from theory and practical aspects of the "span of control," that one person cannot provide effective supervision to or be a leader for an unlimited number of people directly reporting to the leader, termed "direct reports." Ten is a common number for a reasonable upper limit for direct reports. Because in academic libraries support staff generally are one to two times as numerous as degreed librarians (a ratio of one to

7

two per librarian), a 10-MLS librarian library might involve 20 to 30 personnel. With 30 people, there would almost certainly be three levels at least for support staff (staff→department head→director), but among the 10 librarians, there might only be two (librarians→director).

In terms of responsibilities, a certain number of managerial tasks are needed for any library. Some aspects are directly related to magnitude: the time spent managing (communicating with, mentoring, and/or assessing) many people is greater than the time spent managing fewer. Others are simply a quantum, necessary in any size of library, such as preparing a budget, reporting to a supervisor, or handling gift decisions. The smaller the libraries, the more likely it is that directors, while handling directorial duties, will also spend time as "regular" librarians; they will have a dual role. It is only in libraries over a certain size that managerial duties are so numerous that the organization can afford to devote someone full time to them.

Whether the director of a large library does or does not continue to do regular librarian tasks is a different issue. The point here is that the smaller the library, the less likely it is that the director is only a director. This is also the case in reasonably independent special or departmental libraries on very large campuses: the director of an art, chemistry, or museum library generally also has a role as an art librarian, chemical librarian, or museum librarian.

(small) College (library). This book is concerned with small academic libraries, those serving post-secondary colleges and universities. In the United States, most doctoral-level institutions are large (228, compared to only 23 small), master's institutions are evenly divided, large and small (324 and 223 respectively); and most baccalaureate and associates institutions are small, 10 times as many small as large (baccalaureate: 476 versus 53 and 990 versus 87).[1]

Religious or denominational issues are discussed throughout this book as an aspect of organizational culture. Almost 40 percent of master's-level institutions have denominational affiliations, and this is over 60 percent for baccalaureate colleges. A denominational culture can range in strength and intensity. Catholic institutions tend to be master's or doctoral level and comprise about half of all religiously affiliated institutions at those levels, while a

Protestant affiliation is the dominant type at the baccalaureate level, comprising almost 90 percent of religiously affiliated institutions.

The for-profit sector is strongest at the associate's level. In fact, only 4 percent of all associate's institutions are private and not-for-profit.

Director. The word "director" designates the individual who bureaucratically, formally, and structurally has overt responsibility for the library unit on campus. It may be a one-person library, or one with 20 to 30 employees.

Librarian. The terms "professional librarian" and "librarian" refer to a person employed as a librarian and possessing either the ALA-MLS (representing the vast majority) or a similar graduate-level degree that is recognized on that campus as being equivalent. Permanent employees, full or part time, who do not have the MLS are generally referred to as "support staff" (paraprofessionals) and not as "librarians." "Library staff" mostly includes both librarians and support staff; "library workers" refers to everybody who works at a library, whether librarians, other professionals, support staff, or student workers. "The library" is also used as a collective noun to represent the interests of the unit as a whole.

Faculty. When "faculty" means people who teach for-credit courses in a discipline, it is generally qualified as "classroom faculty" or "teaching faculty" because librarians are often also considered "faculty." "Administration" and "administrators" generally refer to personnel who are not faculty or librarians (or employed in offices of academic departments or the library) and who work at higher vice-presidential levels in academic as well as support units such as student services and human resources.

College. For consistency, the word "college" here is always used to refer to an entire academic institution. Sometimes, the word "university" is also used to designate this level, the whole, singular, accredited institution: College of Mary or University of South State. The word "school" is used to refer to an academic grouping that is larger than an individual disciplinary department: the school of health sciences or school of education. "Deans" refers to people in charge of "schools"; the word "provost" is used for the person in charge of all departments, schools, and academic affairs. "Unit" is an all-purpose word that can refer to several levels on the academic side (department and/or school) and administrative side (e.g., purchasing, finances, or human resources).

FORMAT AND CONTENTS

After an initial chapter describing management's theoretical perspectives, the main sections of the book cover the library as a unit (organizational structure), people (personnel recruitment, development and evaluation, and faculty status), and the essential processes of an academic library: planning, budgeting, and managing for teaching, research, and service support.

Stories appear in the text to illustrate features of the issue being discussed. These stories are based on true incidents, generally camouflaged or made composite to guard the real institutions from embarrassment. They are drawn from the author's personal experience as a library director, tales from other libraries, and incidents or situations related in articles. In order to avoid singling out institutions, citations to original articles are not provided when the item being discussed is used generically. For example, an article about reference services happened to describe its setting as an eight-librarian library that had four levels in its hierarchy. This book does not provide the article's research conclusions, which would be plagiarism, nor use its specific wording, which would be a copyright violation since a citation might identify the college.

The annotated bibliography describes some key articles and books that will help the reader more fully understand the concepts and context of managing small college libraries. When a discussion refers to a specific publication, a specific citation is given in that chapter's endnotes.

NOTE

1. These figures are derived from National Center for Education Statistics data from 2006 in the Academic Libraries Survey, which has 70 (associates) to 95 percent compliance rate; religious affiliation and control data come from the NCES Integrated Postsecondary Education Data Service (IPEDS) (100 percent compliance for Title IV eligible institutions). It includes only responding institutions with at least one professional librarian.

2 PERSPECTIVES ON ORGANIZATIONS

Throughout this book, each topic in the management of the small academic library benefits through considering it from perspectives drawn out of general organizational theories. This is not the place for a full examination of each particular theory, especially since all theories or theoretical perspectives have themselves grown, changed, splintered, and recombined over the years. Certainly, no single theory or perspective is complete in itself, and no single theory can really explain what is going on in most circumstances. Each individual perspective tends to leave out important elements and issues.

Even organizational theories that take a "contingent" approach, where levels of communication and complexity depend on specific circumstances of very specific tasks, are in a sense too limiting. Contingency theory is organization centric: it implies that an organization has a known, single, or focused purpose, and that managers and others work with and develop organizational arrangements to match that purpose.

Instead, this book takes a broad, flexible, ad hoc, pragmatic, and diverse approach to the use of theory in understanding organizations. Much of the day-to-day managerial decision-making is done on the fly, from a basis of personal experience, and in response to immediate input and concerns. It is hard to detect administrators, at least academic administrators, working out formal decision trees, practicing decision-making steps, and employing specific conflict-resolution techniques. This is not to say they are ineffective, capricious, or ignorant. It is rather that they work primarily from a variety of assumptions and habits, rather than fitting themselves into the neat categories or innovative models described in organizational research or prescribed by management gurus.

Organizational theory is not irrelevant or unimportant. Instead, its greatest value to managers is when it helps them understand more clearly what is going on in the institution and form more consciously designed plans for success. In this light, having multiple perspectives sheds much more light than one overarching schema.

Many organizational theories have been developed since the original and influential theory of management, Max Weber's description and definition of bureaucracy. In this book, these are grouped into three main approaches: bureaucracy, politics, and human development. A bureaucracy assumes the organization is a rational structure geared to achieve objective ends; decisions are crafted according to rules and data. A political perspective sees groups of employees who have group interests and goals, and leaders who have reputational or charismatic power, along with or in contradiction to formal hierarchical power. The human-development perspective points to the individual aspirations of each person who happens to be an employee: not just a cog, not just a group member, but someone with personal goals, habits, and tendencies that fit those of the organization to a greater or lesser extent in differing circumstances.

BUREAUCRACY

The Encyclopaedia Britannica defines "bureaucracy" as "[a] specific form of organization defined by complexity, division of labor, permanence, professional management, hierarchical coordination and control, strict chain of command, and legal authority. It is distinguished from informal and collegial organizations. In its ideal form, bureaucracy is impersonal and rational and based on rules rather than ties of kinship, friendship, or patrimonial or charismatic authority. Bureaucratic organization can be found in both public and private institutions."[1]

Some key features of the organization as bureaucracy are the existence of policies, clear lines of reporting and authority, and impersonal consistency in product delivery as well as internal organizational activity. That is, much of what to do is determined by a set code of rules. Everyone reports to a specific supervisor (who is responsible for those whom he or she supervises), and changes are derived from rational approaches to decision-making rather than through ad hoc personal choice.

The term "bureaucracy" has an uncomfortable connotation in U.S. society, especially around professional and knowledge workers. The industrial-production model of the assembly line, an object-oriented example of bureaucracy in action, seems anachronistic at best and inhuman at worst. Moreover, specifically in academia, an influential work by Karl Weick argued that the mechanisms in the context of the university are not very mechanical; they have exceedingly "loose coupling." That is, an action or decision taken at one level or unit seldom had a straightforward, predictable relation to what actually happened elsewhere.[2]

Despite its poor reputation, the bureaucratic (scientific, rationalistic) model is not only desirable, but valuable. Whenever impersonal consistency is desired, a bureaucratic approach is necessary. If fines are levied at your library, your offenders want to know they are paying a "fair" and consistent fine. If you include tables of contents in your bibliographic records, you don't want some of your books to lack them simply because the cataloger wasn't interested in them. If you shelve books, you need to follow the conventions of Library of Congress call numbers, however arcane the "decimals only after the first dot" rule is.

Some parts of a library are bureaucratic: impersonal, mechanistic, and hopefully consistent with thoughtfully established policies. In addition, some individuals in a library will react to problems or issues with bureaucratic responses, looking for something impersonal, mechanistic, and reliable for the future. This can be cumbersome, and someone can call it a staff that

Story: Early one fall semester, a new student worker wondered aloud what the order was for books on the reserve shelves. The director, who helped out at the circulation desk, replied aloud, "Oh, they are on whatever shelf is the first letter of the main book title." This got a stern look and quick correction from the circulation supervisor, who knew the reality of full alphabetizing by book main entry (carefully noted on reserve cards) and also had to deal with searching for items that were "lost" only because someone had just stuck them anywhere.

resists change, but it is also possible that the staff simply want to avoid personal caprice and unknowable results.

Likewise, on the campus as a whole, some bureaucratic elements exist, and some people want bureaucratic answers. Auditing and financial control functions necessarily are rules-based. A library manager's personal preference as to when a set of new shelving is a capital or an operational budget purchase just does not matter. Most steps in recruiting and paying personnel must conform to state and federal laws.

In more academic areas of campus, a rules or procedural approach may be more or less in evidence. The faculty handbook or the faculty assembly or senate constitution may be available and short or extensive. If the campus is unionized, there will be a bargaining agreement. Strategic planning or budget setting processes may be explicit, public, or formal.

It's important not to over-generalize, yet it is not inaccurate to predict that the smaller, older, more denominational, and private an institution, the less extensive formal bureaucratization will be. If a college is public, even if it is small, it generally will conform to state governmental expectations and perhaps university-system procedures. In some states, it may be unionized. Some private institutions have strong denominational cultures, which often substitute for formal procedures. Long institutional or personal history, when the same people have been in their jobs a long time, tends to turn decision-making into a personal rather than a formal process.

Situations always have some bureaucratic elements. In one sense, a drive toward organizational development, in the sense of a data-driven approach to rationally improving an organization, is a bureaucratic, impersonal approach precisely because it outlines a reliance upon impersonal and theoretically objective facts.[3] Library directors can always look for which rules govern a situation, seek out data to support evidence-based decision-making, and work to create new policies as circumstances change.

But similarly, there are always parts of the academic enterprise that cannot be effectively understood or dealt with only with a scientific, rational, rules-based approach. The political and human development perspectives add the personal dimension.

POLITICS

A political perspective on organizations does not refer primarily to formal constitutionalism, separation of powers, or voting. It does include an informal equivalent to political parties. In a political perspective, people within an organization use not only formal hierarchical power, but powers and influence involved in personal charisma and in interest groups. In other words, things get done because they are important to greatly respected individuals or groups. Groups in this sense can be both internal and external: faculty as a group, students, alumni, and/or denominational affiliates.

> **Story:** A small college was reviewing all academic programs to see which could be viable, since over the years, student preferences had changed. On the formally agreed criteria for the review, a performing-arts program was clearly identified for closure, as it had extremely few majors or student credit hours compared to the number of faculty. It did not close because some faculty contacted members of the board of trustees and successfully argued that it was part of the history and culture of the college.

A political understanding is important for a small library director in two ways. The first is for understanding: library directors, especially new ones, will be sorely handicapped if they attempt to interpret and predict decision-making by paying attention only to formalized procedures. The second is for effectiveness: as the political element is identified, the director needs to align the library with those influential individuals and weighty interest groups in order to achieve what the library needs. Who and what the library is seen as part of and important to, in a broad cultural and relational sense, will be as important as its formal position in the institution's organizational chart.

HUMAN DEVELOPMENT

Human development here is used as a sort of catchall category for a variety of theories of motivation and social behavior that bring one's perspective down to the individual level. The bureaucratic and political perspectives have one thing in common: they assume that the parts of an organization, either its formal units (bureaucracy) or its interest groups (polity), have goals and intentions tied to the success of the organization as a whole or of a particular subunit.

The human-development perspective corrects this oversimplification with the idea that individual men and women each have their own lives and goals that may be more or less aligned with, but never solely identical to, those of the organization. In the broader field of organizational theory, this perspective developed from the obvious and painful limitations of the scientific bureaucratic approach, the mechanistic treatment: we pay X wage and expect Y actions foundered upon the needs, desires, and boredoms of real people.

The reality of a human-level perspective can be illustrated in two very different ends of the academic-employment spectrum. Even though student workers shelve books, and even though shelving books or shelf-reading (checking for shelving errors) is important and necessary, it is simply not possible to retain employees in the long term, or even achieve reasonable accuracy in the short run, if a student worker is expected to shelve or shelf-read for hours on end. They want more out of their lives. Similarly, very far away in their corner offices, star professors are plotting what institutional moves will adequately allow them to achieve whatever degree of fame and fortune they desire.

> **Story**: At a fall faculty retreat, a nun with a PhD in soci-ology and more than 30 years of teaching made it clear that she considered herself a X College faculty member before she was a sociologist. She was both, but her loyalty was to the institution (which was affiliated with her order), rather than to her discipline. Stars of academia who move from Ivy League to West Coast powerhouses to flagship state research universities are the exact opposite.

It can be seen from these two examples that the human dimension is important at both small and large colleges. Small colleges may not worry about the star professor, but they do need to have a productive group of people and hence those who feel relatively fulfilled. Moreover, the way things are decided at an institution often involves the human element in addition to political (group) considerations ("What's in it for the faculty?") and a set bureaucratic apparatus ("What's the rule about recording overtime?").

Somewhat artificially, to simplify the use of theory in this book, additional useful theories about human or organizational condition or behavior are considered part of this "human-development" group. Maslow's theory of personal fulfillment is considered part of this perspective. External and internal aspects of culture or values also have been intensively studied as part of understanding organizations. Employees bring expec-tations, habits, and motivations from their own family and civil-ian societies. Companies themselves form and pass on their own cultures, as sets of expectations and assumptions.[4] It is im-portant on the one hand to avoid unwarranted stereotyping, "pre"-judging individuals according to group characteristics. On the other hand, societies and cultures are real and are part

Bureaucratic	Political	Human
Impersonal	Group interests	Personal interests
Authority from hierarchical position	Authority from individual charisma or group's perceived centrality or power	Concerned about personal, not necessarily organizational, goals
Rules-based		
Rational	Decisions made to sustain or extend group power *within the organization*	Works with and around other sources of authority to achieve individual ends
Organization-directed		
What the policy says	**Who you know and hang out with**	**What you want for yourself**
I am reliable	People trust me	I like being thought of as a good . . .
I can't do that without a policy	Have you checked with him/her/them?	You ignored me and I'm having a bad day . . .
It's a college: of course it has rules	We are essential to the heart of the college	I like the college and I'm glad I have a good job

of the diversity that is a strength of the American culture itself. These are part of this "human-development" group because they pay attention to how individuals perceive their own goals and proper societal connections.

The rest of this book pays attention to these perspectives in relation to each issue at hand. All three aspects are usually useful. Although each one may be stronger in a given case, in general a manager does well to incorporate each one of them. When it comes to effective leadership, there is no such thing as too much understanding.

NOTES

1. "Bureaucracy." *Encyclopædia Britannica.* 2009. Encyclopædia Britannica Online. http://www.britannica.com/EBchecked/topic/84999/bureaucracy. Accessed June 17, 2009.

2. Weick, Karl. "Educational Organizations as Loosely Coupled Systems." *Administrative Science Quarterly* 21 (1979): 1–19.

3. See a pro-organizational development review in Russell, Keith. "Evidence-Based Practice and Organizational Development in Libraries." *Library Trends* 56, no. 4 (2008): 910–30.

4. Collins, James C., and Jerry Porras. "Organizational Vision and Visionary Organizations." *California Management Review* (2001): 30–52. Developed in more detail in Collins, Jim. *Good to Great: Why Some Companies Make the Leap . . . and Others Don't*. New York: Harper-Collins, 2001.

3 ORGANIZATIONAL STRUCTURE

Organizational structure defines the formal relationships between positions in a unit and between one unit and another. It means people and organizational charts. Someone is a supervisor and others are supervised by that person. One unit's leader or representative reports to a particular position upward in the hierarchy or chart tree. Structure includes which positions are included in or excluded from different meetings or groups. Structure is not limited strictly to command-and-control, where higher positions dictate to lower positions. Decision-making can be based upon discussion, debate, democracy, and consensus, but even in that situation, which positions are included in the debates is a structural issue.

The formal structure is *position*-based, not *person*-based. The director of the library, the head of information technology, the chief financial officer, these positions have their designated spots in the organizational structure. Some people may consider "bureaucracy" to be a negative term implying mechanism and soul-destroying formality. However, an impersonal approach can be a more polite and less confrontational way of managing organizational workflow than a purely personal approach. Say the library director and information technology director need to be involved in a meeting because it concerns their organizations, but Sarah is invited because she's easier to get along with, and no one likes Mary, who bores people with her long-winded speeches. If Sarah is truly easy to work with, knowledgeable, and productive, she will gain the positional titles that fit her appropriately into the organizational structure.

Position-based structure is a core feature of a bureaucratic or rational approach to management and to the exercise of power. Someone's position gives him or her the right and duty to do certain things and, more importantly, to make certain decisions. Positional power is not the only power that exists in an organization, but it is a factor in even the most personal and charismatic situations.

In the small college library, structure seems an overly complicated consideration for a unit that has only a handful of people. Surely it is a simple matter of director, librarians, and support staff. Have all the student employees report to a support staff person (because managing student workers is time-consuming) and everyone else report to the director. The director listens, asks questions, and decides. The pleasure of the small organization is simplicity.

But it is not that simple. Effective management is a blend of the bureaucratic, political, and human perspectives. And even in the smaller library, the smaller but larger than the one-person library, elements of formal structures and different possibilities are very much in evidence. The purpose of this section is to review what the two main alternatives (collegial and bureaucratic) mean and consider their political and human resources implications on three levels. The first level is the director's own role, the second level is the effect on how the library is organized, and the third level considers how the campus is organized.

MANAGER'S DUAL ROLES

One of the first issues that directors in small libraries face is that they themselves play two roles within the library structure: from the start, any "organizational chart" has overlapping boxes, without the neat separation of powers that is a hallmark of a standard bureaucratic approach. Key elements of scientific management are clear reporting lines, fixed roles and responsibilities, unity of command (one person supervising specific people, who are supervised by only one person), and a division between management (decision-making) and labor (doing).

One of the defining characteristics of the small academic library is that the library director has simultaneous responsibilities for *doing* as well as *directing*. That is, these directors spend at least part of their time being librarians: dealing with students and faculty about their information needs, thinking about the development of part or all of the collection, and implementing new technologies. This is not necessarily absent in larger libraries. Many large institutions have a corporate culture that expects that all the people who are librarians will do at least some hands-on librarian or professional-level activity. Nevertheless, the larger the library, the more common it will be that the director's duties will include less and less frontline work.

This feature has both positive and negative effects on the life and managerial role of the library director. The negative effects are thoroughly examined in standard commercial business organizational literature; the positive ones arise out of the non-commercial, professional environment in general, and the academic environment in particular.

In classic company organization, the standard advice for new managers in business is to remove themselves as cleanly as possible from their previous status and responsibilities. That is, no longer try to be a friendly colleague to one's work-mates. Trying to maintain social-professional ties is thought to tempt the manager into micromanaging ("I know how to do that better") and muddy former friends' expectations of the authority and decision-making that is necessarily part of the manager's job. Obviously, this separation is feasible only when there is no need for the manager's labor in actually doing those "worker-bee" tasks.

This perspective is a largely bureaucratic one. The strength of the bureaucratic framework is largely seen as a function of its clarity of responsibilities, both for directing and for division of labor. Continuing personal friendships with formerly coequal colleagues is contrasted with an impartial attitude toward all of those who are now subordinates, and equally subordinate, not less or more important because they are friends or not with the boss. A political approach is generally shunned: what worse situation could there be than for a manager to create or encourage special "in" or "out" groups among employees?

Business managers develop and evaluate employees, determine their compensation, and assign their duties. In the impersonal bureaucracy, they do so with respect to the employees' value to the organization, not their personal relationships with the manager.

Contrast this business framework with the experience of the typical academic teaching department. In a small college, there are generally three to six faculty members in many departments. Very few academic departments will be large enough to have a chair who has no teaching responsibilities. Indeed, not only will the chair teach, but in the three- or four-member department, the chair often teaches full time while doing much of the work that the chair of a larger department does as a sort of overload. The chair may receive a special stipend for this, rather than a reduction in teaching responsibilities. If the stipend is considered hopelessly inadequate, a rotation of the chair's duties among the department members can compensate.

The larger the department, the more the payment for doing chair duty will be compensated for by a reduction in teaching responsibilities, but it is very rare that the chair would not teach at all. Ordinary, non-chair faculty often insist upon this. They are suspicious of a chair who no longer experiences the core daily life of a faculty member.

> **Story**: At a meeting of faculty from several disciplines who were all beginning projects involving portfolios, when people introduced themselves, one person said he had been the department chair and was now "a real faculty member."

Talk of "real" faculty members as those who teach, not those who administrate, reflects a political perspective. Do I as a faculty member want to be managed, to have important aspects of my life such as my teaching schedule and tenure

expectations controlled by someone who is *not like me?* Someone who is not part of my own interest group, the teaching
faculty, is in danger of being seen as someone who is part of
another group, the administration. The fear is that a person
who does not understand fully the life of a teacher may try to
control it in ways that are detrimental.

> **Story**: Promotion and tenure reviews at a small college
> were shot through with suspicion of non-teaching faculty.
> The school-level committees were not elected or selected,
> but consisted of all qualified (tenured) faculty in grouped
> disciplines (e.g., all natural sciences, all health sciences).
> These individuals tended to insist that no candidate could
> be truly evaluated without significant student course eval-
> uation data. They attempted to get this provision written
> into the tenure policies in such a way as to eliminate the
> ability of an administrative-only person achieving tenure
> and full faculty status.

Parallels to this we-real you-manager suspicion exist in other
fields, especially those with professional activities. Doctor-
administrators are expected to continue to practice, managing
partners in law firms still interact with clients, etc. All of these
individuals who are managers consider it vital to maintain their
ties to their own group, the professional practitioners. The
drawbacks that non-professional bureaucratic theorists point out
seem to pale in comparison with the benefits of continued professional allegiance. This is a prime example of how a political,
group-affiliation perspective explains more about how academic
management is conceived than does the rational, bureaucratic
approach.

The human resources, individualistic perspective can be
detected in the distinct lack of interest on the part of many
librarians toward managerial responsibilities. Library school
faculty often report that many students are indifferent or even
hostile toward learning management skills. The ability to exercise control over others does not appear to be a common career

draw for library students, even at the graduate level. This contrasts with those who go into business and in particular those who pursue graduate-level education in business. The MBA is widely perceived as a leadership degree and often requires some post-baccalaureate business experience so that the graduate will have the ability to assume higher roles in an organization. This is one area where the MLS degree bears the characteristics of a classic "profession," based on a complex knowledge base and personal responsibilities, rather than organizational power.

Small library directors have dual roles as managers and as librarians. The first person they must manage, there, is themselves. How do they view their own normal daily professional duties, both internally and externally, within the library and interacting with the rest of the campus?

Externally, the library director will be doing, and be seen doing, professional work. The higher the value the campus population places on that work, and the higher the status that librarians in general possess, the easier it will be for the director-librarian to be seen as a leader on campus. The situation will be seen as parallel to the teaching department chair. On the other hand, if librarians in general are viewed primarily as support or technical staff, the role of the director will suffer correspondingly. Even the administrative responsibilities they have may be considered of not much consequence since, by definition, a small college library director has a small staff. Only lower-level administrators on the administrative side supervise so few individuals.

Internally, the profession orientation, the desire to focus on librarian work, of the other librarians and support staff will be beneficial for the director's relative power. They will be well aware of the director doing professional (librarian) activities, and they may well be content to leave everything else to him or her. The non-director librarians can concentrate on their own librarian activities and leave all of that "administrivia" to someone else. Dictatorships are said to be odious, yet a benevolent dictatorship in which directors divert all administrative work from the other librarians to themselves and leave others in peace can be seen very positively by library staff.

Story: An early textbook on college librarianship insisted that the "librarian" have faculty status.[1] Close reading reveals that this early work assumes that the (male) director of the library is the only one who is called "librarian." No one else working at the library is a "librarian," and none are seen as deserving or needing any status comparable to faculty.

This dynamic can work against the director, though. If "regular" librarians focus their attention primarily on the library, the more they will focus on technical specialty activity, and the more behind the scenes they remain, the more administrative power the director will have as the only person connecting with the larger campus structure.

However, this inward focus will lead to a less positive and even less professional view of librarianship generally on campus. It will lessen the likelihood that the library "department" will be seen as the equivalent of a teaching department. Academic teaching departments are important, even when they are small; each is essential to the entire educational enterprise. Is the library important? Is it seen as important, or is it a one-person show? If library directors are vigorous but nothing else is seen from the library, then they will be only directors of an auxiliary unit, small and marginal. Therefore, diminishing the responsibilities of all librarians to the level of technicians might in the short run make the library director more important, yet it leaves the director in a very weak position on campus. Eventually in that case, even the library staff will notice that the library does not get what it needs.

Therefore, when it comes to the relative importance and power of the director's managerial position compared to professional responsibilities, a careful balancing act involving all librarians is required. Directors need to continue to do professional work, which will enhance solidarity with other librarians and at the same time improve their standing among the academic teaching professionals who typically disdain administrative credentials. Other librarians need to do professional work that is visible within the library and also be visible across the campus, reinforcing their integration with the academic enterprise.

Some aspects of managing the library should include librarians. Administrative responsibilities can be structured in one of two main models: collegial and bureaucratic. In a collegial form of organization, the goal is consensus (or majority opinion) among equals in decision-making. In the bureaucratic form, someone is recognized as being unequal, of having specific authority to make decisions, "because I said so" and "because I'm the director," even if those words never pass anybody's lips.

COLLEGIAL ORGANIZATION

Collegial is a term and a concept close to the academic heart. The permanent "college" is a collection of faculty: note that in Canada, what is usually called a "school" in an American university is called a "faculty." One is admitted to, studies in, and receives a degree from the faculty of X at Y University. The archetypal academic department consists of faculty who feel themselves equal, and who often rotate into (or strive to rotate out of) administrative responsibilities. This approach is often very culturally attuned to religiously affiliated colleges where there is a strong tradition, ethic, or general sense of egalitarianism.

> **Story**: At an Anabaptist denominational institution, when the director was asked if librarians were faculty, she replied that "everyone" was considered faculty. But then, she added, that meant that really nobody, except the classroom faculty, were.

At one end of the collegial spectrum is a situation where all professional librarians are considered equal, one is chosen to speak for the library for a period of time, and this role is rotated equally. A distinguishing feature of this situation is that there will never be a search for a director as such; no one is hired into a formal position of director. People are hired as librarians with some expectations that they will take their place in the library's set of duties, including directorship.

The great strength of this approach is that it conforms the library to the general expectations of a campus, particularly close to academic teaching departments where "chair" is not seen as a permanent nor particularly desirable position.

The problem is that in actual practice, it has internal and external problems. People outside the library, particularly administrators, prefer to deal with a known quantity, and at the outset generally prefer to select for this known quantity to be part of deciding who the director is. People inside the library also find it challenging. It is unlikely that organizational ability (dealing with all that trivia) as well as consensus-making skills would be evenly distributed among the librarians. The smaller the library, the more possible it is that no librarian will be able to handle administrative tasks at any other than a grudging and minimal level, let alone be willing to provide a standout vision or unique leadership.

In addition, the academic library arguably faces a broader, more rapid, and more technical pace of change than an academic department. Changing from blackboards, to transparencies, to PowerPoint presentations, to podcasting is in some ways trivial compared to the size and scope of changes that the library, as a whole, not as individual librarians compared to individual faculty in each course, has experienced. Changes in libraries also require cooperation and collaboration, again a different situation from faculty trying out innovative pedagogy in their individual classes. Providing overall library-wide leadership is challenging in the rotating-collegial situation. It is difficult to create a vision of an exciting future if you know you will be out of the leadership position in two or three years. The only vision that can succeed is one with true consensus and that all librarians who become directors can nourish and make effective.

True rotating collegiality is extremely rare. Three small private colleges tried this in the late 1990s, but after several years, two of the institutions had abandoned it and it was becoming less rotational in the third: that is, some librarians were seen as more able or useful as directors than others.[2]

What is much more common is a "director-plus" model. In this format, the director is set apart and different, with distinct responsibilities. However, in general all of the other professional librarians are equals. Some duties may be unique to some librarians (e.g., cataloging), and others may be universal (e.g., reference coverage or liaison assignments), but there is a sense of the director as first among equals and the others as equals. In this model, the personal preferences and style of the director heavily influence how decision-making happens. It may be brainstorming-consensual, leader-consensual, or leader/listener-follower. That is, the director may determine a course of action by beginning with everybody contributing ideas and then leading them to a consensus selection; he or she may propose ideas that others react to, edit, and agree upon, or propose, listen, and then decide. A manager usually has a favorite style, but it is usually one used most often, not one used exclusively.

Story: A researcher visited a library to talk about some research on reference services. The meeting took place in a conference room with librarians sitting around the table. The director deliberately sat back away from the table. It was clear that she expected the librarians there to react directly to the researcher without needing to clear their reactions through her.

At another library, the director spoke one-on-one with the researcher and then gave a tour of the library without ever introducing the researcher to the librarians working in their offices or at the reference desk.

The collegial approach to structuring the professional librarians is an example showing where politics are considered more important than bureaucratic rationalism. In a collegial situation, the solidarity of the professional librarians is emphasized. The librarians' "we" group is so important that the designated director is primarily a voice for their collective interests. A rotating leadership or leader+equals emphasizes the essential sameness of the professional librarians, with their voices literally having equal weight in decision-making.

Organization Types Hierarchical

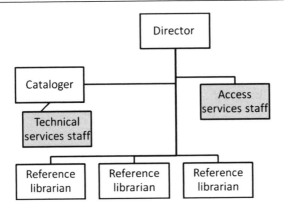

Collegial—One

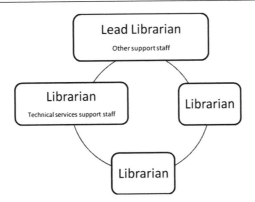

Collegial—Two

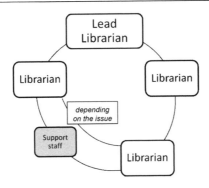

HIERARCHICAL ORGANIZATION

A contrast would be the more classic bureaucratic organization, represented conceptually by an organizational chart, with distinct roles, spans of control, and chains of command. In the traditional hierarchy, people have positional power and specific responsibilities. Someone makes decisions because they are the reference coordinator, the head of technical services, or the director her- or himself.

Some aspects of library organization resemble a hierarchy, and they will be discussed in the "bureaucratic" section below. However, the very smallness of the small college library is a significant obstacle to a strong hierarchical structure. In the 50-person library, organizing people into subgroups is essential. If all 50 are equal, then nothing gets done or everything gets done but nobody knows what exactly (with immense duplication), or huge amounts of time are spent on communication and collaborative activities rather than doing. It is a long way and hopefully a polite way of saying that most small colleges just get by with "reference" librarians and outsource or support-staff their technical service, so remaining professional librarians end up all being reference librarians/equals.

Before the widespread adoption of technology that has made many previously professional responsibilities routine work, librarians often had very separate and specialized roles. Now that much of cataloging and collection management is handled collectively and technologically, there is an increased focus on services rather than collections. More of the librarians within the modern academic library, and especially within the small, personally oriented library, are truly equals in terms of the type and scope of their responsibilities. A director is less likely to be able to plausibly exercise dictatorial command or to divide the librarians into specific narrow niches. More on this is discussed in the chapters on faculty status and personnel recruitment, which includes position evaluation.

CAMPUS CULTURE

It is important for a director to understand both librarian and campus expectations in the decision-making role. The

Story: With the retirement of a very active library director, the remaining librarians suggested to college administrators that a more collegial form of structure be explored. Librarians from other peer colleges came to discuss the issue with librarians and with faculty leaders, heads of departments, and schools. While the college eventually chose to conduct a search for a traditional director, the process enlightened many campus administrators about the professional aspects of modern librarianship.

campus climate matters. While pockets of an organization can develop their own customs, there are general "atmospherics" that have an influence, especially on the small college campus. This is particularly true specifically for the position of director, the position with the most direct and important responsibility for interacting with campus hierarchies and structures.

It is possible to get a good sense of how campus decision-making works by watching how discussion starts about goals for strategic plans or capital campaigns. If people are encouraged to provide any and all ideas at the very beginning, then that reflects a brainstorming-consensual expectation. If people are presented with a list and asked for their input, do people expect that that input will be incorporated into a final consensus (leader-consensus)? Or is the input seen primarily to be simply a means of communicating (top-down) or to avoid large errors (leader/listener-follower)? Do people expect that input will make large differences in the final plans?

Library directors do not necessarily have to change their preferred approach; they may continue to use brainstorming or solicit input. They need to know, though, if this choice is out of sync with campus expectations. Brainstorming and consensus generally take time; campus administrators who are used to a more command-communication method may not allow sufficient time. On a very consensus-collegial campus, librarians may gossip about a command-oriented library director. This kind of reputation would eventually isolate the director by discouraging informal ties across campus.

LIBRARY SUPPORT STAFF

So far the discussion has primarily focused on the level of professional librarian staff. However, non-MLS people are variously classified or termed clerical, staff, hourly, paraprofessional, etc.

The horizontal line dividing librarians and non-librarians is important. In the academic teaching department, there is no confusion between teaching faculty and support staff. There is a small amount of role ambiguity in other campus units with other types of professionals, people like instructional technology specialists, assessment experts, and even some levels of student-affairs personnel such as counselors. However, in the library field, whether all readers of this book agree or not, in general, people remain in the non-librarian category even if, or as, they achieve great technical skill in a specialty area. When they wish to participate in governance, in future-thinking, in directing and leading, it is precisely then that they are encouraged to pursue the master's degree, the essential qualification for "professional" level responsibilities in an academic library.

Support staff nevertheless possess important perspectives and expertise. Library directors would limit themselves severely if they did not listen to and actively encourage the participation of and input from support staff in those areas where those staff members have unique knowledge and contributions. For this reason, the director-plus model can expand for certain issues to include every permanent employee in a library, eliciting brainstorming and developing consensus among the entire staff.

Beyond input, some support staff positions will also have formal bureaucratic power. It is common for support staff to do direct supervision of student employees, and some senior support people may supervise more junior-level support people. This is not entirely at the discretion of the library director. Formal supervisory authority is something that needs to be explicitly described and formalized in coordination with the human resources department on campus, for two reasons. Who has hiring, evaluation, and firing authority over other employees is very important, and also the level of authority in a position relates directly to its rating or ranking in a compensation structure. In a small college, the director needs to work closely with any supervisory support staff to be sure they develop managerial skills; this is usually something the campus human resources office will assist with.

THE DIRECTOR-PLUS LIBRARY STRUCTURE

Given all these considerations, what is the best approach?

Management is about making things happen. This means making decisions in a sea of possibilities. The quality of the decisions depends on good input and good processes. No one person can come up with all of the answers to everything. If librarians do not feel that they are truly colleagues when it comes to the idea stage of decision-making, then the director will simply not benefit from their diversity of perspectives, expertise, and judgments. This is true as well of issues that support staff are the experts on.

And while people may welcome being shielded from administrative trivia by a director who takes care of all that mess, on the other hand, they usually do not appreciate being considered mere cogs in a machine, without opinions or contributions. This is a challenge in libraries large and small. In large libraries, the fiftieth or hundredth librarian has to work hard to escape feeling like a little person trapped in a large organization. In small libraries? Part of the reason why people take jobs at small libraries is precisely to experience a more human, direct, and personal quality in their work lives. If they wanted to be anonymous cogs, they could have sought one of the more numerous research library positions.

With all those factors, a non-rotating but collegial structure for professional librarians offers the most strengths and fewest drawbacks. People can be specialized enough, including specialized at administrative expertise, to excel in certain areas while experiencing enough cooperation to make collective decision-making effective and relatively efficient. Many decisions can be opened up to support staff input, while more professional ones can be discussed in the smaller circle of librarians.

This collegial approach to organizing the small library sounds good. It sounds great. It sounds like it could be perfect. On the one hand, everyone has a voice in and a perspective to add to the conversation; on the other, when there is a specific director, there is a sense of finality and also someone to take care of the more tedious parts of decision-making. Why go further? The next sections will review in more detail nuances that each of the main management theory perspectives contributes to understanding existing or potential organizational structures, and then proceeds to consider where the library fits on campus.

MANAGERIAL THEORY AND ORGANIZATIONAL STRUCTURE

Bureaucracy. A library environment has distinct ways to emphasize bureaucratic features in the organizational structure. This can be very few features even if a more collegial approach is used. It will be more than a little if the bureaucracy is the style of the director and perhaps the campus administration.

One element of the archetypal bureaucratic model that is a poor fit with the library and with many academic units is the line versus staff distinction. "Line and staff" refers to the observation that even within a traditional hierarchy, there are people or positions in an organization who have no formal power, yet have direct communication and contributions to make. These are usually represented graphically with dotted rather than solid lines: solid lines are power, and those who are staff have influence, not direct power. The president's secretary is acknowledged by the wise to have a great deal of situational knowledge and instant access to the most important person on campus and often can grant others access to the president. Yet this secretary possesses no power to make decisions. That is a staff position. These positions do exist on campus. The major limitation of this two-way division is that it ignores professional personnel. The collegial model makes room for people who do not have directly outlined decision responsibilities, but who are frequent participants in decision-making.

Two other elements of bureaucratic theory that are more important and related are the notions of span of control and unitary reporting. Span of control refers to the number of people who directly report to an individual manager. Unitary reporting means that a person is supervised by just one person. Typically, going outside of one's reporting line is regarded as confusing at best and a deliberate strike against managerial authority at worst.

In contrast to a collegial system that emphasizes communicating with a wide range of people, a specified span of control and unitary reporting structure means that managers are supposed to communicate with, and *only* with, their direct reports who are limited in number. Whenever there is an organization chart, it has boxes for departments and managers and lines for authorized channels of communication and control. Each box or tree segment has distinct responsibilities to a limited number of boxes tying to one superior box and no horizontal ties between boxes with different upstream reporting lines. That is a bureaucratic organization that obeys recommended principles of span of control and unitary reporting.

How close a fit can an organization chart be to the reality of life in a small college library, especially given a fluid collegial situation wherein the particular people involved in decision varies by the level and substance of each decision? Is this perspective too rigid? Too alien to small colleges?

In fact, it can be a closer fit to the small-library reality than organizations at some large libraries. This book specifically targets libraries employing at the most 10 professionals, which generally means between 10 and 20 support staff, for a maximum total of 30 full-time workers, and a minimum perhaps of two (one professional and one non-professional), excluding student workers.

In a large library, there are usually designated departments, but the variety and changing nature of library work make it difficult for an individual librarian to exist solely within a single-purpose organization. In any larger library where most or all librarians have formal "liaison" or simple reference-desk duties, they inevitably belong to two boxes on the chart: the one for public or liaison services, and their other duties. These libraries can use different organizational techniques, such as matrices or teams. In those, although each team ("bibliographic control" or "instruction") looks like a traditional box, each librarian often belongs to different boxes (teams) or reports to different people for different purposes (matrices).

In the small library, in contrast, the small number of people involved means that each person can be designated a "department," with as generous or flexible a description of responsibilities as desired. A library director can usually "span" all of the staff directly, at least as far as numbers are concerned. Moreover, the director will usually be considered by senior administration to have "control" over all of the library, so that in the larger campus organizational chart, the library does end up as a very tidy little box. Therefore, at least graphically, the library fits nicely.

But will the library director in every small library truly deal directly with each individual librarian or staff member on each issue? Will there not be areas of delegation or creations of subordinate levels of responsibility? What about "coordination"? If a position is described as "coordinator," how much power does that have?

> **Story**: One medical library with eight professional librarians managed to have a hierarchy with four levels. The director supervised the head of technical services and the head of public services. The head of public services supervised the head of reference. The head of reference supervised three reference librarians.

Bureaucratic types of control (or at the least, coordination) develop in even small libraries in three key areas: technical services, access services, and reference coverage. The structure of technical services will depend first on whether the library director has a cataloging or technical/systems background, and whether the technical-services function is outsourced or otherwise located outside of the library. ("Outsourced" means formally contracted to a separate agency or company; "outside the library" is any other arrangement, such as in a network of public institutions where one central office handles cataloging and processing.) In those situations, the library director will generally be the head of technical services, either by contracting with the outside provider or by supervising staff members. Given the relative scarcity of catalogers, and the relatively low volume of original cataloging required in a small institution, it would be unusual for a small library to have two technical-services-oriented professionals at the level of the MLS, the director and another MLS librarian.

If the library director either has a public-services background or devotes the majority of time to public-services tasks, then it is usual to either have a senior support staff member in charge of technical services or an MLS librarian. Given, again, the small absolute volume of professional-level cataloging work, that MLS librarian will probably also have public-services responsibilities but may be in charge of all technical-services personnel, including paraprofessionals and student workers. Each library, depending on its size and culture, does need to answer one specific question: Who has hiring, evaluation, and firing authority over other technical-services staff? The director needs to ensure that a technical-services supervisor has the managerial skills and desire to fulfill this role if it is part of his or her job. Such a supervisor really does act as a mini-director and needs to act in accordance with campus human resources policies and practices.

Access services, which in an academic library typically means circulation, reserves, and interlibrary loans, is most commonly managed by a person at the staff level. The librarian can either consolidate these activities under the responsibility of a single staffer, or the director (or another librarian) can supervise a variety of individuals doing different aspects of this area.

Again, this may seem like a small point: the people supervised are only a handful of full- or part-time staffers and a few student workers. It has important budgetary implications, though. If a staff person has authority to supervise other staffers (for example, a circulation supervisor might be responsible for selecting not only student workers but night or weekend support staff), then this position will be classified at a higher level of responsibility and therefore (usually) require a higher compensation level. The positive side of this added cost is that this higher-level position represents a small but real potential for staff development and an upward career ladder for non-MLS staff, something that is very limited in a small library.

Reference coverage is a broad term used for the notion that when individuals contact a library, they usually expect to receive help with their questions. It includes, but is broader than, the traditional in-person, walk-up reference desk. "Coverage" simply means that someone does, or will, respond, and that someone will be a professional librarian when appropriate. No small library logistically can provide 24/7 professional librarian reference assistance to its users with its own librarians, so all libraries live with the issue of how to determine the extent, character, and circumstances of its coverage.

This is an area that a director often handles directly, given that many academic library directors come out of public services. Some of the philosophical aspects of coverage can be handled with a collegial approach, as librarians discuss, trade ideas, and come to a common consensus of what their library can/should/will offer in terms of patron assistance. The benefit of collegiality in this respect is very powerful: for those librarians who will be "colleagues" in providing the services, it is vital that they have a common understanding about expectations and responses.

Bureaucracy is a reality, too, though. Who gets the e-mail? Who answers the phone/picks up voice mail? Are questions routed to liaisons (people who work consistently with particular academic departments) or handled by someone "on call"? What happens during school breaks and personal vacations? Who decides, or organizes people to decide, when changes from the Web site design to desk hours need to be made? For the small library, this will be the director, or someone else. If someone else, just as with access services, the director needs to ensure that that person has the managerial capability and support to fulfill what is needed.

Therefore, analyzing library structure through the bureaucratic perspective makes the director aware that there are subsidiary boxes and lines of responsibility and reporting even within the smaller academic library. These boxes and lines need some attention so that everyone has clarity on who is responsible for what, when, and how.

Politics. The lines and boxes of the typical organization chart in the bureaucratic model are intended to outline formal power: who has decision-making power over what and whom? Answer: the office and the officer to whom the person reports. This format assumes that people do not exist outside of the boxes, nor does communication. Of course, this is significantly at odds with day-to-day activity and with common human behavior.

The political perspective understands power. Politics considered broadly, not in national electoral terms but in essence as the method by which resources are allocated, the pure function of power. A key insight of the political perspective is the notion of an interest group. Derived from this are the ideas that people who may not share reporting lines may share commonalities of interests. Staffers can feel "kin" to others in the organization, those not in their own unit (box). That is, they will communicate with those others who are like them, and they may combine to organize pressure that passes around the formal limited spans of control and unitary reporting.

Who gossips with whom? Knowledge is power, and informal communication among like-minded individuals is a way of passing knowledge around. All rules have interpretations. Someone in one department may learn of the best interpretation because someone else tells them. This has been formalized in the often-recommended role of the mentor. "You are or will be like me," says the wise experienced person, "so I will tell you all the things that people like us know."

This sort of internal, informal politicking can be an area of distinct strength for the library. A library and its people by their nature cross the boundaries of many natural interest groups as well as formal units on campus. All academic departments should work with a librarian; therefore, given effective communication between faculty and "their" librarians, the librarians collectively have a cross-campus, cross-discipline, and cross-program perspective on the whole academic enterprise.

Librarians also, necessarily, work closely with administrative units. Libraries house complex forms of information technology. They generate a significant amount of college purchasing. They employ a large number of student workers and student-aid recipients. They are even noticeable recipients of development funds; donors give money more often to and for libraries than to housekeeping services or even information technology.

Given good intralibrary communication, this intercampus communication gives the astute library director valuable knowledge about various activities, desires, and developments on campus. The best way to use this is to keep the rest of campus within and beyond the formal reporting lines aware of library initiatives, contributions, and needs. The best director will also understand how to frame library needs in terms of the interests of other groups on campus:

- Attract new students by having a library that looks as good as or better than the competition (notice when student tour guides compare campus living or recreational facilities to other institutions).
- Attract development money by giving donors a tangible way to contribute to the broad academic mission.
- Support student academic needs so that the faculty's teaching life can be made easier.
- Integrate library computer facilities (WiFi, labs, and laptops) into the campus information-system planning.

The more people know and understand the work librarians do, the more successful the library will be in securing adequate resources, the goal of politics. This goal of greater knowledge and appreciation is separate from two drawbacks of a bureaucratic-only approach: adhering too rigidly to a single reporting formal line and continually trying to deviously circumvent it. Using a nuanced political awareness, library directors propose budget or other requests or decisions through the formal structure, with and through their direct supervisor. When that supervisor needs to make a decision, it is usually in conjunction with, even in competition with, input from the supervisor's peers, those who supervise other reporting lines and have their own proposals or decisions to make. If politics have been used to make these other areas aware of how helping the library advances their own goals, it makes supporting the library's requests far easier than if the library is only one isolated box within one reporting line.

Imagine a provost sitting in a strategic-planning session. Various vice presidents bring up campus strengths and weaknesses. The good provost will appreciate and value the library's contributions. But how much more powerful it is to have more than that one person nodding, and perhaps speaking, when the library is mentioned. The library that is aware of these other interest groups and purposes can work to keep them informed of how the library can serve them, too.

Human resources. A major insight of the human resource perspective in organizational theory is the idea that individuals are not just employees, oriented at all times toward their duties, interacting solely with those in the organization, and focused on external rewards. Employees are humans who have both basic and higher-level desires. Everyone needs a living wage, and most people want more. Autonomy, flexibility, and respect are among the higher-level experiences that people usually desire. For non-profit and public employees, there is the added motivation to contribute to society or to a specific mission.

It is important to consider how a formal organizational structure within a library interacts with the desires and needs of the people who work there. These are both positive and challenging aspects.

The smallness of the small college can be a distinct attraction for people who value responsibility and flexibility. At the least, at all levels, people necessarily have to multitask. There is really no way to sustain confined duties, rigid reporting, and isolated control lines within the small group atmosphere, even if a library director had a strongly bureaucratic preference. When a student needs help, usually it is the nearest employee who responds, from a student worker to the director.

However much the overlap and blurring, there remain distinct and visible differences between different types of employees and their roles and responsibilities. A strong emphasis on the "we" of collegiality may collide painfully with non-MLS employees who view it from a perspective of always being on the lower side of the staff-librarian dividing line. When is the "we" for discussion and decision a reality, and for what issues? Does "the library" mean only professional librarians? Do support staff have a voice? Is the "we" lip service, and if not, how does that complicate things?

The only real remedy for this confusion is to be as clear as possible about various forms of decision-making and the role of each individual in them. The faculty example will be instructive. Teaching faculty usually have "self-governance" structures, with all-campus officers, bodies, processes, and resolutions, but however central faculty are to the university, there are areas of higher education administration that are simply not under their control. Similarly, there are areas of library management and decision-making that are not part of some people's jobs.

The ideal to be worked for is to attract individuals at all levels who are self-reliant, relish personal responsibility, and understand the match between their education, positions, and roles in daily duties and decision-making. The good manager retains, rewards, and develops them through involvement at appropriate levels of input and decision-making. Lack of clarity or agreement on where responsibility and authority lie is one challenge, and will be discussed more in the personnel development chapter.

Another problem is the smallness of the small college library structure. During a person's working life, each begins at an "entry-level" position, gains knowledge, skills, experience, and judgment, is trusted with more tasks and higher responsibilities, and proceeds, as desired, to "better" positions.

For teaching faculty, this progression is taken care of in two ways: formal positions, such as chairs and deans, and ranks. A great benefit of the system of faculty ranks (assistant, associate, and full) is that it tangibly rewards faculty who have gone through that progressive development of getting better and better at what they do, yet does not require them to stop doing it, to teach less so they can administrate more.

Story: A 30,000-student university and a 2,000-student college had the same monetary reward for promotion through faculty ranks: $1,000.

A ranking system is greatly desirable for MLS-level librarians and is available within institutions that have faculty status for librarians. The absence of a ranking system can lead to lower morale, as senior librarians see no recognition that they are different from any newly hired librarian. This rank issue, rewarding senior-level experience and expertise without changing one's duties fundamentally, occurs at both large and small libraries. Even library directors in large libraries need to find ways to reward librarians who are not concerned with pursuing administrative positions.

A more serious problem exists for support staff. In a large library, there are enough staff and staff positions to have either ranks or specific career ladders. In the small library, there is often little to no upward room for that kind of progression for staff.

In order to provide support staff with a form of organizational recognition that rewards them as individuals and provides important human-level motivation, a library director has three basic choices, not necessarily mutually exclusive and not pristine in any case in real life. First, there is usually at least a small career ladder between a position that is open for high school or two-year college graduates and one that requires a bachelor's degree. Second, staff can be encouraged to grow into and develop out of entry-level positions and to consider other options on campus where their skills and maturity can transfer and be recognized. Finally, tasks can be gradually adjusted for what is done in the library to reflect growing expertise and skill on the basis of the staff person. To be legitimate, the last option needs to be accompanied by a reclassification of library positions, so that as higher-level activities are performed, the person is appropriately compensated.

These options require not only encouragement on the part of the library director but also the initiative of the staff people involved. Some may not wish to take on more complex tasks or more responsibility. Some may not wish to leave the library. In those cases, the director and the employee should both be conscious of the decisions that are being made. Human resource frustration exists when people do not believe that their preferences and contributions are recognized.

This is discussed at further length in the personnel-development chapter, but it is important to realize how the individual aspirations of the people working in the library strain sometimes against either a formal bureaucratic structure or the assumptions of a political, "we" group culture wherein some in the library are not always part of "we."

THE LIBRARY ON CAMPUS

Where does the library fit in terms of the whole campus organizational structure? At this level of connecting to the campus, a formal arrangement in terms of an organizational chart is most likely to already be in existence whenever new directors come on board. They inherit what exists. Most of the time, the chart or organization will look distinctly like a rational bureaucratic structure with formally designated reporting lines and areas of responsibility. If collegial decision-making is consciously practiced, it will be within clearly outlined groups and units.

In terms of the library's organizational positioning on campus, there are several items to pay attention to: where the library director reports, horizontal lines of communication (connected to interest groups on campus), and individual capabilities.

Where a library director reports: "Reporting" refers to the library's position in the administrative structure of the college. This is not the only governance or decision-making structure. There are usually faculty-related bodies and committees with formally delegated powers as well, in addition to a host of ad hoc bodies. These are discussed below.

The formal organization of an academic institution traditionally includes the following parts:

- Enrollment/admissions/perhaps retention
- Student affairs (current): advising, residential life, etc.

- Support
  - Facilities
  - Finances, purchasing
  - Information technology
  - Human resources
- Development
- Academic affairs

On different campuses, different elements find themselves in different places. Student advising can be handled by admissions, student affairs, or academic affairs (faculty). Writing assistance can be considered part of academic affairs or student affairs. Institutional research/assessment can be part of academic affairs or support or be a direct report to the president's office. Instructional technology may be part of support/information technology or academic affairs. Even the highest level has some variation. On some campuses, the "provost," whose title traditionally designates the chief academic officer, head of academic affairs only, may be the second-in-command of the campus as a whole, with non-academic units also reporting to this office; on others, the provost is one among equal chief officers.

The single most important question any library director candidate should ask is where the library reports, and within what grouping. The answer will reveal essential aspects of how the library is perceived on campus and how it will work with other units.

In general, a library should be considered an academic unit, for a philosophical reason and two pragmatic reasons. The philosophical reason is that independent inquiry is the heart of higher learning. Anyone can teach from a textbook and learn from a textbook, but only to a very limited and predetermined extent. True scholarship requires information resources and the ability to identify and access them. Therefore, a library is essential to a college's core function.

The first pragmatic reason is that on many if not most campuses, the academic-affairs unit is considered most central to the enterprise as a whole. Colleges teach, after all. Other units are important, but they exist to serve that central teaching/learning function. The closer a unit can get to this center of power, the better.

Admittedly, this may not be the case on all campuses at all times. There are instances in which other areas, such as information technology or finance, do indeed control more resources and appear at least for a time to be more favored at the highest levels. Yet a focus on identification with these areas will detract from the library's identification with the academic-affairs area. Since working with students and, more importantly, faculty, is essential to a library's fulfilling its mission, it needs to keep as close to that central area as possible. Imagine the counterexample: sports. On what big-name campus where the coaches make far more money than professors or even perhaps presidents would or should the library attach itself to athletics, simply because that is where the money is?

The second pragmatic reason is that to work effectively with students and faculty, the library needs to be involved in those structures where academic decisions are made. Every new and every discontinued academic program is something the library director needs to respond to. The library director needs to be at the table when those issues are discussed.

The following describes a spectrum of library-campus structural possibilities, from the least to the most desirable:

1. Reporting to a non-academic affairs unit.
   Possibilities include student affairs (rare) or a facilities group also including information technology.
2. Reporting to a subordinate level in academic affairs (that is, not to the CAO [chief administrative officer] but to an associate dean or assistant vice president).
   This will be rarer the smaller the campus is, because the CAO may not have any subordinates other than unit heads (chairs of departments or directors of offices).
3. Reporting to the CAO, and *meeting in a group* that includes other support units but not academic departments.
   This group may include units such as student academic advising, writing centers, faculty technology or instructional assistance, some ad hoc grant-based programs (e.g., the McNair program), and assessment/institutional research.

4. Reporting to the CAO *individually*, with no regular group meetings other than occasional campus-wide meetings of managers.
5. Reporting to the CAO *and meeting in a group* that includes academic departments or schools as well as academic support units.
6. Reporting to the CAO *and meeting in a group* only with academic department or school chairs.

> **Story**: A library director took a position at an institution where librarians did not have faculty status. Initially, she reported directly to the provost and was in the general deans/academic leadership meetings. With a new provost, the structure was changed so that the provost met more frequently with only academic unit heads, while the library director was relegated to a group of "miscellaneous" offices that also reported to the provost. Since the librarians were not involved in faculty governance, this reorganization eliminated any formal connection to academic discussions.

The reason a direct report to the CAO that takes place only one-on-one is considered less desirable than one that includes meeting with peers is the need for the library director to be a participant in brainstorming, idea-floating, and pre-planning. The CAO and the library director can talk all they want about issues either knows about, but the CAO can't tell the library director what the chemistry department chair is thinking.

FACULTY AND OTHER HORIZONTAL ORGANIZATIONS

In addition to the formal organizational chart that encompasses all units on campus, there are usually other structures involved for both administrative staff and faculty. Among administrative units, horizontal cross-department committees tend to be task-oriented or ad hoc committees. Their purpose is to bring together perspectives on issues that cross multiple separate areas and reporting lines. They function both top-down as ways of communicating administrative plans and requesting input on them and bottom-up as participants bring forth issues and identify and create responses to grassroots level problems. A major responsibility of campus management is to ensure that there are effective bodies of this sort. It is a delicate balance. If there are too many groups and meetings, people will complain about spending time in meetings rather than doing actual work, but if there are too few, organizational communication suffers. "Poor communication" is a common complaint when administration is disliked, although it is difficult to say for each instance whether it is a cause, an effect, or a misperception.

For faculty, most though not all colleges will have a formal faculty governance body as well as additional all-faculty/faculty-led, all-faculty/administratively led, and faculty-staff committees. This is encouraged by accreditation standards that identify the faculty as the primary controllers of the curriculum. In addition, since the faculty is the primary and essential workforce, its input is not only rationally necessary as subject-matter experts, but also politically essential as the most important interest group.

Clarity about what falls under faculty control and what the administration handles is always something that people say they want. Clarity is a changing spectrum, though, and even when achieved may not actually satisfy critics.

> **Story**: At a small institution, faculty were involved in two sets of reviews of existing academic programs. In one case, these were part of an effort to institute a regular rotating program review for ongoing assessment purposes. In the other, financial stress meant program cuts were inevitable. Faculty participants generally desired a role in assessment aimed at strengthening programs. Informally and formally, they attempted to evade any participation in criticism or the elimination of programs.

The two common forms of all-faculty governance are a faculty assembly or a senate. The former includes all eligible faculty; in the latter, a smaller number are elected by their peers. Even relatively small institutions can choose the senatorial format. In some institutions, different schools may have their own bodies but there may be no all-campus organization. In others, some academic activities, based on their type, format, or special origin, may not be integrated into all-campus bodies. This can happen with all-graduate programs, with distance-education programs, and with programs for special populations (e.g., adult learners). It is most likely when these initiatives are new or when they are staffed primarily or exclusively with faculty-administrators and part-time/adjunct faculty with few "line" or regular faculty being involved.

An overall faculty-governance body also generates smaller committees. Some common ones are those concerning student issues, particularly academic discipline or integrity; faculty welfare, such as considerations of benefits or policies on promotion and tenure; and curricular issues. The key point in determining whether these are faculty or administrative bodies is whether their voting membership is elected or selected. If peers elect faculty, then they are faculty-governance bodies. If they are led by administrators (such as deans) or persons selected by them, then they are administrative bodies; and, in general, faculty will consider that they are foreign, perhaps friendly, but not really part of faculty governance.

Just as the question of where the library reports is indicative of the library's position on campus and affects the ability of the library director to communicate with peers on both administrative and faculty sides, a question about where the director or librarians sit on these various governance bodies helps determine how well the library will be integrated into the overall academic enterprise.

At the very least, the library director or another member of the staff needs a seat on curricular bodies. If librarians have faculty status, this will probably be a voting seat, but even if not, an *ex officio* place at the table will allow the library staff to hear and understand what is going on programmatically at the college and be proactive in meeting those needs.

New library directors would probably benefit greatly from filling this seat, particularly if they are not part of any CAO/ provost group of academic leaders. After a while, any experienced librarian can effectively fill this position. Especially in a small library, all librarians should have enough knowledge about the library's general capacities and flexibility to contribute intelligently to discussions of program changes. Adding one more health sciences program, for example, is different from adding the first one.

If there is a budget committee, separate from any reporting-line meetings about the budget, it would be useful for the library director or another librarian to take part. All realistic budget requests need to be placed within the larger institutional context; similarly, without badgering committee members, casual comments about things like periodicals inflation ("Health insurance is going up? Yeah, that sounds like our periodicals bill."), automation needs ("Yes, we're looking at cooperative system purchase too."), and new initiatives ("A new writing instructor? Maybe she can work with our information-literacy-across-the-curriculum coordinator.") build understanding for current and future prioritizing.

All of these areas of organizational participation are valuable for the library. They keep the library staff or library director informed about campus issues and ideas so that the library staff can work beside (not trailing behind) and even lead initiatives. Moreover, in academic issues, the library is probably one of the best-placed units with a broad perspective. Other units on campus also have horizontal contacts and seats on various committees, but the library is one of the few units to have systematic formal and ongoing contacts with academic departments in three different forms: special-purpose committees, broad faculty-governance bodies, and liaisons.

Not all campuses will incorporate librarians as peers or "ordinary" participants within faculty-governance structures; it requires at least some level of faculty status, although it can exist without other elements of faculty status, such as tenure or sabbatical eligibility. When librarians are included in faculty governance, regular "line" librarians will sit in the same meetings as regular "line" teaching faculty, hear their concerns firsthand, and be seen as part of any answer to problems.

Another venue for communication and connection is the "liaison" concept, in which a specific librarian is the designated contact for each academic department. In the fullest implementation, one librarian would exclusively handle all of collection development, advanced reference questions, and user instruction for a group of departments. Even in smaller institutions with much collegiality among the librarians, this sort of designation is commonly used to help faculty feel a stronger connection to the library in the individual relationship with "their" librarian.

This liaison structure, beyond the simple functional purpose of fulfilling library services needs, works extremely well on the political level for the library's position in the overall campus structure. Liaison librarians are in a position to communicate frequently with the most formidable interest group on campus, the faculty. As librarians talk with one an other about what is happening in "their" departments, they all benefit from a campus-wide knowledge of academic happenings that few other units can achieve.

INDIVIDUAL CAPABILITIES

Some people think that the most important thing in work life is who you know, or who you are, and that this is more important than what you know or how good you are at your job. They believe that no formal structure explains what *really* goes on. In contrast, the bureaucratic perspective is impersonal by design. Faced with each situation, it strives to apply or to create a general rule, to guide behavior rationally and impersonally: the embodiment of the rule of law, not men.

Reading stories of how libraries or other organizations became unionized often proceeds from the who to the rule. Managers are seen as capricious and unreliable, pursuing personal agendas. Union work roles and procedures are intended to eliminate the erratic and arbitrary with agreed-upon and transparent rules, bureaucracy writ strongly, to the point of suppressing individual decision-making and, often, initiative.

Somewhere in between an unrealistic mechanistic view of the entirely pre-planned organization and paranoia about erratic people, there is an inevitable reality to the idea that who a person is does affect power within an organization. People get reputations; a reputation begins from the first day on campus. Others react to those reputations. People are respected, or not. When openings occur higher up, some will be considered, or not. The library will be respected, or not, depending to a large extent on what people think about the librarians themselves, not impersonally as "librarian," but as Kim or Mari or Jon.

> **Story:** A small campus had two libraries: a health science library and a main library. The director at the main library noticed that a number of health sciences students were showing up at the main library's reference desk with questions. It became evident that health sciences faculty had reservations about the "branch" library librarian and directed their students to the main library. The health sciences library director retired and his energetic and proactive replacement revitalized personal faculty connections with the result that the health sciences faculty and students began fully utilizing "their" library.

The campus culture will have a strong role to play in the balance between a personal or a formal approach to power. Some small campuses are strongly affected by individuals with long experience and extensive connections. Others may feel for reasons of mission or faith that taking an impersonal approach is just not the way they work or should treat people.

The dark side of a personal approach is that sometimes people get into situations for which they are truly not suited. For example, more often than professional librarians would like, people are placed in libraries for reasons completely unrelated to their knowledge of librarianship. Or, people may have such respect for a library support staff member that they misunderstand the limits of her responsibilities, and ask her to do advanced research or instruction.

> **Story**: The résumé of a candidate for dean of faculty included a year as a government documents librarian but no MLS. When asked how that job came about, the candidate explained cheerily that the director of the library, a history professor, thought she would be good at it.
>
> At another library, an older purchasing clerk was losing effectiveness as he resisted learning the new computerized systems; the head of finances suggested that the person be transferred to work in the "stacks" of the library.

It is really important to pay attention to the issue of individual capabilities in two ways. First, the fact that what a person achieves on campus is affected by his or her own personal abilities and initiative as much as formal responsibilities and structures emphasizes the crucial role of selection and development of librarians. A wonderful formal structure or an exciting and important list of duties won't mean much if the individual is not well suited to them and will be unable to achieve and maintain a good reputation. Second, elsewhere on campus, the library director needs to investigate, identify, and handle with respect those who are really influential on campus. These individuals and their wisdom and goodwill are invaluable, far above their formal structural responsibilities.

NOTES

1. Lyle, Guy Redvers. *Administration of the College Library*. New York: Wilson, 1944, 1st ed.; 1974, 4th ed.

2. Lesniaski, David, Kris MacPherson, Barbara Fister, and Steve McKenzie. "Collegial Leadership in Academic Libraries." In *Crossing the Divide: Proceedings of the Tenth National Conference of the Association of College and Research Libraries*. Denver, CO: Association of College and Research Libraries, 2001. The libraries were St. Olaf College and Gustavus Adolphus College in Minnesota and Davidson College in North Carolina.

II
PEOPLE AND HOW THEY FIT TOGETHER

4 PERSONNEL RECRUITMENT

The key: Every new person: an opportunity to review and renew.
The future is created by good library staff.

The chapter on organizational structure was primarily concerned with how "boxes" representing positions and units were arranged within a library and connected the library on campus. However, it concludes with the essential truth that individuals and their personal capabilities, attitudes, and contributions have a huge impact on the success of a library. If management means how to get things done, then one recognizes that it is people who do the doing. These people are not simply positions, faceless technicians, or impersonal professionals. Library staff do many things, complex and simple, and innovating and boring. The whole culture they create by their preferences and choices, and their soft skills in dealing with the campus as a whole, greatly affects how the library is viewed on campus. Everything flows from this. Even the most library-friendly campus administrator is likely to start ignoring the library if it does not show itself worthy of a minimal level of respect.

It is important to have the right people around. It is also impossible under the most common circumstances for new directors to completely "stock" a library with their own picks, even assuming that those selections would be perfect. Quick personnel turnover is a bad thing, both for efficiency and as a disturbing signal that something is wrong with the library as a workplace. Slow turnover means a slow process of maintaining or building a staff with the "right" people, one by one by one. Some will be new hires and some will be existing personnel. Some will be those who are already excellent and others who can become excellent. Development of existing personnel is covered in the following chapter.

This chapter discusses the issues that are involved in getting new people right, personnel recruitment:

- Position review, approval, and description
- Legalities and logistics
- Interviewing
- Internal candidates
- Deciding: weighing characteristics

These steps involve the library director, other library staff, and other units on campus, in particular the direct supervisor of the library and the campus human resources department. Bureaucratically, the library director needs to make a rational case for the position. In terms of human resource considerations, the position needs to be attractive to the right kind of person; the person picked will become part of the political landscape, inside and connecting to the rest of campus. Again, *what* the library can accomplish, *what* people think of the library, and how successful the library is will depend heavily on *how* the library staff, both professional and support, behave in both technical and interpersonal ways.

POSITION REVIEW, APPROVAL, AND DESCRIPTION

Recruitment is always precipitated by change. Either someone already working there has changed (resigned, retired, etc.) or the director believes changes at the library warrant an additional position. In either of these cases, in the small library, an essential step is to recognize that change and take the time to review *all* positions at the library.

"No decision is a decision." If there is no review of positions, then that is in effect a decision to simply continue the current position with a new incumbent. It is a decision that everything is perfectly fine, no responsibilities or expectations need adjusting, and everything is expected to stay the same for a minimum of one year. It is one year because that is a rough estimate of how long it takes any new person to truly master a new position, whether support or professional.

Reviewing only the new position is too limited. In a small library, what any one position does affects everybody else, from formal shared responsibilities, to backups, to pitching in when things get busy, or changing entirely when new needs come along. It would be unusual to have any changes in one job's position description be so minor or self-contained that nobody else at the library is affected.

Position review. Position review is easy, essential, and ties into other planning processes. Reviewing positions at the time of change (retirement or resignation) is comparatively easy on the personal level for both the director and other staff because it can be viewed, even if it seems a little artificial, as an impersonal effort. This review does not criticize or seek to change an existing employee's habits or capabilities, but focuses only on what is desired in the new position and hence in changes that might happen to others through no fault or inadequacy of their own.

The next chapter covers personnel evaluation, and it is a managerial responsibility to work with each employee to see that responsibilities assigned and activities to be carried out are a good fit for library needs. Weaknesses are identified and strengths are built upon. However, managers will also acknowledge that this is personally quite difficult. Actually confronting the weaknesses of any existing employee, face-to-face, is not easy, and even reviewing the duties of an existing position can be seen as threatening by an employee. With a new position opening, the review becomes impersonal, separated from individual personnel evaluation. Therefore, it is a golden opportunity to sidestep this awkwardness because the review of positions becomes separated from existing employee performance. It is the fact that someone already has left that is the trigger. Hiring new staff happens relatively frequently and hopefully often enough to keep the library up-to-date on duty assignments. For a typical library career of 20 or 30 years, in a 20-person library, such a review would happen roughly every one or two years.

This review and time of change gives others in the library an opportunity to mention their own goals and changes in their preferences. Perhaps the nighttime supervisor is leaving. The daytime circulation person's children are older now and she would welcome a change of hours. Perhaps the access manager is retiring, and someone else thinks she can handle part of the interlibrary loan process. The career ladder in a small library is short, but revitalization can also be accomplished by a form of job rotation and redefinition.

This is the human resources aspect of new-position recruitment, not only to prepare a good fit for a new person, but to enhance the quality of work life for existing personnel.

Finally, reviewing a position and others in the same unit is bureaucratically essential because that becomes part of justification for hiring. In some colleges, *any* open position is subject to a review to see if it is still necessary. In most colleges, open positions need approval from superiors to be filled. In all institutions, the human resources department must understand enough about the position to ensure that it is classified correctly for compensation purposes, which also fits into budget planning. All of these require the library director to know and be able to exactly articulate the responsibilities and requirements of the position.

With respect to position review, one small practical and political consideration may affect some colleges at some times. In some circumstances, the library is in a position where the director needs to avoid adverse attention from supervisors. That is, they fear that supervisors will not so much listen to the library's explanation of the position's importance as see it as a simple opportunity to save money or to impose their own limited understanding of what librarians do. If that is the case, for replacements only (this cannot apply to new positions), the library director may seek to simply refill a position as quickly as possible without signaling any kind of review because that review may result in a negative consequence for the library.

When might this happen? It might apply in the unhappy situation in which administrators are looking for cost savings and have an insufficient appreciation for what is necessary in the library. Not filling an open position is the easiest personnel cut of all. Under those very limited circumstances, if the library director can refill the position and judges that greater discussion (review) of the position might lead to greater skepticism that it is needed, it may be best, for that one hire, to proceed quietly.

This extreme case should definitely be an exception. If others perceive that the library director is either unwilling or too lazy to review positions, that may make the director look like someone who is not "with the program," who is not trying to help the institution with cost-savings, who is concerned only with his or her own turf, and who distrusts administration.

In the long run, this would be very damaging for credibility, especially if the whole institution is facing financial difficulties. Politically speaking, directors who seem to separate the library from campus goals and needs become isolated and eventually powerless directors. Given this consequence, directors should choose to fill a position without public review only when they reasonably foresee that the library may be targeted for disproportionate cutting or their supervisors are unfavorably disposed to the library. In that case, getting the position filled quietly may be the best temporary solution while the director makes efforts to improve the library's position with respect to campus decision-makers.

A reason for reviewing all positions is that this is a vital part of long-range planning. A permanent position is a long-range commitment. A library director should always be thinking about strategic planning, not just when planning is formally being conducted for accreditation or other reasons, and not just when campus hearings are held and administrators request all units develop strategic plans. Library directors should think about position review all the time, even in that "lull" year right after a five-year plan has at last begun. The thinking that everyone in the library puts into reviewing positions is exactly the thinking that nourishes strategic planning: what are we doing now and what do we want to do in the future?

This position review applies to both professional and staff positions. It does not need to include student workers, as they generally make up a relatively homogenous labor pool. Librarian and support staff duties can all be subject to rethinking. As technology and skills adjust, the responsibilities of librarians and staff also adjust, such as the development of copy cataloging and the position of "cataloging assistant" and the hotly contested job category of "reference assistant," officially recognized by the College and University Professional Association for Human Resources (CUPA-HR).

Position approval. After the internal review of library positions, the library director is well prepared to make the case for a new position, to defend the continued need for an existing position, or to propose a new configuration of responsibilities with existing and new staff. The chapter on budgeting notes that, in general, library directors do not have independent authority to switch funds from the regular personnel category to other needs such as materials, fees, or supplies, or back again. Campus administrators view personnel different from all other expenses. They keep track of overall headcount and view a full-time or permanent part-time position as a significant commitment. It can be a larger commitment than the library director realizes. In some cases, fringe benefits do not show up in the library budget, yet cost the institution considerable money.

The position needs approval in two offices: that of the direct supervisor for the library and in human resources. The most important thing in both offices is to have the position classified correctly. The director needs to be very alert to any changes that might happen during the posting process. Just as some see an open position as an opportunity for a neat cut, they may also see an opportunity to change it to a less expensive classification. Faculty librarians might be replaced by librarians classified as staff, a salaried support staff position might be reclassified as hourly, or vice versa.

> **Story:** On a small institution's bulletin board, faculty positions were always posted on cream-colored paper and staff on plain white. A replacement-librarian position was initially posted on white paper. While this was quickly corrected with no argument, it was interesting to find out that the human resources specialist responsible for the posting did not understand that librarians did possess faculty status (not new to the institution, but apparently new to her).

The library director needs to understand the exact extent of the approval. This includes a specific starting date, but also a time frame to fill the position before the "right" to fill it expires. Failed searches usually prompt some degree of reexamination. These issues will depend on the institution's current financial situation and also the timing with respect to the fiscal and planning cycles. Library directors may also need to work with their supervisors and the human resources departments so that everyone agrees on a search timed to when the best candidates are likely to be available. If someone retires in March, it would be shortsighted to insist on a quick search and demand a start hire by April when better candidates might finish school (high school, LTA program, or MLS) in May.

Position description. For both staff and librarian positions, a position description will be necessary for advertising. The goal of the description is for the director to understand and articulate what the library needs and for prospective candidates to have an accurate sense of what expectations exist so as to make a reasonable choice about applying for the job.

For support staff positions, the director will work especially closely with human resources personnel. It is important to follow legal requirements and campus policies. In particular, the level of details to be included in the ad or description need human resources input. For example, a library director may not think to include "must be able to lift 20 pounds," but it may in fact be necessary for that particular position. HR people also will know the standard wording used to indicate different levels of responsibility and, in the best cases, will know what kinds of applicants tend to be attracted by what positions.

Story: In the mid-1990s, that is, prior to the widespread use of the term "information literacy," a library director sat with a human resources staff member to go over copy for a reference librarian ad. "But what if they don't know what 'bibliographic instruction' is?" she asked. "We don't really want that person" was the answer.

Library directors have two main areas to be concerned about. First, they need to provide accurate library-specific language and control the level of specificity. For example, does the director want to require knowledge of a specific automation system or just experience with any library automation system? Which parts of the automated system: the public interface, circulation, or acquisitions/budgeting? Second, the fact that the library is part of the academic or teaching-and-learning part of the campus, not administrative support, means that library staff positions may have educational requirements higher than other clerical positions on campus. In particular, if a library staff position involves providing reference assistance, a bachelor's degree may be desirable. This may not be obvious to the human resources staff. The final, advertised position description is essential in ensuring that a position is articulated correctly, that its requirements, expectations, and compensation, and, consequently, the quality of candidates, will work together for what the library needs.

For professional librarian positions, how the description is handled varies. In many situations, if librarians have faculty status, that means librarian recruitment would flow through the provost's office. Human resources would be involved to a varying degree. They generally handle all demographic, equal-opportunity requirements, and data-gathering, and may provide assistance for interviewing logistics. For librarian positions, there are three key points for the advertisement or description: librarian degree requirements, qualities required compared to those desired, and how the wording signals expectations.

The director needs to be careful and deliberate about the degree requirement and one element in particular: "ALA-accredited MLS . . . *or equivalent.*" In general, for academic libraries, the position requirement can legally be restricted to simply "ALA-accredited MLS," as a bona fide, non-discriminatory relevant professional qualification. Even though the wording, "or equivalent" is commonly seen, there are reasons to avoid it, unless a particular state has specific regulations to the contrary.

First, there have been few times in academic library recruiting history where a full-time professional position cannot be filled with candidates who have ALA-MLS degrees. Second, even for the most geographically isolated or place-bound, the growth of accredited online programs means that talented persons wishing to pursue academic librarianship have realistic means of achieving full preparation through an MLS program. Thus, "and equivalent" is not generally needed because genuine ALA-MLS candidates are readily available for small college needs.

The main problem with the wording is that it can be interpreted in two ways. In some circumstances, it may mean, and only mean, a library science degree from a foreign country where their education is considered equivalent to an ALA-accredited master's program (foreign meaning not American or Canadian). Those with these truly do have a degree equivalent in library science to an ALA-MLS.

However, it can also be interpreted as any somewhat-related master's-level degree. Typical examples are master's in education, in information science, or in computer or instructional technology. The less candidates know about what an ALA-MLS degree is, the more likely they are to reinterpret "or equivalent" to mean any master's degree.

What the library director needs to focus on is avoiding the dilution of understanding of what a librarian is by an accident of wording. If the library director and staff really feel that for a given set of duties, preparation in teaching or technology is truly what fits the need, then it is appropriate to specify those types of degrees and to be as explicit as possible about what program other than an MLS is acceptable. If "or equivalent" is taken to mean that "anybody" at a generally master's level of education or lower can be a librarian, that would considerably weaken the professional respect shown the librarians generally.

> **Story:** Common comments reported by SLIS students when their friends learn they are pursuing an MLS: "You have to go to school for that?" "You have to get a master's for that?" and, for public library people, "I thought librarians were volunteers."

The list of, and division between, "required" and "preferred" characteristics of candidates will depend on each institution's goals and on the candidates it believes it can attract. A library may need someone with knowledge in the sciences. Should that knowledge be from SLIS coursework? An undergraduate major? A second master's degree, or even a doctoral degree? That depends on what the library director wants and what is available for any given subject field. The librarian population has many liberal arts majors, and comparatively few science majors. A library director may really want someone with a second master's in chemistry, but should decide before advertising whether to insist on it. The most flexible arrangement is to list such items as "preferred." In that case, a search can legitimately end up hiring someone without the item, assuming that candidate's strengths outweigh the missing elements.

The final purpose of the advertisement wording is to signal expectations. To the discerning eye, a job ad or position description can give many valuable indications of the type of place the library is and therefore the candidate sought. "Dynamic" and "innovative" are common buzzwords. "Good communication skills" and "flexible" often are important. Some adjectives speak to what you hope the applicant will bring, and others to what you will offer the candidate. Terms like "team-oriented" signal a collegial managerial approach.

It is especially important to take a step back from formal lists of initial qualifications and duties to ensure that the ad attracts people who can succeed in the long run. If the library has a system of review and tenure, are those requirements represented at least broadly in the ad? In particular, if tenure involves professional service or research or publication, it is wise to incorporate that into the ad. Using the term "faculty status" will be one screen for some applicants, particularly those who are experienced in academia. Many librarians who dislike faculty status do so because they feel research or publication are not desirable or achievable, or are distractions from "real" librarianship. Others believe that faculty status means greater autonomy, closer work with faculty, and greater integration into governance. Since "faculty status" can have many different manifestations, it is usually best to include at least some specifics, such as "librarians have faculty status and candidates will be expected to participate in research and teaching."

LEGALITIES AND LOGISTICS

It is important to work closely with the campus human resources office on the legalities and logistics of advertising a staff or faculty position. All accredited colleges are subject to affirmative action and equal employment opportunity rules. One area human resources people will be particularly knowledgeable about is denominational expectation. For religiously affiliated institutions, a faith position or particular faith practices may be legitimate requirements for all employees. In most institutions, an appreciation of the institution's specific mission will be important. These are issues that the human resources department is very familiar with on both the staff and faculty levels, and they can ensure that the processes and wording that are used conform to both the law and the institution's particular preferences for diversity and mission commitment.

Advertising. Logistically, the human resources department will be familiar with general academic advertising, both at the staff level and for administrator and faculty positions. The library director can add to this a special library-related perspective. The most common venues for advertising academic librarian positions, and therefore the ones where most candidates will look, are the ALA JobLIST Web site (which has largely replaced print advertising in *College and Research Libraries News* and *American Libraries*), the *Chronicle of Higher Education* (print-online combined), and general academic job sites.[1] Particularly if librarians have faculty status, it is important that their procedures use the same techniques as faculty searches.

Two important points should be considered when comparing local (newspapers or location-specific sites) to national advertising. The first is that the level or geographic reach of advertising is something that reflects the institution's seriousness about and commitment to a position. A national search reflects a desire to compete in the largest possible pool of candidates. At the other extreme, if a full-time librarian position is advertised only locally, especially if degree qualifications are loosely worded with many "or equivalent" phrases, the advertisements will miss many of the best candidates and attract people with weak qualifications.

On the other hand, local advertising added to national advertising has two strong points. First, it emphasizes to the local community the fact that the college is an employer that is a vital part of their economy. Second, even in the era of Facebook, LinkedIn, and other online networking venues, there still exists the "grandparent network." In other words, a grandparent may notice an available position and mention it to a relative living far away. If a college is geographically isolated, it is often difficult to interest people who are unfamiliar with the area. Local advertising has the ability to generate word of mouth to reach people who know the area but may have moved away. This is particularly valuable for those who are not currently job-seeking and hence may not be looking at national advertising.

The visit. The details of the application review, candidate interview, and selection processes will vary according to whether the position is clerical or professional, the campus's usual procedures, and where the college is located. For all but the most technical or specialized staff positions (few of which are found in small colleges), recruitment is primarily local, which simplifies and speeds along the process. Typically, the campus human resource department will receive and process applications. Either all applications or only those that qualify will be given to the library director (or the position's direct supervisor) for selection of the top candidates. In-person interviews can usually be done in one-half day and involve primarily the human resources department and library staff.

One practice that human resources persons usually prefer is for clerical-level candidates to be interviewed by only a limited number of people directly involved in supervising the position. This is a bureaucratic, rational perspective, which envisions each clerical person filling a defined role in an organizational chart, with clear lines of supervision and control. It minimizes a teamwork aspect. If the library is generally run on collegial lines and many decisions involve both staff and professional personnel working in groups, the library director may need to make a specific case that the interview process itself must try to assess how the person might work in those circumstances.

For librarian positions, the library director should be aware of the elements used in filling both administrative and faculty positions, especially when the desired pool of candidates is not entirely local, which is the usual case for faculty hires. The more a librarian position is public-services oriented, the more it will resemble a faculty search. Since in a small library most librarians are involved in public services, the closer the process follows the usual faculty processes the better.

A typical recruitment sequence for a faculty position includes a search committee reviewing all applications (letters, résumés, and other requested materials), telephone or professional conference interviews with 4 to 10 individuals, and campus visits for two or three. Each visit is extensive, consisting of meetings with potential colleagues, tours of various areas on campus, meals with representatives of various interest groups, at least one formal interview (questioning) with department chair and other faculty and/or a search committee, interviews with higher administrators, and at least one public presentation of research or teaching demonstration or both. This cannot be done all in one day, nor does it usually make sense to fly someone in and out for one day, so usually the candidate is brought to campus for at least parts of two days and in some cases three days.

Two logistical points here are vitally important when adapting this structure to a librarian position. The first is that faculty interviews generally involve a wide range of people. It is even more appropriate that librarian interviews do so as well. Librarianship touches many areas on campus. It is important to show candidates those other areas, and in this way the visit schedule may resemble higher administrative positions in introducing people to units such as information technology or student services.

It is particularly valuable for candidates to meet experienced faculty and conversely to introduce the candidates to the faculty. Meeting a sequence of sparkling, excited, and visibly competent candidates can do wonders to revitalize the campus's appreciation for librarianship. Having candidates give public presentations on innovations not only helps the search committee assess their skills, but it is a cheap way to enhance everyone's knowledge of what libraries can be.

The second point is also that interviews generally involve a wide range of people, which means scheduling can become a nightmare. Interviews should involve higher administrators, especially on the small college campus. Simply setting up times where at least the provost and possibly the president can meet candidates is both important and exceedingly challenging. The library director needs to nail down dates and times and will expend a great deal of effort on this seemingly mindless task. This timing issue is a pervasive problem in the recruitment process. The time it takes for a committee to meet jointly, find compatible open times for administrators to meet with each candidate, and make a decision and have it approved up the chain of command means that librarian searches may take weeks and often months. If the position that is open is entry-level and hence will attract people new to academic librarianship, it would be wise to directly advise applicants and particularly the best candidates that the process will take a long time and a delay does not mean that they are being ignored.

Managing schedules is something that in the small library will mostly fall to the director. When planning a search for a professional position, the director needs to be aware of how time-consuming and vital this part of the logistics is and be proactive about getting details finalized.

References. The process of contacting references can be used either as a screen before choosing people to invite to campus or as a confirmation or clarification at the final decision-making step. Checking 10 candidates' references prior to the final cut is obviously more time-consuming for the search committee or director than checking those for three interviewees. However, inviting someone who is really weak is also a great waste of time and money.

How useful will information from references be? That is a vexing question and there will not be any really satisfactory answer, particularly for marginal candidates. The strongest candidates will have people as references who know them in work situations that have similarities to the position for which they are interviewing. For new graduates, library school faculty such as teachers or advisors can provide some information. Almost more than formal grades, a student's attitude toward learning and his or her visible relationships with fellow students and faculty can be good indicators of the kind of intellectual curiosity and service and team orientation that will be valuable in the librarian's future career.

References pose two big problems. The first is whether references can, and the second whether they will, be able to provide truly useful information. Not all people asked for references know everything about the person they are recommending, nor are all equally articulate.

> **Story**: Applicants for a master's program in education were required to have a letter of reference from their principals. More than a quarter of these letters had grammatical or spelling mistakes. The admissions committee did not penalize the teachers for the errors of their supervisors.

One approach is for the person who is talking with the references to try to probe for quality and not quantity in their input. Some standardized references forms include 10 or 20 characteristics that each reference person is expected to evaluate and even comment on. These forms are more common the lower the level of position or experience desired, yet it is just those new or entry-level people who may not have one single reference person who has in-depth knowledge of that wide range of characteristics. Other times, when a letter and not a form is used, those writing references may use such broad and generic language that it is virtually impossible to tell the difference between a candidate who is genuinely wonderful and someone merely described as "good" and "great" and all the other positive adjectives of an affirming society.

It is more useful for the people being asked for references to be asked to describe just a few but far more concrete examples of characteristics that are relevant to the job at hand, either positive or negative. This has a couple of advantages. First, more detail allows the search committee to make its own judgments about the candidate. A manager saying a call-center person "didn't press the customer enough on products they could purchase" is more useful to a library search committee than one saying "this person was okay but not outstanding" because the meaning of "outstanding" for this referee is not the same as for the library position.

The second advantage is that more concrete examples may help mitigate a prevalent problem with references, which is the reluctance of people to provide truthful but negative information. *This book does not give legal advice.* A library director should be aware of what an institution itself feels can and should be disclosed. However, respondents may feel more comfortable talking about very specific situations without trying to provide and justify broad evaluations.

"I would absolutely hire this person myself if we had openings" is the best thing to hear about a recent school graduate from an internship supervisor. Sometimes, references really can make the difference.

INTERVIEWING

The interview is the key step in gathering information needed to make a decision about whom to hire. If a library's quality and effectiveness are dependent upon the quality and effectiveness of its librarians and support staff, and they are, then this is the key element, the crux of the whole process. Résumés and cover letters help screen for the large issues and do provide some indications (e.g., degrees) and assertions (e.g., "strong communication skills") about quality. References are important, too. But the interview is central. It takes a lot of time and effort, and so should be treated very seriously.

It is useful to view the interview through the lenses of the three organizational theory perspectives: bureaucratic, political, and human resources. Thinking about these three aspects can strengthen the process so as to make the final decision the most informed possible.

Bureaucratic rules are intended to provide consistency. This happens in the search process when all candidates are treated equally. Equal does not necessarily mean identical. Bureaucracy is impersonal, and before any interviewee is selected, the library staff impersonally determines a set of issues that it needs to know about each and every candidate. For the support position, "the library" means the director and the position's supervisor (if different). For the librarian, "the library" means the director and usually all other professional librarians.

The set of issues will be the same for each candidate (equal), but the questions asked may differ (not identical). For an entry-level position, one candidate may have preprofessional experience, another might have internship experience, and a third may have covered the concepts in coursework. Based on those differing résumés, candidates should be given the opportunity to address the same issue by explaining their own thinking and background.

Bureaucratic rules include important legal issues. This is where even those who dislike "faceless bureaucracy" the most have no choice but to conform. For example, discrimination on the basis of race or family structure is usually both illegal and inadvisable. Thus, questions about childcare, partner relations, or personal health are out of bounds. All those participating in direct interviewing should have a refresher from the human resources department on forbidden topics, even for faculty positions.

Story: The nun who chaired the religion department had to be repeatedly reminded not to ask candidates about their families even when strolling in the hallway as opposed to the formal interview room. "But we want to know if they'll be happy here!" she protested. You can ask if they will be happy there, but not presume that information about their spouses helps *you* make that prediction.

What is the political aspect of interviewing, group identity, interests, and the flow of power outside formal bureaucratic positions? First, making librarian interviews as like faculty interviews as possible advances the goal of librarians being seen as part of that group. That is, regardless of who any individual candidate is, or what his or her specific duties are, if librarians are faculty, then it is important to conform to what faculty candidates do. Faculty give teaching sessions. Public-service librarian candidates should demonstrate one or more varieties of library use instruction; technical-services librarians can explain how their areas of expertise contribute to the campus. Faculty talk about their research, and any librarian candidates can be asked to describe new ideas or techniques in their own areas of expertise. Having a shared interview experience is one part of being part of the faculty-interest group. That is a matter of the format matching group expectations.

Second, the interview process needs to involve important people. In the bureaucratic model, only those formally involved with the librarian would be part of the interview process. Politically, however, involving faculty and influential campus people, perhaps from information technology or instructional technology in either open sessions or informal meals, is an opportunity to strengthen bonds between them and the library, reinforcing cross-campus political connections for existing librarians as much as laying the groundwork for the new hire.

A human resources perspective asks what the candidate as well as states what the library director want out of the interview experience and the job itself. It is in this human context that interviewing shows itself most clearly as a two-way street. It is very easy for directors, librarians, and existing campus personnel to become completely focused on what the person can do for them and what roles they can fill. But any candidate, however outstanding, has to agree to become part of the organization.

What does the candidate think? Here, it is more than the answers the candidate gives that is important. The questions candidates ask are a valuable glimpse into how people think and what they think is important. Can you tell how much background study they did? If they are creative? "Stock" questions like "what is the role of a liaison at this institution" or "what does faculty status mean here?" or "what support is there for professional development" show diligence; relevant but unpredictable questions show autonomy and independent-thinking. Some candidates, particularly for entry-level jobs, may be nervous; can they overcome that? Have they prepared the most basic questions? Can they avoid known pitfalls from asking about vacations to whether staff are married?

What will candidates think about the institution? When the committee starts with a huge heap of 10 or 50 or 100 applications, each saying that the applicant wants the job, it is easy to forget that good candidates have choices, too. You don't just choose them; they must choose you.

On the individual, personal level, there needs to be a good fit between the candidate and the institution. The person will be moving their work life to that college, and may be moving their personal life to the community. A lot of matching and adjustment must be done beyond simply marking whether someone has claimed to have and can reasonably prove the existence of the job qualifications listed in the advertisement.

How can the library director and others help with this matching process? How can they find out about personal preferences, soft qualities, and the fit with the whole campus culture? Forbidden questions remain forbidden, but talking is not outlawed. When library or campus employees talk about their personal lives in between meetings and during tours ("Most people think this area has the best schools; my children go to the charter school across town"), they provide information and send cultural signals without putting the candidate on the spot.

The more geographically isolated the college and the more distinctive the local and campus cultures are, the more important this is. Tell a candidate about how you travel to the big city for theater or enjoy community theater. Chat about when students are invited to their professors' homes or how holiday parties are organized. What community projects are library staff involved in? Talk about how you met people in town when you were new to the area, or about how people drive or fly to get to conferences or to visit extended family. These topics will provide the candidates with information about what their lives might be like if they accept the position.

People will stay in a job because they need it and can't get another, or because that job and the whole situation meets their needs. It is worth the effort to provide as much information as possible about local and cultural aspects. Interviewing is expensive and exhausting for both candidate and college, and the best technical ability on the part of new librarians won't help if they leave after a year.

INTERNAL CANDIDATES

Sometimes there are internal or known candidates for a position. This category consists of people who are already working on the campus or who are known to those who work there. Examples include a reference librarian applying for the director position when the current director retires, a human resources clerk desiring to become a library circulation clerk, or the wife of the newly hired director of college development seeking a position, hopefully with an MLS and years of experience!

In some organizations, especially public colleges and especially those with unions, it is expected that all openings will be posted and available for internal applicants before any external search is made. At others, the openings are public and available on the same conditions to both internal and external candidates. And in small institutions, sometimes position openings and hiring may not follow any visible procedure at all. In these cases, what should be done with candidates who are already known to the library or to the campus?

This is not about changes to the positions of people already in the library. Library staff both professional and support are almost constantly adjusting their responsibilities, and from time to time, their positions will be formally reviewed or reclassified. That is covered in the personnel-development planning chapters. Here the question is an *open* position.

An internal candidate for an open position presents a very delicate situation because it is by definition personal, very literally, as it relates to a known person. Every bit of the bureaucratic, impersonal, rules-based approach to filling a position is colored by the human being involved. Things change even if the library consciously decides to proceed with a standardized format and a competitive search because a decision to *not* consider personal contacts is a decision itself, with its own consequences.

Many different kinds of internal or non-standard applicants may apply with a range of unqualified, minimally qualified, qualified and competitive, and so qualified you are lucky to get them. A shortsighted, tactical approach to the situation would be to proceed according to the characteristics of that individual at that point. If a candidate is unqualified, insist on a standard procedure that will thankfully and inevitably weed out this person. If this person is minimally or adequately qualified, think about whether it is likely that outsiders would be more qualified, and weigh that against the cost of simply hiring the available qualified person. If the person is highly qualified, hire immediately and consider the library to be lucky.

The problem is that only one of these options really works in the long run, that of following standard, competitive procedures. In one instance, someone is clearly outstanding and can be hired with confidence, even without looking at any other candidates. But nobody can count on that happy situation to happen every time an internal candidate is presented. And then the library director will have lost his or her best argument for imposing standard procedures that will weed out unsuitable candidates. That is the normal process.

It is best to treat all internal candidates in no way different from external candidates, with an open, competitive search. This has support in all three organizational perspectives.

From a bureaucratic perspective, following a set, standard procedure means legal and ethical consistency in personnel decisions. Affirmative action and equal employment opportunity-monitoring personnel will be best pleased with a process in which all applicants, internal and external, are treated according to established norms rather than an ad hoc "just for you" preference. Procedures are rigid, but they will not inconvenience the truly qualified person. They will impersonally weed out the unqualified internal applicants along with the weak external applicants. Consistently relying on a bureaucratic sequence will avoid a very difficult attempt to suddenly put it into place when a particular internal or known candidate appears.

Politically speaking, it can seem that hiring someone known or desirable to someone already on campus, such as the semi-mythical dean's wife, might be considered a smart move. However, this fades when taking a close look at the essential interest group orientation of the political perspective. Who fills positions based on personal connections? Everybody? Or only positions seen as peripheral? Do new deans' spouses get positions in admissions or development? Are they put into tenure-track faculty positions? The library director should try to match the practices used for faculty and senior administrative searches. To bend in an attempt to please one individual might secure that one person's gratitude, but in the long run, it would portray the library as a convenient parking place for people the administration wants to appease or to shuffle out of the way.

Finally, looking at the situation from the human resources perspective shows the value of an impersonal procedure from the point of view of the applicant. It's true that most human beings would really just love to be hired without any of the preparation, labor, and anxiety of applying and interviewing. But in the longer run and larger context, when internal candidates go through a truly standard and competitive process, they can begin the job confident that they were truly the best candidate and that their future colleagues have tested and now trust them.

Some objections to a competitive search may surface when an internal candidate is available that the director should be prepared to handle.

- Internal-only searches are less expensive in time and effort. This is one reason why some organizations always start searches internally. In this case, the director should be prepared to argue, if true, that important positions are never solely filled internally: new faculty, new senior professionals, and new administrators.
- Qualified people may be difficult to attract; this person is qualified. The more specialized the institution, the more common this will be. Like barnacles, painful memories of past failed searches may clog campus administrators' minds. They may not be as optimistic as a library director might be about the ability to attract outside applicants. This can be especially difficult for institutions with significant religious employment requirements or that are physically remote. One problem with using the "we can't attract" people argument is that it sometimes is used as a cover for other issues, such as salaries that are not competitive. The library director would be wiser to probe into why qualified outsiders are not attracted than to give up on having an open search. The library job market is open enough that it is generally not realistic to suppose that no outsider wants to work at a given academic library.
- An outsider might not stay; the insider already knows and accepts whatever the local situation is. This can be very tempting, but a good interview process should alert any candidate to the major issues in working at that library and living in that place; and the library should be conducting good interviews. It is generally considered a bad idea for an academic department to be too inbred, and for any organization to hire only from a narrow pool. Diversity in preparation and background will strengthen the library as a whole.
- X important person wants this to happen. . . . This is normal. . . . This is important to make Y happy.

All of these can certainly happen. This might be more common at small institutions, but it is not unknown at larger ones, especially in the classic case of the trailing-spouse issue. The problem is that while a hire in this situation might immediately make a particular person happy, it too easily can put an under-qualified person and the library staff in a very difficult situation. The basic decisions the library director needs to make are: Is this spousal hire or internal preference truly normal for this campus? If it is not, then the library is being singled out, and that is never a good situation. Will the person who wants this to happen continue to care about it, particularly after the first few months? Maybe not in the case of the "important person"; maybe so in the case of the spouse elsewhere on campus.

If library directors decide on an internal, non-competitive hire, they should immediately ensure that the person hired becomes a normal part of the library with normal expectations for job performance and also a normal path for development at the staff or faculty level. All library staff members have areas of strength or weakness. Any weaknesses in a new hire should be addressed through the normal way that the library develops its staff.

The internal candidate situation has multiple red flags; but the internal candidate can also be the culmination of a managerial success story, especially when an existing staff person has grown out of one position and truly is qualified for a higher position. The best human-oriented personnel development will help each employee grow and improve; and it should be the rule, more than the exception, that library staff should become truly qualified candidates for higher or better positions in the library and elsewhere on campus. If they are truly competitive, then they will be successful in an open search and then confident of their fit with the new position.

MAKING A DECISION

Write the ad, distribute the ad, review applications, and identify and interview the top candidates. That is how you add good people to your staff. If you do it right. Or if you do it well. Or even if you don't do it well, but things turn out well or badly depending on circumstances on the campus, in the local economy, and in people's lives.

This chapter so far has described important steps, essential considerations, and useful perspectives when considering both how to structure the process and issues involved in each step. They range from the pragmatic yet vital tip to nail down meeting times to reviewing how the involvement of different units or people on campus affects how the library is viewed within the academic ecology.

Finally, the decision points come. Is there a suitable (even exciting) candidate? Are there multiple suitable candidates? Does the search need to begin again? Will a chosen candidate agree to come? At the end of the process, whether the small college library has one, multiple, or no suitable people they would be comfortable hiring depends on the characteristics of the position, the availability of candidates, and a very nebulous but real "risk" factor.

If advertising is reasonably widely distributed and yet produces a very small number of qualified candidates, fewer than 10 for an entry-level position, this result should be interpreted as a sign that there are problems with the position itself. The library director needs to rethink the job and the phrasing, and the phrasing and the job. What does the library director really need and want in this position? Does the ad wording accurately reflect it? If it does, maybe its wants are unrealistic. Does the ad wording make some stipulations that are really not as important as more basic responsibilities?

Here a small library can often be in a better position than a large university library. In a university library, there will, from time to time, be very specific and narrow needs: a music librarian, an expert in preservation, a law librarian with a JD. The small college library will often use generalists. Those aspects of academic librarianship that are exciting and new and technical and cutting edge are also things that both now and in the future will become part of an ordinary generalist librarian's repertoire. Working with database vendors is now a routine assignment. Designing instruction for distant students is no longer the province of specialists. Thinking about digitizing special materials? Again, this is something that is moving into the mainstream. Someone who is a generalist and is capable of learning can do these. Ad wording that is too specific can discourage capable generalists.

Candidates also will be more or less available for reasons entirely out of the control of the library itself. If a campus has specific denominational requirements, that limits the qualified pool. Whether the campus is unionized (or not) may attract or deter certain applicants. Geographic isolation, or being in the middle of a busy metropolis, again has effects on the desirability of a position. Here, the library director would be wise to work closely with the human resources people. They will be very familiar with these general issues and will help as much as possible with attracting candidates who are compatible with the college's situation.

The economy will have a huge effect. If there are many library positions open, the small college may have difficulty competing; if there are few, the library is in a very desirable position, an employer's market. This will be seen immediately at the support staff level. Any turnover in support staff represents an opportunity to attract very qualified candidates who may be without a job through no deficiency on their part.

The length of professional library education complicates the match between labor supply and demand, usually producing a gap between economic conditions and candidate pool size. In a recession, college graduates both recent and those laid off often turn to graduate education both to increase their credentials and to wait out a slow hiring time. If the economy improves before they finish, library directors are in the happy position of having improved finances on their own part and then having a relatively large pool of candidates from which to select.

Risk comes into the final decision between two or more qualified candidates. Deciding between alternative candidates usually depends on a combination of their personal qualities (initiative, spark, seeming to fit with cultural expectations, ability to learn, curiosity in questions, creativity in answers, and diligence shown in preparing for the interview) and their formal qualifications, such as a second master's degree, undergraduate or graduate training in a specific desired area, or particular types of experience. It is impossible to predict or to advise here about the relative weights of these factors.

Two major errors should be avoided. One is an unconscious, or at least unacknowledged, error. One is connected to the issue of risk.

One situation that is often reported on after the fact is for a hiring committee to be intimidated by or to subconsciously avoid someone who seems too qualified. It can be as blatant as simply not wanting to hire someone who will make existing librarians or staff look weak in comparison. This is difficult to detect and few will admit to it as it is happening. A more open form of this is wondering whether someone is overqualified. It becomes an easy and acceptable excuse because overqualification does happen, especially in a weak economy where people may take jobs they don't really want and will leave as soon as they can.

The director needs to be very self-aware and try to guide everyone to see the benefits of hiring a really outstanding person. Maybe that person will outshine existing librarians, but maybe his or her light will reflect well on the library as a whole. The image of a library on campus generally depends on how well each librarian is perceived, not by colleagues, but by others. The better the librarians hired, the better the library will look.

The other error is a belief or feeling that the person is too different. Much of this book reflects on the importance of campus culture in a small college. A lot of warnings have been provided about how someone needs to accept being part of the peculiarities of that particular small college ecology, which is in fact a very concentrated and inward-looking small town. But the desire to identify people who fit in can lead to not seeing the benefits that someone who is different can bring.

Diversity exists in many forms and reaches beyond the general categories of ethnicity or other protected classes. Intellectual, political, and aesthetic diversity also exist. Age, digital comfort levels, and educational backgrounds also vary. Because a library needs to serve an entire campus and also because a library is a place where the diversity of human knowledge is provided to users, it really needs a proactive stance toward diversity in individuals. A candidate who seems different in some way can be a more creative and fruitful addition to the staff than someone who seems just like the existing staff, who fits right in, and who might enable the library to stay just the same as it always has been, which is not a good idea.

Risk. Is this person perfect? Is this person right? Do you know? Do you hire only someone whom you *know* will be successful? Deciding between candidates who have it all, and then some, who are creative and intelligent and have everything you've asked for, is easy. If the final pool consists of people who have this or that shortcoming or lack of preparation or seeming mismatch, is that a reason to reject them? Sometimes it is; but sometimes, especially in a college without huge applicant pools, the director of the institution needs to think about the virtues of taking a risk: not hiring someone who cannot do the job, but hiring someone who should be able to but you are not yet sure about.

> **Story**: A small college in a plains state stated to a job applicant in an interview, "We know that some people will leave us in three years. We feel that that is our contribution to the profession as a whole."
>
> Another college, in a metropolitan area and with a religious affiliation, stated that if someone who had been hired failed to perform as expected, it was the college's fault. They had not hired well, and they were obligated to keep that employee.

For example, job ads that stipulate three years of experience are an attempt to eliminate risk. Colleges want to see a successful track record. Librarians should remember their own frustration with these sorts of ads when they graduated with a shiny new MLS. They knew they could be good librarians, but who would give them a chance?

The flip side of taking a chance is the necessity of having a hard-hearted determination to set reasonable expectations, provide appropriate assistance, and then assess whether it is indeed working out. Chances don't always pan out; the nature of risk is that sometimes there are failures. That is a hard and difficult thing to contemplate. It is worth contemplating, it is worth taking a risk, because risks have upsides as well. Harvard doesn't take risks; most of its junior faculty are only temporary and senior faculty are recruited after they've proven themselves elsewhere. Other rich and prestigious institutions can get by with this, but that's not the case at all small colleges. For the small college with a small budget and less attractive location, taking a chance can be a key way to get really good people whom larger institutions had the luxury of screening out of their larger candidate pools.

The final step is to make the offer and have someone acceptable accept it. Prior to making an offer, it is wise, as noted above, to educate applicants about how long the process is likely to take. Too many stories are floating around about companies who simply never respond to applicants. To not receive a response means to be rejected, but in an academic search, someone could be a viable candidate and still have to wait weeks and even months.

A library is in both a better and a worse position than academic departments. Hiring classroom faculty is strongly conditioned by the academic year cycle, with most decisions made in spring for fall starts. A faculty candidate who isn't in place when the semester starts is someone who has been skipped for a season or a year. Libraries can be more flexible; librarians can start any time of the year. If possible, they should try to be more nimble. This can present a comparative advantage in a contest between institutions for good librarians. If a small college can make a decision sooner than a large university, it may secure someone who the university really intended to get around to at some point. If the library is following faculty hiring procedures and working with people mainly in the faculty area (deans/provosts), the director may need to be proactive in urging a quicker decision process than the other participants may be used to.

In the end, someone who can be successful in the position joins the library. This is not an ending, a comfortable "now that's taken care of" point to fill existing needs with new labor. No, now the real process begins. The person has to become used to his position, to the library, and to the campus. This will take weeks for a staff person and months for a professional librarian. And then, the future is ahead. The hiring mindset cannot become fixated on a particular job description or needs and an at-this-time fit. Libraries change, or should, and librarians and support staff will change, or will let their institutions wither. Personnel development creates the ongoing library of the future.

NOTE

1. Applegate, Rachel. "Job Ads, Jobs, and Researchers: Searching for Valid Sources." *Library & Information Science Research* 32 (2009): 163–70.

5 PERSONNEL EVALUATION AND DEVELOPMENT

The key: The position description: keeping it accurate, evaluating against it, and keeping the person and position moving forward

Hiring a new employee is exciting. Someone new adds a new dynamic and (most of the time!) new ideas; but you can't wait to have new ideas only when there are new people. Day to day, year to year, the good library director and good librarians bring in and implement new ideas and new directions, and all this happens with existing staff. Existing staff will change in themselves and in reaction to changes in the library, on campus, and in the environment. Change is not something to learn to "deal" with; it is the water everyone swims in, the air that everyone breathes. Even a decision to resist a given change is a reaction to it. Someone who becomes ossified, who retreats, who rejects, has changed in reaction to demands and developments.

The good library director helps the library change for the better. It becomes more responsive, more valuable, more informative, and deeper in resources. It changes with the better when new ideas are incorporated and new teaching methods are adapted for ever-new students and new technology. It changes for the better when it leads change, as good librarians come up with the best new ways to help their constituents.

This chapter on personnel development goes through the processes in employees' professional lives that the manager shepherds:

- Learning opportunities do take place on the fly, but in development, the focus is on formal learning, which the manager needs to arrange.
- In periodic personnel evaluation, manager and employee communicate about expectations, address problems, and plan for the future.
- Retention or firing decisions are the ultimate evaluation of how someone is doing overall.
- Student workers make up a significant part of the labor force of an academic library and need special consideration when it comes to development and retention.

This chapter presents the concepts in generic terms that most of the time apply best to support staff, not to faculty librarians or to student workers. Personnel development, evaluation, and retention are roughly similar for librarians who are considered administrative staff, and the general guidance here will apply. A separate section at the end covers student workers. The processes involved in faculty contracts, review, and tenure decisions are so different from staff processes that they are discussed in a separate chapter. Throughout, however, the most important principle is that good managers communicate frequently, clearly, and constructively with everyone they supervise, something that applies across all employee types.

Two of the three perspectives on organizations are particularly relevant to this chapter: bureaucratic and human resources. Briefly, bureaucracy means a set of processes, formalized expectations, explicit measurements, and rationally selected consequences that are framed in impersonal terms and relate to specific static job functions. The strength of this approach is that it is intensely work-related and consistently avoids favoritism and position-creep, in which what people do changes so much over time that they end up spending the majority of their time on responsibilities that appear nowhere in their position descriptions. The human resources perspective focuses on how individuals interact with their job responsibilities and how they perceive and fulfill those responsibilities in relation to their individual perspectives. It views workers as complete humans who have their own individual goals and challenges. The strength of this approach is that it understands and even encourages personal growth, which in itself helps keep the organization relevant and not stuck in antique formulas.

A political perspective is primarily group-oriented. Some elements of small college library life relate to groups on campus. For example, many individual support staff will compare their own situations to those of similar staff elsewhere on campus. Formal staff councils or other groups may provide a voice for people outside of their hierarchical reporting lines. These features are relatively limited by size. A large library develops a culture of its own, dividing into subgroups. In the small college library, people are more isolated as individuals because they tend to have somewhat unique duties and roles. In some ways, professional librarians can more easily form a group of peers than can support staff. MLS-educated librarians are roughly similar to one an other in many ways. The support staff who make up approximately half to two-thirds of a small library's staff may differ from one an other far more than the MLS librarians, and so each individual may be more isolated.

Remember that the term "support staff" is used for permanent non-student workers who do not have an MLS degree. In a small library, most or all support staff will be considered "hourly," not salaried or "exempt" employees. In the small library, most supervisory or professional duties are handled by librarians, and there is often no opportunity for support staff to occupy salaried positions in the library. Librarians who are not considered faculty will generally be classified as salaried/professional/administrative (exempt) staff. This classification may apply to all librarians or only to some, such as technical-services librarians.

SUPPORT-STAFF DEVELOPMENT

Three considerations should be noted when planning for professional development: what is offered on campus, library-specific needs (especially for changing technology), and employee motivation. A good library director will take a thoughtful, deliberate approach in planning for staff development, budgeting time and direct expenses, and considering personnel development's impact on filling and changing library positions. Thinking long term is important, since there will not be enough money or staff free time for everyone to receive development at every opportunity.

On-Campus Professional Development

What development is considered usual, customary, and necessary for staff on a particular campus? Much of this depends on either job titles or formal classifications or levels, such as "administrative assistant I" or "office manager" or "clerk." Even in smaller and less formal colleges that don't use an across-campus structure for classifying hourly personnel, there are usually some jobs that are considered similar to each other and also some competencies that cross over, applying to all or a large number of people. These can range from procedural training for those who supervise student workers to education in the mission, history, and stated values of a particular college.

It is important that library support staff take part in these. It will help both the employees themselves and the library as an organization. Cross-campus training helps library employees see their own tasks and roles within a larger context. This is especially important for public-service expectations: one of the strong marketing advantages of a small college is a personal approach to students, staff, and visitors. Participating in technical skills training, such as general database use or the campus's academic budgeting or student-information systems, gives library employees contacts across campus. The acquisitions clerk at the library may have no one else in the library who accesses the purchasing system but, through shared training experiences, the clerk can communicate with people in purchasing or other departments.

The library benefits in one obvious way and in other, more subtle ways. The direct bureaucratic advantage comes from staffers who improve their skills at a relatively low cost. On a human level, allowing library employees be able to take advantage of resources equally with their peers in other units helps reinforce the idea that they are valued members of the college community. From that external point of view, having library people participate in training in which they describe what it is they do helps people at their level in other departments, the trainers, and those in the human resources department understand better what goes on in the library, with its specific and often quite technical demands on hourly staff.

> **Story**: A teenager says to someone in library school: "Oh, that's probably a pretty quiet job, good after you're retired, so you can just read and shelve books." Many people may not realize that, except to help out at peak times, neither librarians nor, in general, support staff spend their time shelving books. Most academic libraries use student workers or sometimes people with developmental disabilities to perform routine tasks; routine tasks are a very small part of librarians or support-staff duties.

Two mistakes can cause library directors to miss this opportunity. First, they may not know about general staff training opportunities, especially if they are new. Also, library staff may not have participated in the past. Such training on this small and less formal campus may be going on, but nobody informs the library about it. It is important to be proactive in seeking out opportunities and even creating them. The HR department may not realize there are needs that are not being met. The starting point is group staff-level general orientation for new employees, but it should not end there. Both experienced and newer staff after their first year usually will have developed needs that campus training can meet. This is true even on a small campus.

The other error is imagining that non-library training is not relevant. A library is a special place and definitely has specialized demands and tasks. However, there are a number of staff-development areas that are common across campus, such as interpersonal skills with regards to customer service. Because most staff, no matter how technical their position, interact informally with prospective students, parents, and community members, all can benefit from in-depth orientation to a particular institution's history, mission, and current characteristics, including how to refer people to appropriate offices. Information technology in terms of updated office productivity programs as well as campus student or budgeting systems is constantly evolving.

Each small library needs to budget for these in-house staff-development opportunities. The budget involves costs in terms of time (absence from the library) and (rarely) direct training fees. The library should take advantage of an appropriate share of "seats" available in college-provided training. It also needs an equal share of campus funding provided for off-campus development.

The major cost for campus training is time. This is particularly important since the small library doesn't have redundancy with overlapping responsibilities or coverage among support staff. For staff whose tasks can be postponed, the director needs to ensure that this is accepted with no penalty, avoiding sending the message "you still have to get your work done" even if you've lost a day to training. Budgeting training time is part of setting expectations for the quantity of work done. For service providers, the director and other professional librarians will need to fill in for support staff. This is something that is good for several reasons. Filling in helps professionals, particularly supervisors and the director, get a good look at how frontline jobs are performed. It also is a tangible way of demonstrating that the librarians not only understand but value the staff and support their development.

It is important to remind campus trainers to schedule opportunities at times when library staff can benefit. The library has more extensive hours than many other services on campus. An evening or weekend staffer may have just as much need for training as someone who works only within a conventional nine-to-five framework. The crunch times for the library are often different from other departments, too: student affairs is busy at the beginning of a semester, library at the end; admissions in the spring, library in the fall.

Library-Specific Professional Development

Library work comes with very specific development needs. Technology changes, proliferates, and subdivides. That technological marvel, the card catalog, was far more uniform across academic libraries than any of its successor systems. Each library uses a particular system for representing information, for providing access, and for communicating with its populations only until it is replaced with something that is hoped to be better, and definitely is different.

This affects support staff as much or even more, on a daily basis, than professional librarians. The library houses technology for patrons to use. Staff use technology in back offices and design and deliver technological tools for information retrieval. Anywhere in the small college library building any library person, staff or professional, might have to field basic questions from passing students such as "Why won't this print," "Why doesn't cut and paste work," and "Google doesn't tell me where this book is." In the technical-services office, virtually all functions behind the scenes of the modern library depend on very specialized software. Even for patron interfaces, staff support reference librarians in maintaining Web pages and other patron tools.

These specialized needs may not be obvious to people outside of the library. Assisting students in a computer lab is likely to be the only one that is readily recognizable. At one time, organizing information-technology (IT) consultation and assistance was a prime area in which the library director needed to negotiate with campus IT services for its associated computer labs. Whether there are paid computer assistants or student workers onsite in the library and whether they are hired, trained, or supervised by the library staff or campus IT was an acute question that is still being wrestled with at large institutions. In the smaller college, the spread of basic skills among all students and among staff means that dedicated staff may not be an issue for much longer.

Non-generic, library-specific systems will be more foreign to non-library administrators, but for better or worse, the mystique that still surrounds information technology will be an advantage. Campus administrators who are accustomed to paying high fees for student and accounting systems (PeopleSoft, Banner, SCT, etc.) will not find paying automation fees strange, and when they cope with the complexities of their own systems will generally agree that the library technical infrastructure comes with training needs for staff. The library director needs to place library-training needs in the context of general information-technology changes and developments.

> **Story**: A library-school intern at a small college library set up a specialized page as a guide to resources for a special student-support office on campus. Her supervisor declined to pay $120 a year for a dedicated Web site so the page had to display the advertising that was placed there by the free site.

Professional development on technical issues can take formal and informal forms. Listservs, blogs, discussion boards, and company Web sites do a lot to keep people informed of issues as they arise. A library director needs to emphasize to employees that spending time reading these sources is appropriate; it is part of the job, not a distraction from it. To focus staff attention, having an internal way of sharing things read, an internal wiki, group e-mails, or a day each week to get together to chat focuses staff attention and reinforces the importance of keeping up.

Formal training will be available through system vendors and through local, regional, and national user organizations, from library consortia or network partners to WebJunction and any other librarian-organized venues. Online learning is valuable, but in-person meetings can also be especially useful. In-person workshops are ways to meet with others who work with the same systems or who have the same problems. That is a problem for people working in small libraries. They do not have colleagues or co-workers on-campus, so it is even more important to connect with their peers elsewhere.

Employee Motivation and Personal Development

Professional development has a role in employee motivation. How do individuals feel about their own job, about how it might change, and about what kinds of changes they want to make? How does training and education and development fit into what these people view as the future for their job and role? Thinking about this usually is formalized within the periodic performance review (annual evaluation), but it is part of every professional-development opportunity, whether taken or not.

Some people value their library positions for their stability. They may see themselves remaining in a particular position or role and don't envision much change, not a change in careers and not much change in their jobs. At the support-staff level (not the librarian level!), that desire for steady expectations and responsibilities is acceptable *if* it also comes with an understanding that any job and any role will change with technology and changes in student learning and library resources. Doing the exact same tasks does not work out in the long run. Even when staff members have no ambitions for a higher level or classification, they have to accept that ongoing development is necessary for working in a library.

Other library staff are not committed to a particular position or job. They view their positions as entry level and look forward to moving onward and upward, proceeding up a career path. This situation has benefits and challenges in the small college library and on the small college campus. "Small" means that there are relatively few opportunities for promotion within the library or even elsewhere on campus; simultaneously, "college" means that there are a wealth of opportunities for further education. A supervisor can encourage development for all employees in three contexts: the specific technical, job-oriented level; preparation for other jobs; and career development that goes beyond the library.

First, whether people are staying or are moving on, they need to keep up with skills relevant to their current positions.

As described above, these include cross-campus competencies such as communication, technology, and public service, as well as library-specific training. It is self-defeating and damaging to the welfare of the library in the long run for library directors in general to be hesitant in supporting training based on a belief that a particular employee is bound to leave the organization. Employees will bring the benefits of training back to the library while they work there; even if they leave, the library benefits. It benefits because it becomes known as a place that nurtures its staff.

Library directors also need to consider if their own staff will be able to move on to and up to other positions, internally or elsewhere on campus. Whether this can happen will be affected strongly by two things: the characteristics of the existing library staff and campus personnel policy.

A small library has few employee positions, which makes for very short career ladders under any circumstance. Some libraries may have senior employees who are near retirement. This can inspire other staff members to think about moving into those positions. Will they be ready, or will they have been so consumed with their current daily responsibilities that they are not prepared to move up? Just as with current-needs training, development that allows someone to stretch does indeed benefit the library, both immediately and in the long run.

Personnel policy refers to a situation on some campuses that allows for within-position "ranks," with titles such as junior or senior, assistant or associate, I, II, or III. These are especially useful in motivating people when changing to a different job with a higher title or when classification is not possible for most employees. A good ranking system recognizes effort and experience and rewards enhanced skills without requiring the person to move to a different position. When this system exists, the library director can work with individuals to help them develop so as to match the expectations of the higher rankings.

The small library remains small. Movement upward through retirement or rankings is good but limited. Other opportunities for staff will involve change from the library to another unit on campus, from the small library to a larger library, or from staff to librarian.

This is especially relevant to any staff who work at a college. Tuition remission, the opportunity to take college classes at little or no cost, is one of the primary benefits that most educational institutions, private or public, offer their employees. This is a very low-cost way to attract and retain employees; it often is a strong compensation for salaries that are lower than those in business and for-profit organizations.

With tuition remission, a person who starts working at the library with a high school education can gradually achieve a bachelor's degree. The long-term issue is that at that point, they are overqualified for the job in which they started. This is the flip side of professional development when it provides personal not professional development that benefits the individual but not the organization, at least not directly.

Employing someone who is overqualified for a position has drawbacks, and not just for the library. Does a college really want its undergraduates to see college graduates working as clerks? That does not send the right signal about the value of a college education or the opportunities available to graduates. Another problem comes when people want their position reclassified to reflect the new education level. That may benefit them at the moment, but does it really reflect skills and duties needed by the library?

What to do? The library director needs to work with each employee to make the best match for their personal circumstances and for the library's needs, a match not ignoring one or the other. The library director needs to be thoughtful, honest, and clear in what the expectations are for each position. It is not always possible or desirable to change a position's duties simply because the person has developed beyond them. On the other hand, the director should not discourage employees from personal development, from gaining education that qualifies them for better positions outside the library. If people do want that higher level of position, then directors can give them good recommendations and help them spread their wings. Your reputation as an encouraging employer will help you refill that position with a new high-quality employee.

That advice is good for the general support staff member who looks for a career in a variety of fields. What about library work? There, the question is how to identify the transition between support and professional work: the library director helps the library support person identify the differences between types of library workers and understands the paths that exist for progressing in the library field.

Library staff in academic libraries fall into three broad categories: general and entry-level workers, specialized paraprofessionals, and professionals. Entry-level or general workers can be hired without any library experience; they learn their library-specific duties on the job. Given appropriate professional development and on-the-job learning, they can progress into a specialized support-staff position.

Recognition of support-staff skills and experience in academic libraries is generally informal or specific to a particular campus. One method for both developing and identifying support-staff skills is certification. The American Library Association has created a voluntary but nationwide system for support-staff certification (Library Support Staff Certification, LSSC). This is a very flexible program that can be built on and incorporated into existing professional-development opportunities while providing a structure that, over a certification period, provides externally validated confirmation that a particular individual has core and specialized ability or knowledge. The core areas are foundations of librarianship, communication and teamwork, and technology; specializations relevant to academic librarianship are reference, cataloging, collection management, and supervision/management.

Some support staff want to work in, or work up to, professional positions. Here, the small college library director and librarians are in an excellent position to identify and encourage their best employees to consider moving into the professional level; online and in-person MLS programs make it physically feasible for most people. Librarians do not have to argue about the tired stereotypes of support staff who "think they know it all," or "only want to get their card punched," or "think the MLS is overrated." If a library director, the professional librarians, and the MLS program itself have a good, solid, advanced sense of the leadership, innovation, and forward-thinking aspects of their own profession, then whatever support staffers think when they begin, they will have a solid understanding of the field when they finish the program.

LIBRARIAN DEVELOPMENT

Goals for professional development for librarians start off similar to those for other staff generally. Each librarian needs to keep up with changes in library techniques and technology just to maintain a level of value to the institution: a librarian who is not learning is someone who is falling behind.

Each of the organizational theories applies to librarian development. Improved skills is a rational, bureaucratic, and instrumental argument for development: it helps the machine run effectively. At the professional level, moreover, librarians should be encouraged and even expected not only to learn new things, but to be leaders, to be the ones to create new ideas in addition to learning from the ideas of others. Politically, the more innovative and competent the librarians are seen to be on campus, the more respect "librarians" in general will receive. Stereotypes and assumptions can be positive (and accurate) as well as negative. Finally, most professional-level librarians did not choose librarianship just to have a job. Other jobs pay more and are easier to get. Instead, they are generally people who enjoy developing their skills and becoming more adept and proficient, the human-development perspective.

The most important factor in thinking about appropriate librarian development is whether librarians follow a framework of tenure review. The classic model for teaching faculty is a period of six years of employment during which they strive to meet institutional expectations for teaching proficiency, research productivity, and service as defined by their college. By the middle or end of the sixth year, a decision is made as to whether the person is suitable for indefinite employment. The common phrase is a "seven-year clock." However, in most cases, people who are not awarded tenure are notified during the spring of their sixth year and then have a seventh year of employment during which they can seek another position for the following year.

Development for librarians who fall into this tenure framework is discussed in the section on faculty status. It changes the dynamic considerably. Impending tenure review generally is stronger at encouraging development prior to the award of tenure and weaker afterward. This section will concentrate on librarians who are considered to have academic, not faculty, status.[1]

Support-staff development can be considered on a very individual and ad hoc basis, adapting to the experience of each individual, their own goals, and where the library is developing needs. This is especially true at the small college. Again, each library support staff person at the small college is usually a group of "one," the only person holding a particular position. Moreover, even though support staff often have great longevity at an institution, there is more of a sense of long-term commitment with salaried people and with faculty than with hourly employees.

Librarians make up something of a homogeneous group. The MLS provides a reasonably similar background for all of them. Except for specialized technical-services librarians, most librarians in a small library have roughly similar roles. Therefore, it is useful to think in a more structured way about their development. Long-term librarian development passes through three phases: the first year, a middle period, and a senior period.

First year. For most hourly and some salaried positions, one month or six months are considered sufficient trial periods in which to orient someone to a job and to evaluate them to see if they are really working out. In contrast, professional positions are by definition complex enough and their hiring processes expensive and extensive enough to make an academic or calendar year a better fit. A year is necessary for the new librarian to fit in and become a fully capable professional. It is important in this early phase for the director to ensure that a new librarian is oriented to the campus as well as to the library and to any specific responsibilities.

Formal or informal mentoring is useful. Library directors may need to think creatively here. In the small library, it can be a little too easy to assume that wise, experienced directors are able to provide all of the mentoring necessary, and of course they have specific responsibilities for some of it. It is also easy to assume that the close working relations with the rest of the small group of librarians will also be sufficient. Nevertheless, in order to become as successful on campus as possible, ties outside the library are invaluable.

It would be particularly useful for librarians to be involved in new or ongoing classroom faculty orientation or training when available. While some things like student advising are very specific to teaching faculty, learning about course-management software and the mission of the institution are things that all academics, librarians included, need. Sharing the experience of new faculty training can create bonds with other people. This is possible even when librarians do not formally have faculty status. The director can point out to administrators how each specific training session or meeting (such as one on campus history, or how to relate to the new generation of students) is relevant to the new librarian's work with faculty and students. In general, faculty training is more valuable to librarians than most training for other salaried staff, which is often geared more toward supervisory responsibilities than the academic environment.

A clichéd question for interviews is "Where do you think you will be in five years?" Whether or not someone can really answer that in an interview, especially for an entry-level position and especially a new graduate, that question is very good to revisit toward the end of the first year in a new librarian position. The new librarian has spent the previous year learning about the institution, about how librarianship is really practiced, and about living in the new community. Institutional fit is very important for both sides. A year will be enough time for someone to be more knowledgeable about how he or she will fit in to the institution and the local community, or what changes or opportunities would make the fit even better.

Usually by the end of the first year, the director needs to make a decision on retaining the person. Here the director needs to consider the factors described in the section below on termination, to follow the general evaluation procedures for the librarian position/classification, and to be sure to do interim probationary evaluations on schedule, such as after one month or one semester. This is a really important checkpoint.

For personnel on longer-term contracts, such reviews are necessary to avoid renewing someone who is not suitable, and even for non-contracted at-will employees, it is still an important stage in evaluating their long-term suitability. Not renewing or not extending the contract of a relatively new person is certainly harder than not hiring the person, but much easier than trying to terminate someone later. The director really needs to be confident that the present level, at the end of the probationary period, of enthusiasm, competence, initiative, and general performance are really up to expectations. All the way through the first year, the director needs to give as much support and feedback as is reasonable, to help the person achieve perfectly satisfactory work performance. "Reasonable," because handholding and assistance and advice are needed and useful in the beginning, but the library needs librarians who can be independent.

The library needs good librarians, not just to do the work of the library, but to strengthen the position of the librarians. Even when librarians do not have faculty status, that condition might change. Faculty status can be both lost and won. Someday, the library director and staff may be able to change librarians' status from staff to faculty. If this is ever to happen, the librarians at that moment must seem to the other actors on campus, particularly the classroom faculty, to be worthy of faculty status. Keeping someone who is performing at a marginal level will inevitably damage any proposal to change, because those proposals are not just about abstract concepts. They become rooted in people's experiences of real librarians. Every real librarian conjures an image of an active or passive person; an academic or a tradesperson; a professional or a cloistered technician.

If librarians are not working out as desired, they leave when their contract or employment understanding lapses. It is expensive to research a position, and it can be dangerous to leave a position vacant for a long time. That causes extra strain on others and also might make administrators think the position is not that important. However, it is vital to emphasize that the library director and staff have, and are intent on upholding, high standards. A sufficient supply of good librarians is available, and it should be possible to refill the position without too much trouble. Keeping someone on who is a poor performer or even who is just passive or barely marginal is more damaging in the long run. A library is its staff and librarians, their quality, and its quality.

The first-year transition period is relevant whether the librarian is new or has professional experience. Even when someone has experience in a very comparable position elsewhere, there is a period of adjustment. More experienced persons need something the entry-level person does not, to learn what from their past is or is not valid and useful in the new situation. Someone with experience elsewhere can be a very invigorating addition to a library staff: new ideas, new comparisons of your troubles with troubles elsewhere, and built-in, full-time, cross-institutional networking! There is a balance here: some experiences and suggestions will be valuable, but others will be based on different cultures and resources that make them inappropriate in the new situation. In other words, experienced people need to learn and unlearn, to teach and to listen, to share the good and new, and to let go of what does not fit in the new situation.

New librarians who have extensive non-professional experience are in a similar situation and an even more difficult position when it comes to unlearning. They should be able to master systems and procedures more rapidly than someone new to the field as they understand libraries, although this varies depending on their previous staff position. If they are from a larger library and had specialized duties, they may not be as familiar with the entirety of the library as people in small libraries must be. Then, through the MLS program and crucially in this first year, they need to learn the nature of a professional-level approach to responsibilities. It is easy to stray in two directions, to assume that the MLS means merely a better title and pay ("I already was as skilled as they are. I just needed the credential."), or to assume that being an MLS means avoiding non-professional tasks. In the small library, people need both to pitch in and to be confident about rather than defensive of their professional status.

Middle period. The middle phase lasts from roughly after the first year up to about the fifth year. What makes this period distinct? It is not a coincidence that it corresponds roughly to the probation periods used for faculty, for licensing periods, for lawyers and accountants heading toward partnerships, and even for doctors in residencies. An extended period of development allows the new, adequately skilled librarian to become the fully proficient librarian. The MLS program imparts skills and knowledge about librarianship generally; the first year teaches the person about the institution and library. In the second through fifth years, the librarian builds on those bases.

It is important to keep building. In surveys, some of the lowest levels of interest in professional-development activities are from librarians in the first to fifth years of service.[2] Possibly they believe that they already know what they need to know, and it is only after five years that they begin to perceive a looming sense of obsolete skills or that change is "dangerous."

It is best for the library manager to be proactive about this period. A tenure-review system will motivate probationary librarians to accumulate evidence of professional development in order to make their case for tenure. In the absence of the timing framework of tenure review, it is primarily up to library directors to encourage, to enforce, and to be open to development activity on the part of the new librarian.

Encouragement and enforcement can come in two ways, informal and formal. "Informal" is a somewhat inaccurate phrase. By this is meant a general daily appreciation of professional development and encouragement by the director on a personal basis with each librarian. It can involve something as simple as mentioning interesting Listservs or blogs, or expecting librarians to regularly share (and therefore find out) something new in their areas. It also means organizing staffing and budgeting to allow for attendance at local, state, and even national groups and conferences, making them possible for the library staff as a whole and also conveying the idea that they are important.

Formal encouragement and enforcement can also take place during annual performance reviews. This bureaucratic procedure is taken more or less seriously on different campuses, and more or less seriously by library directors and other department heads. Even if support staff or other clerical employees on campus are reviewed, reviews may be more loosely enforced for salaried professionals. But at its best, the review is an annual checkup in which a director and librarian talk about ideas and plans for personal professional growth in the context of goals and objectives, present and future, for themselves and the library. "Enforcement" comes from seriously evaluating the employee on real professional-development progress. "Encouragement" needs to be tied to real resources. It will not do much good to say, "You should," without understanding how that is to be made possible.

During this early professional period, the entry-level librarian should develop a habit of professional development that will last. When faculty face tenure review, they are expected to have demonstrated "trajectories," track records that not only prove the substance of activities for the past several years, but promise more of the same. Professional development for librarians is essential because information and the ways it is organized, stored, and mediated for users are in constant flux.

The already-experienced hire and the hire with preprofessional experience should not be neglected with respect to development opportunities. The worst situation would be where either of them, especially if they did limited professional development in a previous position and perhaps, specifically, because they came to the present job with knowledge and experience, now believe that they are fine without the need to add development activity. This is not at all inevitable. Even if they did little professional development in the past, these experienced people can now be grateful, pleased, and eager to take advantage of what a new situation should offer them.

All of the above was primarily expressed in terms of what library directors can do to or with or for employees. Equally important is how library directors respond to initiatives coming from librarians. New librarians routinely complain that management does not address their needs (very contented librarians are seldom heard from). Sometimes this is phrased in a sort of generational or intergenerational inevitability. Managers do not understand Generation X, or older people do not understand younger people.

Five-year plans: In Soviet countries, five-year plans were the norm, and because they were top-down and took no account of input from consumers or citizens, they were rigid and ultimately unsuccessful. Some personnel-evaluation procedures involve five-year goals. Some people may indeed have definite ideas: I will be the director of a library, I will be a department head at a research university, I will get a second master's degree. Others simply don't know enough. They know enough to know they want to be librarians, but they need experience to know what future experiences could be. Hopefully, many of these and others are in a third category: people who know they cannot know, that the future is changing and that therefore they need to be aware of possibilities as they develop, and that the only really wrong answer is, "what I am doing now," where "doing" is very specific and settled.

When these complaints are based on structures ("I'm in a very junior position and nobody listens to me") and assumptions ("Nobody wants to hear what I know about new students"), they are less of a problem in a small library. No librarian at a small library is simply a cog in the machine. Nobody can be anonymous or ignored. Every librarian matters, for good or bad. That said, it is still important for the more experienced people at the library, who hopefully are already used to listening to one an other, to listen to newcomers. However much newcomers have to learn or have to unlearn from other positions, they always have something valuable to teach and to ask about.

Therefore, library directors need not only to suggest, but to be open to suggestions. The enthusiastic, energetic librarian is a precious asset and needs to be encouraged as long as the enthusiasm is for the benefit of the library and the college. That's not hard to do; there are almost limitless possibilities for any library to interact with its users and its parent institution. Since one role of library managers is to know the larger campus context and to effectively communicate broad issues, they will be sharing those perceptions with the enthusiasts while being visibly open to the reactions and ideas of enthusiasts in return.

Middle-phase retention. If you read job advertisements for librarians, some phrases tend to crop up: "three years' experience" for the not-quite entry-level position, or "five years' experience" for a department head.

> **Story**: At a relatively small research university in a remote city in a plains state, the director of the library said she understood that new librarians might simply use the position as one in which to gain experience and thus be more qualified for more desirable positions elsewhere. She said she accepted this role in the academic library job food chain; the benefit was that she got bright and eager people who appreciated a truly entry-level opening and were confident or brave enough to move a long distance.

What this means is that it is in this early professional period that librarians think seriously about significant options for their futures. They can remember the anxious feelings when fresh from library school: so many jobs weren't open to them without that all-important experience! But now, surely those numerous openings are theirs to pick and choose from.

Will a librarian leave? How does this affect professional development?

In the most negative bureaucratic stereotype, the Dilbert-Catbert model of human resources management, a supervisor should ensure that workers are capable of being adequate in their position while not qualified for a position elsewhere, so that the library benefits from their work without worrying if they will leave. Besides not being a humane approach at all, it is self-destructive. The director so Machiavellian in that respect will almost certainly not be effective at providing a workplace that anyone would choose to work in, which itself leads to the workplace being populated by those who have no choice. Any attempt to produce "just-qualified" people will end up with unqualified people.

Happily, the reverse works. The director of a library where people truly learn, grow, and change is not only developing those who could get good jobs elsewhere. Those people have an attractive place already. The better the librarians, the better they are currently for your library, and the more likely they are to believe they are better off staying there. Even when life events inevitably lead people to leave, if librarians leave happy, then their positive word of mouth will help your future recruiting.

Senior stage. The next stage, beyond five or seven years, is when the habits of the past meet the ongoing challenges of the evolving library. The practices of the early career are still relevant. People need to continue to keep up with developments in librarianship and in academia, in methods of research, forms of information, and modes of instruction. The need for professional development becomes even more obvious.

A reward and encouragement system for long-term staff members needs to be in place so they continue to provide valuable, timely work. Especially in the small library, they may not change or be able to change their formal titles. The role of "rank" is discussed in the faculty-status section and in the support-staff position. Even in the absence of faculty status, an equivalent system can be very important for motivating and rewarding continued development.

More significant opportunities for professional and career development exist, too: advancement in education, advancement in management, and aspirations to different positions. Some librarians will be interested in pursuing additional graduate degrees. This can be done in-house, as most colleges offer free courses to their employees. That would generally be valuable for the library. Additional graduate degrees will informally enhance their status among faculty and librarians, but even more practically, they would gain an inner perspective on the graduate programs offered at the college. Learning about "student" needs would be intimate and very current. This is an attractive and low-cost employee benefit. Precisely because library hours are extensive, librarians have flexibility in scheduling so as to accommodate almost any on-campus class attendance needs.

Some may be interested in master's degrees at other colleges. The smaller the college, the less likely it is that it will offer a specific suitable program, so the librarian will look elsewhere. In that situation, time off and funding would generally be the responsibility of the librarian to arrange, whether for an across-town or online program. Even more than with the in-house program, having librarians have multiple graduate degrees (the "subject master's" degree) is generally a good thing, although not necessary at many colleges.

The most ambitious may want to pursue a doctoral degree. This could be directly supported by the library or college. That would happen most often in the case where librarians are considered faculty with the same benefits and opportunities for development support as other faculty and where the administration is interested in raising the number of faculty with doctoral degrees.[3] A librarian's request for support for doctoral education might be considered in the same pool with other faculty applicants.

Why have a doctoral degree, and which doctoral degree should be chosen? Librarians may have several choices. They could pursue a doctoral degree in the subject of an existing subject master's: a PhD in English or history or education. They could pursue one in a cross-disciplinary subject matter such as leadership or higher education, or they could pursue a doctoral degree in library science or a closely allied field such as information science or instructional technology.

Pursuing any doctoral degree at all is a significant commitment of energy and resources by librarians. Will this be a distraction from their responsibilities? A library director who values the librarians' creativity and initiative manages an attractive workplace. The human resources perspective suggests this creates a good place to work where a bureaucratic rational perspective might not see anything specifically of value for the library.

This issue has an important political dimension. When librarians have their doctoral degree, they look more like regular faculty. Even though the doctoral degree is not universal among classroom faculty, particularly at small colleges and in professional disciplines, there are always people with PhDs around, and a librarian with a PhD looks a lot more like "one of them."

In this light, librarians and their advisors or director should consider carefully *which* degrees are best to pursue, particularly with respect to non-traditional programs or formats. If the librarian is the first person on campus to have an online doctoral degree or the only one to have a doctorate in "leadership" or "change management," faculty with more traditional backgrounds may be hostile to or dismissive of the accomplishment.

This is advice similar to that given to job-seekers when they ask, "Is my online degree okay?" It depends on the degree's reputation with a specific employer, and in this situation, it depends on how that degree is viewed on campus. Degrees are by their nature shorthand. People use them as broad-brush indicators of intelligence, preparation, and experience with research. They assume that someone with X degree has roughly "X" thing. They do not individually examine each element of "X" thing. Therefore, even if to get that online doctorate someone reads broadly and critically, produces a top-quality dissertation with an extensive and important literature review, an innovative and compelling research design, extensive data and analysis with real depth, something indistinguishable from a dissertation produced at a top-10 research institution, people won't know that. They will go by the most visible thing: you have X degree from Y institution.

Therefore, *that* a librarian has a doctoral degree can usually be a good thing in enhancing librarian equality with teaching faculty. However, *what* doctoral degree a librarian has also matters.

Will the doctoral degree affect the library itself? Few library directors or their staff insist on a degree as an entry requirement. Will the content of a librarian's doctoral program or research really have an impact on the daily life of a librarian given that the normal working qualification for librarians both new and experienced is a master's degree? Yes, in several ways.

- A librarian who has a research doctoral degree will have a much better grasp of what "research" is, and that will be helpful in assisting faculty, particularly on liberal arts campuses, where research is more important for faculty. Unfortunately, some library-school students believe that "research" means "look stuff up in a library" or "find out what has been done" or possibly, "synthesize what others have written on a topic."
- A doctoral program or a specialist (post-master's) degree can be a place to acquire high-level and very current technical knowledge. This would be most applicable to programs in education, instructional technology, or library science, in other words, programs that are most closely "about" what it is that the library does.
- A doctoral program specifically in library science is a way to reconnect with or discover the depths of librarianship as a science. Doctoral programs are both broad and deep. They culminate in a dissertation that is a project representing focused attention, but also involve an extensive, critical examination of the field's past, its methodologies, and its future prospects. All this gives the librarian a deeper and fresher perspective on library practice.

A special note should be made of managerial, business, or leadership programs. These include MBA (master of business administration), MPA (master of public administration), management (such as for non-profits), and leadership. People in these sorts of programs should be deepening their knowledge of managerial skills and attributes of leadership. This would be most valuable for those aiming at managerial positions, particularly within larger libraries and in academic support units. In central academic areas (the provost or deans), "leadership" degrees are relatively few as more academic administrators have subject doctorates.

The next area for potential advancement is in management itself. Many if not most librarians are very focused on a professional path. They are librarians, they do library work, and that is the direction they wish to take. They are and remain uninterested in administrative opportunities.

> **Story**: A male librarian at a small college had to continually fend off suggestions or insinuations that he was headed for the director's position. It is true that men are overrepresented in leadership positions in academic libraries relative to the gender balance among all librarians, but it does not mean that men always want management or that women always avoid it.

Every librarian, especially on a small campus, needs to understand and appreciate his or her leadership role. Librarians represent the library, and, as professionals, they manage themselves. They are the leaders of themselves, and along with other librarians and faculty, they are part of the leadership of the institution.

But there will be those who are indeed interested in formal management and becoming a library director or head of a department themselves. A discussion in the personnel recruitment chapter specifically addresses internal candidates. That would be when a library director retires or otherwise leaves, a natural opportunity for someone to make the case to move up. The strength of that argument will depend on how proactive the internal candidate has already been on campus, how much of a collaborator, and a real cross-campus participant, as the director must be.

Most of the time, though, moving up will mean moving out. Except for the head of technical services, small libraries do not offer much in the way of career ladders; but could someone really move into an administrative position elsewhere? This gets back to the issue of whether the library should encourage staff in development that marginally benefits the library in the present but significantly benefits the staff person in moving elsewhere. Again, the same argument supports encouraging people's growth. At the moment it gives the library better people who appreciate working there; and if they move, it will create and enhance the library's good reputation. The library community can be very small when it comes to rumors.

The way to help librarians acquire managerial skills is to involve them in small steps. Besides being active on campus, this includes membership on search committees (both in the library and out), small-scale supervision (supervise at least some student workers directly), and substantial work on campus projects, such as preparing for institutional accreditation, writing major grants, or doing strategic, master, or capital-campaign planning. These involve real work, not just providing an opinion at meetings. It will quickly become apparent if the aspirant manager really can work well *with* others, a quality that translates relatively easily into working *over* others. Moreover, the librarian gains professional references outside the library, which would look very valuable to prospective employers.

The final category is aspirations to a different position. Someone who becomes ambitious at the five-year mark is probably someone with at least an idea of an upward trajectory. Someone who becomes restless or ambitious at the 15-year mark may simply have done enough. This might be more likely at the small college where most librarians have roughly the same set of responsibilities even if their format is constantly evolving.

Will a new position (excluding director) be available in the library, or does it mean a move elsewhere? For the "move" scenario, recall the advice about supporting people's personal preferences because that makes for a more motivated workforce. Sometimes radical changes are possible within the library even though it is small. When anybody retires or moves or any new position is added, any change in who is doing what, that is the time to listen to people talk about what they might like if things were different. Things *can* be different. And if nobody moves anywhere for five years, it is a good idea to have the conversation anyway.

All along, from that early career period right into "mature" librarianship, librarians have been keeping up, have been changing, and have evolved along with technology, users, and information. It may have been small and incremental, but there has been constant change. The final question is whether there is a large, revolutionary, personnel-sized change that could or should happen. "I'll be the distance librarian." "I think I can be the systems librarian and manage the institutional repository too." There may be big changes, or maybe not, but raising the idea for discussion has an invigorating effect.

Faculty status can be a change in status of a completely different sort. It does not involve different reporting structures, moving to a new institution, or having new duties. Faculty status for librarians means placing librarians, *staff at the professional level in libraries*, into the same group (for most purposes) as classroom faculty. Faculty status comes with its own trajectory of personnel development prominently in the tenure-review process, but also in expectations for levels of engagement with research or service or teaching. A primary bureaucratic argument for faculty status is that it imposes an easily understood, even if stressful and erratically applied, structure on personnel development that moreover places the impetus for improvement on the candidate.

Faculty status is discussed at length in its own chapter. Of note here is that a faculty status system can come or go. About half of academic libraries seem to have some system of faculty status, half do not, and while the proportion has not varied much over the years, the exact institutions on either side do not remain constant. Any change in this sort of status will have significant implications for personnel development, and personnel development will have significant implications for the likelihood of the change. If librarians with "academic" (non-faculty) status have been working with the most minimal expectations of academic staff for adequate professional development but nothing more, certainly no leadership role, the requirements of faculty status will seem very foreign.

An important relationship exists between the concept of faculty status and the reality of annual, daily, professional development for librarians. Some people argue that faculty status, especially when formulated in the classic "publish or perish" mode, detracts from real librarianship, diverting attention from full-fledged library practice. That argument starts out reasonably, but it is in danger of becoming a caricature of itself. The academic-status librarian can and should focus just on being a good librarian, and "good librarian" is defined as just doing one's job day to day. Instead, the Association of College and Research Libraries (ACRL) guidelines for "academic" status reflect most of the essential elements of "faculty" status, and the professional-development activities of a truly dedicated and thoughtful academic-status librarian will not be all that different from those of someone with faculty status.

The point for all librarians is to reach farther than today's needs. That benefits the library as well as the individual, whether chasing change in their own jobs, thinking about further education, dreaming of management, or considering bigger opportunities.

ANNUAL EVALUATION

In most organizations, people are scheduled to be evaluated by their supervisors on an annual basis. This book will not go into any details about forms or processes involved. No one book can be complete, accurate, and up-to-date with regard to the many forms that personnel evaluation can take. Several manuals on personnel evaluation with respect to library work are available for librarians. What is different about an academic library as compared to a public, special, or school library is that it does not independently create its own formal personnel procedures. Every academic campus will have its own procedures, policies, and customs for evaluation at all levels of personnel, including faculty.

Campuses that use merit-based pay will have especially detailed processes for evaluation. Other colleges may rule out pay distinctions entirely other than for longevity. Some may avoid serious or systematic evaluation altogether. These reflect reality for an academic library that it is part of a larger academic environment.

Rather than looking in a generic librarian manual for details, the first step is for library directors in small college libraries to educate themselves about the campus procedures and take advantage of campus training for managers. Each member of the library staff needs to be evaluated in a way compatible with or comparable to others at that level on campus.

> **Story:** Merit pay is often more an aspiration than a reality. At a small college, at one point fewer than half of managers were completing annual personnel evaluation forms. The director of human resources changed evaluation timing to spread review dates throughout the year, and also tied each supervisor's own annual merit pay evaluation to whether all subordinates had been evaluated during the previous year; managers got their own raises only when they had completed evaluations for all subordinates.

Library directors follow those procedures and add the essential details about library-specific aspects of each job. What good library directors do is to energetically pursue whatever processes do exist and create informal annual reviews even if they are not used elsewhere on campus. Being proactive, accountable, and prompt in this very central managerial responsibility brings internal and external benefits. For higher administrators, it shows directors to be dependable and responsible managers. Supervisors of library directors will appreciate not having to hound them about this chore that so many try to escape. Internally, staff can see the library director as a personal champion and a communicator because above all, evaluation means communicating, to each employee, from each employee, and up and out to the campus as a whole.

Whether or not the process is used for setting pay, annual evaluations have three main purposes: they are a systematic method of providing feedback to employees on how the supervisor thinks they are doing; they allow employees to express their own ideas about their position and plans for any personal development to their managers; and they provide important input into longer-range personnel planning.

The key elements of annual evaluation are:

- Description of responsibilities
- Evaluation of quality of performance

- Special accomplishments (or problems)
- Personal/professional plans for the next year (or more)
- Changes needed in the position's description or classification

Even though these elements can be listed separately, they all work together. The bureaucratic formality of description/evaluation interacts inevitably with the person's individual goals and what is happening with his or her position in the library.

The most important element at the beginning and end of the process is a thorough, concrete, and yet flexible position description. It is only in the context of what a staffer should be doing that you can say that this person is really doing well or badly in his or her position. Staff who have ideas about their positions should be free to discuss them with their director throughout the year, or at the least, in an annual review format. Once a year, the manager and the employee can talk about what the person actually does and needs to do. If the position description were to be created that day, what would it say?

The manager talks about, and documents, quality, quantity, and accomplishments, with the staff member's input, however that is arranged. This backward-looking process then leads to the question, "What next?" What is needed or desired for the year to come? Does "more of the same" mean the same professional development or different training for changes in the position? Does the staff member have different responsibilities because the whole job environment has changed? Five-year or strategic planning is hard. Taking a good look at the past year and thinking about one year in the future is not too difficult.

At the end of the manager-employee discussion, each should share a common understanding of how employees have been doing, what needs to be done to improve, what they can look forward to enhancing, and what other changes may be on the way. Library staff come from educational and experiential backgrounds that are different from library directors who have to communicate well, both listening and speaking, and check to be sure they are well understood.

Even after employees and supervisors agree, there is another step, that of documenting change. Minor changes in a position description need to be filed with human resources. Major changes may mean that the position needs to be reclassified. All staff positions exist at a certain level of responsibility, complexity, and pay. The library director is responsible for following through with the next step, which involves organizing agreement among human resources people and the library's administrator about the value of each position.

This has monetary consequences, and that is discussed in the budgeting chapter. However, it is a part of honest management that if the college or library really cannot afford a more-advanced position classification, then the manager and the employee really need to scale down their expectations for the position. Sometimes, a position description will be of what the library can afford, not what it might like or what its people are really capable of doing. The alternative is to run a library on people who are undercompensated for what they are asked to do.

TERMINATION

Hiring is one decision; firing is another, and it is far more painful and difficult. Even though in hiring the director rejects several, maybe dozens, of good candidates, in firing, this concerns only one. Rationally, both hiring and firing involve a fit between a person and a position. Bureaucratically, the position wins. The person fits or does not fit, is hired or is let go; but the person is a person, and this becomes personal in a way far more humanly intense than hiring. New people are still unknown; they come from a pool of candidates who are not already colleagues. Existing persons who might not be working out or not working adequately are anything but faceless, not only in the library, but on the small college campus, where people are known everywhere.

The chapter on personnel selection goes over the process and considerations involved in hiring someone for a new or newly open position. The budget and planning chapters describe the rational, impersonal procedure of reviewing positions in the case that monetary cuts are needed and layoffs are the only answer. Here in the personnel development chapter, firing does not refer to a situation in which the library is having money problems. The position still exists, but the person occupying it is not doing so to an acceptable standard.

What does "acceptable standard" mean? Good annual evaluation processes show what this means. A position is described, and someone's performance is measured against its expectations. A position description can and should include not only concrete tasks ("process books as they arrive"), but soft skills, such as "timely attendance" and "cooperation with colleagues."

Human resources policies generally build upon an existing framework for personnel evaluation when it comes to considering termination. In between annual evaluations, managers should be communicating with employees. For individual incidents or failures to do certain things, managers warn the employees about the problem with that situation. They then make a note in their file. Notes are extremely valuable, and managers should consider making a note even in a first, informal conversation about an issue. A memory of "I know I mentioned this to you before" really doesn't count. For a warning to be real, it has to be documented. If managers want to start with something informal, the manager has to understand that the "warning" really has not occurred until it is formalized. If an informal discussion doesn't have the desired effect quickly, a more formal warning needs to be done.

It is very important to consult with human resources on this process, particularly but not only in unionized situations. Library directors don't fire many employees. They can't have the depth of experience or education on this process that human resources professionals have. Further, every single actual termination comes with legal and financial consequences, from eligibility for unemployment insurance to discrimination complaints. Directors should not fear that HR will "take over" the process. After all, if directors do value that employee and want to fight for him or her, directors wouldn't be exploring termination or discipline at all.

For overall inadequate performance, an employee's personnel file should consist of annual performance evaluations that show there is a problem. With the rare exception of incidents of spectacularly poor judgment on an employee's part, a termination process fits very poorly with generic, bland, or even positive evaluations. If all employees are "above average," directors really should mean that. They shouldn't think about firing an "above average" employee; therefore, there was something that should have been said all along.

Evaluations then should state clearly where and to what extent the individual was not meeting standards and would lay out clear expectations and a time frame for improvement. If and when the improvement was not made, the person would be terminated.

Of course, that is idealized. Realistically, that kind of step-by-step description, warning, follow-up, warning, etc., is unlikely to be fully followed except in a very formal environment. Small public colleges that are unionized may well operate in this exact fashion. In those situations, library directors at all times must be aware of how to interact with staff in terms of performance. Any library director in a very structured environment needs to conform to campus practices.

Story: In one small college, an administrative assistant preferred to work a four-day week, even though students at the commuter campus used the library heavily on Fridays. In this situation, union processes needed to be followed to document a need for the person to staff the hours she preferred not to work.

In a non-union small college, a shelving clerk was regularly observed sitting around or taking very long breaks; when all shelving was completed, he did not volunteer to help with other library tasks. In that case, his hours were cut to match the hours of work he actually had been producing. Since the position then became a part-time position, he left to find full-time work. A new employee was easily able to do all of the work during the part-time hours.

Most small libraries are at private colleges, and most private colleges are not unionized. Many have personal, educational, or religious cultures that weigh against very formal processes, and others may be so small (the one- or two-person library) that evaluation consists of a supervisor's general sense that one is doing a job adequately enough to be better than attempting to hire someone else. Even so, private colleges are subject to state and federal rules on employment.

Between those two extremes of the thick personnel files and a vague sense of "well, she's doing okay," the effective library director needs to remember why the general rule for documentation exists at all (at least for non-lawyers). That is, effective personnel management has to mean that supervisors and employees have a shared understanding of what a position requires. Then, if necessary, it includes how the person in question is not meeting expectations. Whether or not the campus requires paperwork in a particular format, the director really needs to make clear in any way possible, to both him- or herself and to each employee, just what is necessary and what is wrong.

How can directors arrive at reasonable expectations? One technique is particularly available in the smaller library: they can directly observe or even do some of the person's assigned tasks for a while. This is most commonly possible in technical or processing tasks, such as processing periodicals or shelving books. It is common in a small library for all staff to pitch in when things get busy. This makes it very normal to see directors doing some of these tasks. And there's a reality to first-hand experience that is hard to come by in other ways.

A step back from that is observing staff persons when they work, even asking for verbal descriptions. The strength of this approach is that it is even more important to know what an "average" employee can do than to know what directors can do. Directors have advanced degrees and a high level of professional and occupational skills and might be able to do something far faster than would be reasonable to expect of an hourly employee.

This kind of explicit examination of the details of the job are especially valuable when the director has a general sense, for the annual evaluation, that things are not going well, but does not have enough concrete details to be specific in expectations. The first step then becomes finding out and agreeing between the employer and the employee just what needs to be done, in what way, and in what time.

Quantity, speed, and accuracy may seem too rigid, too bureaucratic for many library responsibilities that often involve patron interaction, working with others, and exercising judgment. Nevertheless, it is useful to include specific concrete details where they do fit.

Employees often have the same sort of performance level through all of their tasks. Doing well or poorly in some measurable matters probably goes along with doing well or poorly in other areas.

For many staff, punctuality and attendance are also easily measured and compared to campus expectations. The library has one specific problem, though, staff who work non-business-hour schedules. The single most effective method of ensuring punctuality or documenting its lack is for the library director to periodically personally check on arrival and departure times. It is tedious but effective.

Other work aspects are not so easily quantified as items processed or hours kept. They are not impossible to observe, though. On all campuses, library staff should treat visitors (students, faculty, and others) with courtesy. If a visitor is rude, the visitor should be referred to the director, not answered in kind. On small campuses especially, any staff person is part of the entire college's atmosphere. Staff should be encouraged to learn how they can be helpful to all campus visitors.

> **Story:** One afternoon, the evening support staff person came to the director confessing that he had brusquely told a difficult student off by saying "talk to the hand" when the student complained about an overdue fine. The director was impressed with the staff person's honesty until the human resources director pointed out that the staffer was going to be "caught" anyway since the student complained and that the staffer wanted to preempt any discipline.

It is possible to observe or record most of what a library employee should be able to do or how they are behaving. In the small library, there are not many areas that the director can't observe. Furthermore, good employees usually welcome the chance to show how much they are accomplishing and thus how important they are. They do not view this as a threat because they are proud of what, how much, and how well they do things.

> **Story**: One human resources director rolled out a new form for evaluating hourly personnel. All objectives were to be stated in these terms: Person will produce X in Y amount of time. Most library processes were reactive: ILL requests can't be processed until patrons generate them; overdues can't be processed until they occur. The format was a poor fit for real-time customer service.

Interpersonal habits may be the most difficult to talk about—except that everybody knows they exist. If everyone nods when someone says "that grouchy guy," then you have a problem that everyone recognizes. How do you handle it?

The first step is to decide if it is actually necessary to deal with the issue directly. If employees have trouble with their interpersonal qualities such as friendliness, cooperation, being proactive, learning, and developing, they often have trouble with quantity and quality, too. Those will be enough to suggest that these people would find a better employment fit elsewhere.

If someone has clearly adequate performance on quality and quantity measures, then the director has to consider if the problems in interpersonal qualities are important enough to ask the person to change how he or she behaves or face termination. Three important considerations make problems important enough to address directly and back up with a threat of potential termination: public service, intra library morale, and change.

Libraries exist to provide services and resources to their communities. More than that, they receive all of their funding from their communities, which for academic libraries is their parent college. They sell nothing, they make nothing, they charge for nothing more than copiers or late fines. They will thrive and survive only with the support of their particular public. Each staff member in a position to interact with the public becomes part of the face of that library for that community. Each library's image rises and falls with the actions of each individual staff member, and each member of the public deserves respectful and helpful service.

If a support staff person has some problems in public service, a good solution is to ask the college's human resources department for help. They will be concerned that the entire campus embody attitudes consistent with the institution's mission and values, and good human resources personnel will have much more experience in encouraging growth among hourly personnel in interpersonal skills than the typical library director, who supervises a relatively small number of individuals. They also know impersonal and neutral language in which to frame specific expectations. No modern director is going to say, "act ladylike," but how else can one get across the desired concept?

Morale within the library itself, among the staff, is also important. Few things are more damaging to the morale of co-workers than having one person who is visibly less diligent, courteous, or helpful than others. The most ideal situation for any manager is to lead a team made up entirely of self-motivated individuals who each strive for excellence and collectively move the library forward. Not every person in every library acts like that. Some treat the job as just a job, and they do a reasonable, honest day's labor. Those people have value, and they do contribute. What is really damaging is someone who takes advantage of the campus or library culture to be less than diligent or respectful of others. Someone working hard at the library will not be happy when someone else slacks off with no consequences. Firings are traumatic to everybody, but if the staff can see that the employee in question had a genuine opportunity to do a good job and failed to live up to expectations, a firing can be a short-term crisis that leads to longer-term satisfaction.

Change is the final issue. Some people will always think that libraries are just places where books are neatly arranged.

Others think of libraries as quiet, peaceful retreats for employees as well as scholars. The reality is that the small college library exists not for its own sake but to serve its campus, and it does so by remaining as close to the cutting edge of information and technology as is feasible. The academic library is a place of continuous change, growth, and development. If the "problem" with problem employees is that they resist learning new things or changing what they do, then the library director needs to look at more than one day's particular issue, because there will be changes coming that year and the next and the next. Change is inescapable, and the attitude has to be to accept it, even if not with wild enthusiasm.

Fortunately, this particular personnel problem sometimes can correct itself. To make that happen, the library director makes very clear what new thing has become part of an existing job and spells out the reality that adapting to this and the next and to all new things is part of a particular position. Nor are these changes cause for reclassifying a position. Mastering a computer rather than a triplicate typewriter for sending overdue notices is not cause for moving a circulation clerk into a higher compensation bracket. The library director stipulates each time what new thing is necessary to do for that position. Adapting to change cannot be considered optional. The person who is truly resistant to change will soon learn either to bend to each necessary change as it comes along or to find work in a field not so dependent on technology.

All of those steps and elements are most applicable to support staff positions where the evaluation regime consists either of annual evaluations or an informal promise of continued employment if no major errors are made. It is a different situation with professional staff.

If there is a performance problem with a professional librarian, how it is handled will depend on whether the librarians are considered staff or faculty. In the first case, the above procedures and principles are the same. Spell things out, make performance evaluations candid and specific, and follow through with consequences. It will be more difficult because the nature of professional work is that it includes judgment and discretion, and librarians often do their work very independently, the one-on-one meeting with a faculty member, the in-class pre-sentation, and the encounter at the reference desk. Nevertheless, the library director can still observe and more importantly can communicate with people in a position to know how the librarians are doing, the faculty with whom they work. If they are public-service librarians and have no relations with individual faculty, then that is also a problem that can be pointed out.

If the librarian is considered faculty, that process is covered in the chapter on faculty status. There is a very different dynamic when evaluation is embedded within a peer group structure and an up (approved for tenure) or out situation. Post-tenure review is a difficult issue as well.

The main point about termination is that the library director above all needs to ensure that all staff members are performing at least adequately. That's the bureaucratic perspective, jobs that are defined and the people who fill them. Jobs change, people conform. Professional development is essential. Beyond ensuring basic adequacy, good annual reviews inform thoughtful development activities and lead to personal growth. Good, competent employees are the creators of the future, not just submitting to change, but leading it. Recognizing and rewarding that human element makes the library a success.

STUDENT WORKERS

What is the relationship between the student workforce in a library and formal career development? These people are not in any sense "professional" nor even permanent. Usually, new students are hired on the basis of good generic work skills (being dependable and polite) and whether their course schedules fit library needs. Students are trained on the job and do tasks that do not take extensive training. Large libraries sometimes have formal training programs, with learning objectives and specific goals, but in the small library, these are primarily accomplished one-on-one or in small orientation groups.

Nevertheless, good student workers who begin as freshmen can have four or more years of library employment ahead of them. Many institutions have two tiers for student wages, with a higher rate for students who supervise other students, for students who perform more technically advanced work, or for students in hard-to-fill positions. In all of these cases, the wages are often lower than they would be for people on the "outside" hired for similarly complex tasks. Many student workers are potentially of higher quality than people hired from the community at the rate that students are paid (minimum wage or only somewhat higher). A job at minimum wage with no benefits would normally not attract any college graduates in the community, while student workers are right in the middle of becoming well educated. They are college-graduate-level people in many respects.

This high level of ability means that library student workers can provide benefits to the library far above what their wage rate suggests. The good, smart, energetic student worker can develop over four years into someone who can handle significant responsibility and technical skills. Some may even be able to propose special projects at an advanced level or internship level, although the library needs to make sure they are scheduled such that they can be completed. The library student workforce is not permanent.

The library is usually a desirable employer for student workers. Students like library jobs because they are part of their financial aid, they are convenient, and they usually have pleasant working conditions. Library directors and staff can enhance this advantage by considering ways in which students can use their library experiences to increase both soft and specific skills for their future careers. Students often underestimate how important for their future meaty entries in a résumé and enthusiastic references from supervisors are. The library staff should make an effort to educate their student workers about the link between what they do in the library and their future careers in whatever field.

Student workers have had a monopoly on one specific area for the past 20 or so years: frontline responders to information-technology issues. The first line of the IT help desk in many colleges and universities is staffed exclusively by students. This has important consequences for the library and its employees: who they attract, what skills they can develop, and how they train their own workers to fit within the library's processes.

When the library seeks to fill its student worker positions, it is in competition with other positions on campus. The library often doesn't have the authority or the money to compete on wage levels. What it can control is the potential for development in a library position. Because of this, it is important to involve students in some high-level work in addition to the necessary and dull tasks of shelving and shelf reading. Interesting work attracts and retains more interested students. Training on specific library tasks such as interlibrary loan procedures or cataloging item entry should emphasize the similarities to non-library work, such as process control and database maintenance.

In just the same way that the library director specifically budgets time and resources for staff development, student worker supervisors need to budget training and other forms of education for longer-term student workers to enhance their skills and retain quality employees. If students are first responders for IT, are they the first information-desk contacts in a library? The chapter on managing for teaching support discusses various models for reference service. This is easier to handle and to monitor in the physically small library. Students at a circulation or information desk will usually be observed closely by librarians. It is important that whatever the method of staffing reference, even the most informal or one-on-one training for any student workers include policies and examples of how to handle patron questions. This is especially true because students see students answering IT questions elsewhere on campus and because other students often approach them first.

Library student workers really need to know the ways in which library questions are similar or are different from IT questions. In the small library, the student worker may indeed be able to handle computer questions, but it is all too easy to mistake that for a role in handling all questions. When library-science students themselves need to be specifically educated about the complexity of reference work, it is a mistake to presume that undergraduate students will understand what is involved.

Story: A bright and experienced circulation-desk student answers the phone: Does the library have a copy of the U.S. Drug Pharmacopeia? The experienced student of course knew how to look up materials in the library catalog. "No," she responded, "You're welcome," and hung up. What's wrong? The library did not have that particular reference work but was well supplied with drug reference manuals. This was probably not a simple known-item search. Thus the rule: student workers can say *yes* but cannot say *no*: they must refer questions.

Educating student workers about what "real" librarians do in public service has multiple benefits. Internally, this kind of educating ensures that library service is consistent with what the library really wants. That is, if what is wanted is to have a librarian first-response model, or triage, or appointment model, student workers need to know enough so that their casual encounters with users really follow the desired pattern. Externally, student workers are students. They share their experiences with fellow students. Tell one student how reference really works, and other students might learn something, too, by word of mouth. That will raise the general knowledge level, perhaps not a lot, but at least more than assuming that students know what the different types and levels of reference inquiries are.

The final point about developing student workers is that they could be the future of the profession itself. Precisely because library science is a graduate-level program, academic librarians are in a tremendously important position to recruit the next generation of librarians. Few people are better placed to help students understand what professional librarianship is, in many different formats, than those who work with student workers on a daily basis. In the small college library, these student workers can get a sense of the whole range of academic librarianship. The troublesome student worker who keeps on going beyond a "student's" role can be encouraged to channel that enthusiasm toward becoming a librarian.

One important note though is that the majority of librarians do not work at small academic libraries. When talking with student employees, librarians should take care to represent all of the possibilities. Most academic library jobs are at large libraries; many librarians work in public libraries; librarians work in private and public organizations and in schools.

That a library is its people is not a prediction, or an aspiration, or a philosophy, or even just a tired cliché. Instead, it is a cold-blooded and completely accurate description of the situation. How big Harvard's collection is, what cool articles on Google searching and data curation are published, and what new books on "cybrarians" matters much less than what happens on each college campus. What happens depends on how librarians, staff, and student workers behave, grow, develop, and change. They will be the measure of success for the library and the library director.

NOTES

1. Association of College and Research Libraries. "Guidelines for Academic Status for College and University Librarians." http://www.ala.org/ala/mgrps/divs/acrl/standards/guidelinesacademic.cfm.

2. Long, Chris Evin, and Rachel Applegate. "Bridging the Gap in Digital Library Continuing Education: How Librarians Who Were Not 'Born Digital' Are Keeping Up." *Library Administration and Management* 22, no. 4 (2008): 172–82; also, "Marketing Survey," American Library Association, Library Support Staff Certification Project, unpublished data.

3. Technically, however, even librarians with formal faculty status are not included in the common calculations of the percentage of faculty who have doctoral degrees, just as provosts or other administrators, who may also be tenured faculty with doctoral degrees, are excluded. Only people who teach 50 percent or more of their time are included in the "Common Data Set" definition of faculty. Therefore, having a librarian acquire a doctoral degree will have no effect on the college's percentage.

6 FACULTY STATUS

The key: Librarians working effectively with instructional faculty

This is the longest chapter in this book because:

- Faculty are the heart of the university. They conduct research, perform service, and teach.
- Students are the most numerous library users, but their use of academic libraries is determined by their academic needs. Their learning experiences are designed and driven by faculty.
- The relationship between faculty and the library is conditioned by the relationship between faculty and librarians. Two things matter:
  - Person-to-person individual competence and respect.
  - Ideas and expectations about what librarians are and can do.

The status of librarians on a campus will determine these things:

- How the library attracts, develops, and retains the right librarians for its mission. This is the foundation of personal respect.

- How the librarians interact with faculty corporately, in governance structures. This is the primary way librarians have a voice in and can effectively respond to academic program planning and delivery.
- The process of personnel and professional development for librarians. Librarians who are considered administrative staff experience an annual cycle of personal goal setting, development, and evaluation; those who are considered faculty experience the promotion and tenure structure and cycle. Research is an important component of faculty status itself and of meeting tenure and promotion standards.

Finally, the characteristics of faculty, and the nature of faculty status, are not as monolithic as many people assume. Important variations from college to college exist, and they are most acute at small colleges. Therefore, this chapter will discuss the issues of:

- What "faculty" means
- What the common elements are that make up "faculty status"
- How faculty status works within a small college library and between librarians and the college

DEFINING FACULTY STATUS

Faculty status refers to a group of benefits and responsibilities that members of a defined group on campus have because they are considered "faculty." The most basic items in this group are lifetime job tenure after a probationary period and an independent, non-bureaucratic role in campus governance concerning curricular and sometimes other matters.

Having an entire chapter on faculty status, something that other management guides spend little time on perhaps including only a paragraph, a page, or a section, is a reflection of its centrality to academic life. This chapter discusses faculty status and librarians at small colleges in detail and at length. It is given so much attention because faculty status affects the careers of librarians individually, it has significant effects on how a library relates to the campus at large, it is subject to more change than is often supposed, and it is especially acute, personal, and significant in the small college environment.

Faculty status or its alternatives are a set of benefits, review procedures, and functional designations; therefore, it defines much of the working conditions for a librarian on a particular campus. It is part of what attracts or repels candidates for job openings, it determines how they progress through their career, and it affects their relations with the rest of campus on a daily basis.

The power of faculty status derives from the unusual power of faculty within the academic organization. More precisely, an academic organization is unusual among organizations in vesting power in a group that is formed and operates separately from bureaucratic hierarchies. In some ways, this resembles the format of a professional partnership, making faculty parallel to doctors, lawyers, and accountants in group practices. Yet some of the powers that function within professional partnerships are diminished. Faculty do not have control over their practice interactions or bill their customers independently. Except for some stars, few faculty can walk away with their clients if they don't like their cut of the partnership's income. Academic faculty depend upon the college structure, but that structure also depends on them.

In recognition of the centrality of subject expertise expressed in teaching, research and service academic organizations have developed both bureaucratic hierarchies and simultaneous parallel governance structures in which faculty exert their influence on subject matter but also across all facets of the institution. Because this parallel structure exists, the status that individual librarians and the library director have affects the library's placement within the formal organizational chart and also librarians' participation in the advisory structures.

The status of librarians on a campus is not static. Just because librarians have faculty status at one time does not mean that will continue, nor that if they do not, that they cannot achieve it. No empirical evidence has developed that convincingly demonstrates a trend either toward or away from faculty status for librarians. For decades, its presence and absence has fluctuated nationally around 50 percent of academic librarians. On each campus, every change in leadership, particularly in the offices of the president, head of human resources, head of academic affairs, and head of the library, means a new decision-maker who may have a different attitude about the status of librarians.

The importance of faculty status is especially sensitive for smaller institutions because of the number of librarians, the size of the library as a unit, and the character of the teaching staff. In a small library, each librarian makes up a large percentage of the librarian staff. What the library means, what librarianship means, and what being a librarian means are embodied in the actual librarians at a library on a campus. In their actions and attitudes, they affect the attitudes of people, administrators, and groups on campus about where librarians fit into the academic universe. Librarians, in a sense, "are" the library, and this is true of large as well as small libraries; but in a small library, the potential or change that comes with the retirement or replacement of any one librarian is huge. When a new librarian is one-third of the staff, what the library looks like is altered more than when a new librarian in a large library joins 100. Each new librarian similarly represents a proportion of budget commitment and that is much more noticeable when it makes up 33 percent of personnel spending than, say, 1 percent in the 100-librarian library.

The small library is also small when considered as its own unit. In a large university, the unit of the library or system of libraries means a robust professional cohort with its own internal structures, mentor and colleague relations, status of its leadership, and weight in campus affairs. A handful of librarians simply cannot have a complex internal structure, and the director's position is affected by that. A library director in charge of one or three or seven others is not the same as the "dean" of libraries, who commands a staff of 100 or more.

Finally, the differences between librarians and teaching staff are distinctly different on smaller as compared to larger campuses. A small college teaching faculty member's qualifications, daily responsibilities, and status differ more from faculty at large universities than a small college librarian's qualifications and responsibilities differ from those of librarians at large universities. In several important ways, librarians on small campuses are more like the traditional faculty on that campus than librarians at research institutions are like traditional faculty there.

The detailed pros and cons surrounding faculty status laid out in this chapter might be seen as tilting in the pro-faculty status direction; that is for the reader to agree or disagree. Whatever a library director's stance on the issue is, what is universally important for the effective management of small college libraries is to understand the issues themselves and how they may affect individuals within the library and elsewhere on campus, and how the different forms of status affect how the library is administered and how staff participates in bureaucratic and political governing processes.

The culture of each particular library and the attitudes of its librarians are to some degree fluid and to some degree self-perpetuating. Each retirement and each new librarian brings someone else's ideas, but it is also the case that if librarians care about this issue, they will choose workplaces that offer the status they desire, whether that means they are considered the same as faculty, or different from but parallel to faculty, academic staff, or administrative staff.

FACULTY AND FACULTY STATUS

The classic conception of a faculty person at a university in the United States is that individuals hold a research doctoral degree in a specific discipline. They are hired to perform duties that include teaching, research, and service. Their employment begins with a probationary period that lasts a maximum of seven years; at some point before the end of the period, a decision is made as to whether they will be given tenure. This is understood as an agreement to employ them until they choose to leave or retire, as long as they fulfill basic responsibilities without major scandals. The American Association of University Professors has laid out this schema for decades. While there is a great deal of discussion about trends and threats to tenure, in practical terms at most colleges, any tenure crisis has primarily involved the quantity of tenure-track slots (how many people begin and acquire this status) rather than to the substance of tenure itself for those who are hired into the process.

Benefits of Faculty Status

This system has two primary benefits, one human resources oriented and one tied to the culture and nature of academia. In human resources planning, it is believed that this system with its ultimate offer of security attracts the best candidates. This is the most common reason given for college administrators to choose this rather than a more creative alternative.

The most vocal proponents of alternatives to tenure tend to be at the top or the bottom of the academic labor pool, not in its well-stocked middle. Super-star professors, at the very top of the academic universe, are wooed by institutions and do not need job security. Adjuncts, particularly in professional programs, often have "day" jobs and see teaching as an attractive supplement. The majority of people who teach in academia tend to value permanence, the same as those in other professions and jobs.

For librarians, this argument about needing faculty status and tenure to attract good candidates is neutral. Librarians value permanence as much as other people do, but they may feel that they have as much job stability in an annual-contract situation as with tenure. Moreover, librarian jobs without tenure are as numerous as those with, so they have fewer of the expectations for tenure than a new PhD recipient would have.

The more academic and philosophical rationale is more widely advertised, academic freedom. A university is by its nature a place where novelty and innovation are explored. Research involves the creation of new knowledge. In teaching, this is passed on to others; in service, it is applied to community needs. New knowledge by definition differs from an already accepted norm. The intellectual independence case for tenure asserts that:

- Administrators would often, too often, or at least some of the time base retention decisions upon faculty's scholarly opinions, making job stability dependent upon conformity with whatever the administration finds suitable. This would seriously damage two aspects that define the university itself: subject knowledge and knowledge innovation.

- Administrators are not subject experts; at the least, they do not act as subject experts when they act as administrators. Therefore, they are incapable of accurately judging faculty on the content of their scholarship or the quality of their innovation. Only peers can do that, and peer review is an essential element of faculty tenure.
- If faculty were subject to administrative approval, faculty would censor themselves rather than take the risk of annoying people on whose good opinion their jobs depend.

This is very relevant to the argument for or against faculty status for librarians. Academic freedom is clearly relevant to the knowledge work of faculty. When categories of people do not have formally protected academic freedom, it is often because they are not seen as needing it. For instance, on most campuses, counselors and coaches do not have faculty status; on some they do. The work of college librarians in public service and in developing collections is intensely affected by intellectual freedom and needs protection as much as faculty scholarship.

Story: On a large and bureaucratic campus, a student who had a work-study job as a housekeeper was reading a book during a break time; the book depicted a lynching on its cover. Another housekeeper complained that the action and picture were racially harassing. In the ensuing extensive debate, nobody claimed that housekeeping itself was an activity that required intellectual freedom.

Given safety and hygiene concerns, innovation and novelty on the part of individual housekeepers in relation to their work would be something to be discouraged.

After job security and intellectual freedom, the next question is much broader. Are librarians like faculty? What does it mean to be "like" faculty? What does it mean to be faculty, and what elements of that are common across faculty members and what are different or the same with librarians?

It is important to break down the individual components of the classic framework. However different librarians may seem from faculty, there is also a tremendous amount of variety within the faculty group itself. On no campus do all people who have faculty status share equally in all of the aspects of the tenure track or model for teaching faculty. It is easy enough to see where librarians are different and it is equally important to see where faculty differ among themselves.

Faculty Characteristics

Degree

The first element is that the faculty member has a research-based doctoral degree. Saying "research" means distinguishing a doctor of philosophy from other possibilities, professional doctorates, and other doctoral degrees such as the EdD, DNS, and DLett. In reality, not all faculty and not even all tenure-track faculty at any college may possess a classic PhD research doctorate. At community colleges, master's degrees are very common, even in the general education or transfer curriculum courses. In some fields, particularly professional areas, there may be a few research doctoral programs nationally, but a given college may be unable to attract any of its small number of graduates and so master's-prepared candidates may be the best it can hire. In some fields, a "terminal degree" other than a doctor of philosophy is recognized. The oldest example of this is the master of fine arts for arts faculty; the proliferation of professional doctorates in pharmacy, physical therapy, nursing, and other fields is likely to produce more teaching candidates who have those rather than a PhD, particularly since there are comparatively few PhD programs available, and because teaching as a career in those fields is generally less lucrative thus less attractive than practicing, so professionals often find that pursuing a research-based doctoral degree does not make financial sense.

It is important to determine at a particular college how common it is to have a research doctorate, including in what disciplines or units of the college. In some cases, people who are truly considered tenure-track faculty with full privileges uniformly possess doctorates; others who teach but don't have the doctoral degree will not be full faculty on tenure tracks. If that is the situation, it will not be feasible or rational to expect librarians who have master's degrees to be considered equal to the full-fledged tenure-track faculty.

Information about the prevalence of doctoral degrees is available by looking at credentials listed in catalogs or departmental materials. While some college guides give the percentage of instructional faculty with doctorates, sometimes that category does not have sufficiently clear distinctions between doctoral, terminal, and professional degrees. That can make it hard to determine just what the level of qualifications actually is.

The other technique is to review lists of faculty in the college bulletin or equivalent, where degrees are specified. A problem with the college bulletin or Web site is that it may not indicate precise tenure status or academic standing. Some who teach or some administrators may be on yearly or continuing contracts not in tenure tracks but may be referred to by faculty titles. Job ads for new faculty will generally be precise about what is required or what it is expected the average candidate will possess. "Or equivalent experience/degree" is a key phrase.

A college where more than 25 percent of instructors have something other than or less than any type of doctorate or terminal degree is one in which the master's degree of librarians will be reasonably comparable with faculty credentials. Research doctorates are most common in the most traditional arts and sciences disciplines; they are least prevalent in professions, ranging from health professions to education and business. If people are considered "faculty" in the business school without PhDs, librarians will have a claim to equivalence between MBA and MLS levels of preparation for academic stature.

Specific Discipline

The desired level of qualifications and much else about a faculty or staff member's responsibilities varies according to academic discipline and how that discipline is seen on campus. The more traditional and narrow the discipline, the more easily the faculty member will receive academic respect and recognition. This is related to the issue of research (below), but is a separate issue as well.

Much of the more-traditional or more-prestigious relationship comes from the long-standing and worsening relationship between faculty supply and demand. In most of the classic humanities fields, there are far more people receiving research doctorates than there are traditional tenure-track position openings. It may be a two-to-one ratio, or worse. The supply is so generous that on the demand side, colleges stick to requiring the research doctorate, the more traditional the better.

The fact that the small college has a small number of faculty can mean that each faculty member has to have a broader teaching range than at a larger institution. This is especially true where instead of handling basic courses with very large lecture classes plus labs run by teaching assistants, the more personal smaller college uses full faculty in direct instruction of smaller classes with no doctoral students and no teaching assistants. Also, departments may be conglomerations of areas kept separate on larger campuses. For example, one department might include classics, philosophy and religion, history and political science, or sociology and social work. Finally, small colleges that are flexible and value innovation can create new programs and interdisciplinary areas. All of this means that faculty members in small colleges are not so strictly bounded by their traditional disciplines than someone at a mid-sized or research university.

If administrators in a college that has a large number of professors whose highest degree is the master's wish to increase the number of doctoral faculty as part of general improvement or as preparation for offering higher degrees, there are two ways to do it: hire them or make them. Hiring is expensive and slow, so the "grow your own" tactic encourages existing faculty to complete higher degrees. It can be very difficult for working faculty to enter traditional doctoral programs in traditional disciplines when the college is not in a major urban area. An alternative is a doctoral degree in a general field such as "instruction," "leadership," or "organizational development," available in online programs, rather than a PhD in a traditional discipline.

All of this adds up to the fact that the issue of the doctoral degree for faculty and hence for librarians is much more diverse than is often assumed, particularly when the assumptions are based on the situation in large research universities. In all but the most selective and wealthy small colleges, the bright line between doctoral faculty in disciplines and librarians with master's degrees turns out to be very fuzzy indeed. Many academic librarians, almost half in some surveys, possess a subject master's degree and may actually have a greater amount of graduate education than classroom faculty. Also, library science is a well-established field with a decades-long history. The proportion of people who do not consider it a "real" science has probably remained constant through the years, which gives it an advantage over some newer fields, viewed often with great skepticism by more traditional faculty.

Duties: Teaching, Research, and Service

Teaching, research, and service are the three traditional responsibilities of the full-time and particularly of the tenure-track faculty person. Some universities, particularly larger ones, have full-time but non-tenure-track instructional personnel. These people are usually called lecturers or instructors and they concentrate primarily on teaching. Sometimes they focus exclusively on assigned courses and sometimes have more broad responsibilities for student advising, internship supervision, and other curricular or student-centered activities.

It is the specific mark of tenure-track faculty that they do not just teach but also are expected to do research and perform service even if the other areas are emphasized more or less. Does this set of duties exclude librarians? Just as with the doctoral degree, it is important to know about situations in which people who are definitely considered faculty do things that do not fit the classic ideas of each of those roles.

One form of teaching is leadership of a "for-credit" course, in which the faculty member designs, designates, or delivers the content for a given group of students, assesses student achievement, and certifies the level of mastery. They are the sage on the stage, guide by the side, someone teaching and someone learning. This archetype has captured the attention of many academic librarians who then focus on the one aspect of academic librarianship that seems the most compatible, information-literacy instruction.

This is too narrow. Faculty do educational things other than delivering content and assessing mastery in formal credit classes. In many professional fields, there are field experiences ranging from observation to clinical placements to student teaching. Faculty are the ones to organize and supervise these experiences. Even in small colleges, some faculty-side administrators such as department chairs or supervisors of various programs devote large amounts of their time not to classes or didactic course delivery. One of these coordinators, directors, or mentors can spend a considerable amount of time in closely guiding a small number of students in learning through experiences such as research or internships.

Working with students individually like this is much more comparable to most of what a public-service librarian does. A librarian doesn't just present sessions to groups, but spends much time guiding and teaching students one at a time through the library portion of their academic work. Reference work in an academic library almost always involves an intimate instructional experience, not handing over an answer, but showing that student how to find, retrieve, and evaluate information. In this way, the roles of internship supervisors and reference librarians have many similarities.

Faculty occupied with more administrative tasks can be a different situation. Even though making contacts with placement sites, distributing evaluation forms, and logging hours and experiences are all vitally necessary for good student learning, the less individual and more bureaucratic a process, the more the person doing the process will be seen as a bureaucrat and not as a teacher. Teaching a class means the librarian is a faculty member. Scheduling classes is a task for a mindless or even malevolent dictator. Advising students is considered a good thing, but making sure students are advised is the dark side.

The administrative duties of some faculty can make them seem more foreign to a regular faculty member than any difference between faculty and librarian. At some colleges, people whose duties are at least 50 percent administrative in nature and carry a formal course load that is less than half of the "regular" load may not be considered for tenure; if they already possess tenure, when they become administrators, they may lose their seats in all-faculty bodies.

The same may happen to research and service. At a typical research university, research can take up half or 90 percent or even all of someone's time, and they are considered faculty. However, at a very teaching-centered college, designated effort on research or service might be viewed as distracting from the *real* purpose and character of *real* faculty.

The more classroom-centered the faculty culture on a campus, the more difficult it will be to have librarians considered faculty. It would be seen as a dangerous move politically if librarians can be faculty, then perhaps administrators would claim to be included, too. It is the opposite problem with the doctoral degree. The more emphasis on doctoral degrees and research, the less librarians will fit the model; the more classroom centered, the more librarians can only emphasize one aspect of their role, library user instruction. The broader the understanding of learning and of teaching on a campus, the better librarians will be able to fit within the assumptions of what "faculty" means.

In some university systems, librarians have an explicitly defined status that is parallel to or a subset of the faculty structure; faculty exist parallel with librarians with faculty status. In these systems, the professional action of librarians takes the place of the "teaching" component. When a small public college is part of a larger system with these designations, librarians will work within this structure. It benefits them because defining librarian activities is politically easier when backed by the relatively large group of librarians that forms when all are pooled across the system. It can be a problem when details favor the conditions that exist at the larger institutions, which inevitably will employ more (voting) librarians.

If a campus is very classroom focused, trying to translate librarianship into that model has some serious difficulties. The problem is that relying on an educational equivalence between information-literacy instruction and classroom instruction leaves out much of what many academic librarians do, especially in a small college. Public-services librarians spend much of their time doing collection management, Web design, and one-on-one work with faculty and students. Technical-services librarians may not do any instruction at all. This is especially likely if the small college has extensive archives needing high-level cataloging skills or has a dedicated system's administrator rather than outsourcing its system maintenance to a consortium. It is often not possible to include instruction in every MLS librarian's duties.

The research component poses less of a difficulty at most colleges than the teaching component. Just as research doctorates are not found across the board on all college campuses, so research activity varies and is not at a high level at many small colleges.

Librarians might be better off when it comes to research than classroom faculty. Compared to faculty teaching in traditional disciplines, librarians often have quite promising opportunities for research. It is librarians in the field, more than library school professors, who publish a significant percentage of research on academic librarianship in respected peer-reviewed journals. Librarians also often have robust state and national organizations, and presentations at conferences are often considered a form of research or scholarship.

Service presents no special problems for librarians. What service means varies greatly from college to college, but librarians can work professionally and in the community in ways that are recognized as service in the faculty mode.

If administrators are familiar with the classifications and groupings used at large institutions, they may have experience with non-teaching faculty. There is the category of "research faculty," or less formally, faculty who spend most of their time doing research rather than teaching. Some places value research, devote resources in terms of dedicated faculty time to it, and consider research-oriented faculty to be peers with and indistinguishable from classroom faculty, as far as faculty status and governance rights, as well as intangible respect.

At some institutions as well, the term "faculty" has been extended not only to include teachers and researchers, but also a wide range of roles such as academic or psychological counselors, people who run writing centers, athletics staff, and museum curators. The more diverse the pool of faculty, the more it will seem that what the librarians do is essentially similar to what "faculty" do. Compared to counselors and curators, what librarians do is more obviously tied to student learning (reference and instruction) and faculty research (technical services, database management, and electronic tools) than other functions on campus, which again makes librarian "duties" fit that much more comfortably within the definition of "faculty."

> **Story**: At a small denominational college with an egalitarian ethic, the director said, "We all have faculty status—everyone who works here. Except that when everybody does . . . no one, except the classroom faculty, really do."

Probationary Period

Seven years, in for life, or out is the classic time line of the tenure system. The promise of lifetime tenure is so dramatic that often outsiders misunderstand the "or out" part. That is, those who fail to attain tenure must leave. They cannot simply remain in place on a year-to-year basis. Any institution following the traditional American Association of University Professors (AAUP) framework for tenure consideration is discouraged from changing the initial employment bargain. Success means lifetime tenure, failure means termination. People who are hired to provide instruction at colleges are either hired as tenure-track faculty, or not. Non-tenure-track faculty include those hired for individual courses, or on an ongoing contract without tenure, sometimes called adjuncts, part timers, or lecturers. The AAUP encourages institutions to provide expectations of continued employment after an initial probationary period, and these people can sometimes have the same titles as tenure-track faculty and play similar roles in all aspects of faculty governance except tenure review itself.

When a campus has a well-established framework for non-tenure-track faculty, it is possible that librarians will be considered part of this category. The important thing to notice about rolling contract faculty is that this means that the classroom faculty themselves are not some monolithic block when it comes to probation and tenure. Not everybody who teaches has the same seven-year probationary period and then security. A multitude of possibilities exist and librarians can be fit into many of them.

System and Campus-Specific Faculty Qualifications

Faculty qualifications and expectations are affected by whether a small college is small and independent or small and part of a larger formal system. Colleges that are public and small often are part of larger systems. Those systems will have a set of definitions, expectations, and procedures that apply to the system as a whole with some subsets of definitions that apply to particular campuses. "Small Town College" may be a campus of "Big U," but its faculty in general are not like the faculty of Big U. Examples of this exists in Indiana with its four-year regional campuses but its "flagship" in Bloomington, and Penn State University with its regional campuses. They have different working conditions, different pay, and almost inevitably, different requirements and expectations. Faculty can and often do argue that the expectation-reward system sometimes works backward. For example, students at regional and smaller campuses often enter higher education with more limited preparation and qualifications than those at the more selective flagship research institution; this makes it more challenging. Paying regional faculty more because teaching is harder just does not happen.

When comparing small college teaching to flagship research institutions, the life of faculty members at the small public college may differ from their counterparts at larger institutions more extensively than the life of librarians at the smaller institution differs from librarians at larger institutions. Faculty members in smaller institutions may have a higher teaching load, be expected to work more closely with students, and have lower research or grant-writing expectations. General librarians will have a set of library instruction, public service, collections management, and other duties that are roughly similar. The small college librarian will more often be a generalist than librarians who are specialists at larger universities. Both will have roughly comparable abilities to be innovative and advance professional knowledge.

Other variations exist. The larger university may recognize a category of researcher or scientific faculty with faculty titles, faculty representation, but no teaching duties. Regional or small campuses have professional directors, practitioner-teachers, and other types of positions keyed to their specific local missions and programs.

How the differences between larger and smaller colleges within a single university system impact local campus thinking about what faculty status means can be both positive and negative for librarians. Like faculty at small or regional campuses, their librarians may have difficulty making their voices heard; faculty status may be seen as possible and useful at the smaller campus, but the system as a whole may take its cue from the large research university, where librarians differ more distinctly from doctoral faculty. Or, system requirements may place an emphasis on teaching, something shared by classroom faculty at both larger and smaller campuses, a unifying element for them and one that excludes librarians.

This is an element where the perspectives of politics intersect forcefully with bureaucratic rationality. There is no compelling evidence-based argument, from either prevalence or causation, that would lead a scientific conclave to enact librarians-as-faculty (or not). Instead, there is a political idea that librarians are like faculty, or not. Faculty are the larger body; do they gain strength by adding librarians?

A political group, a special-interest group, has strength both in numbers and the centrality of its position in the organization. Traditional faculty are central to the academic enterprise. Libraries are essential but as support systems. Do faculty generally feel that librarians are like them? If there is a strong positive feeling about librarians as suitable for a status like, or parallel with, or in coordination with, faculty, felt on a system-wide basis, librarians at an individual smaller campus do not need to make their case. They are already part of a powerful interest group. If there is a negative feeling, then librarians who might be successful locally are in a difficult situation. Without support at the least from librarians at the larger universities, they will not be successful.

The degree to which a public college has autonomy with respect to various elements of faculty status varies from system to system and state to state. Librarians need to delve into the details, because even systems that appear monolithic may have some deviations that administrators may consider minor but that may be applied in a certain case. Non-tenure-track instructional personnel—lecturers, "associates"—may or may not be part of faculty organizations on a campus-by-campus basis, even when a system has definitive rules for lecturer rights and responsibilities. The library director needs to be familiar with the rules and guidelines for the system, for her campus and for other campuses as well. Arguing for local rules will take place in the larger context that every system has to wrestle with constantly—the degree to which there is coordination, centralization, and customization across all issues, not just a specific campus on the specific issue of librarian status.

> **Story:** In a relatively centralized state university system, librarians have a distinct, defined academic status. They have tenure and representation in faculty governance, but have different expectations, centered on professional work and not research. This is uniform throughout the system, but the specific expectations vary by campus, and within the system, the role of non-tenure-track faculty in faculty organizations varies.

Unions

Some colleges have unions. Labor organization combines the forces of interest-group politics and systematic bureaucratization. Without rehashing the history of the labor movement, broadly speaking organizing appears when workers combine to secure economic and non-economic benefits (wages, working conditions) and also to exercise a defined degree of control over managerial decision-making (work rules, hiring, firing and promotion decisions, etc.). Members of a union forcefully consider themselves a specific interest group that uses the power of its numbers and its role in an organization to achieve decisions in its favor. They are born in politics and enforce their goals in explicit bureaucratic rules and procedures.

Unions are extremely rare in private colleges, because of two significant court cases. In the Yeshiva University case, the National Labor Relations Board for federal legal purposes determined that faculty exercise a role in universities that is sufficiently managerial that they do not qualify as "workers." In another, courts exempted religiously affiliated institutions from collective bargaining. Because many small colleges are private and denominational, very few are unionized.

Public small colleges can be organized, however. Under state, not federal, law, public employees may be allowed or encouraged to organize. This makes unionization in higher education geographically concentrated, with unionized colleges common in the Northeast, Michigan, and California. Small public colleges in these areas may have labor unions for faculty, for administrative staff, and for other groups.

Librarians can be part of a union. Which union depends upon the job designation. When a campus is unionized, the status and relation to a specific bargaining unit of each job or position on campus is something that is carefully and explicitly defined with no gray areas. If change is sought, it must be sought openly. It has to meet legal requirements, such as which library roles are managerial and which are teaching, be acceptable to at least one union, be compatible with other unions or union units existing on campus, and must be recognized by the administration.

One key element will be whether the library's director will be considered part of management or middle management or faculty. Unions need to examine the degree of control that a director exercises. If faculty are unionized, are department chairs considered management or even middle management and thus not part of the faculty union? This may vary if a chair position is rotated, or if there are only two librarians, or three faculty members in a particular department. It may make little sense to divide such a small group. An alternative can be to formulate the "director" position so that it does not in fact exercise managerial duties, but is more of a consensual coordinator. That preserves unity within the library, but at the expense of moving some library decision-making out and into the hands of non-librarians. However, as stated earlier, this will be dictated by the definition given by the bargaining unit and any changes must be approved.

When librarians are part of the faculty union, the equality of status between librarians and classroom faculty is reinforced. If their union is separate from that of the faculty, the status of librarians will be seen as operating in a separate realm from faculty organization at both the union and college levels.

Different labor unions exist on campuses. Bargaining chapters of the American Association of University Professors are concentrated at four-year institutions. Faculty at community colleges are more likely to be represented by the American Federation of Teachers and the National Education Association.[1] At other campuses, librarians have been represented by the United Auto Workers or the Communications Workers of America. This has an inevitable effect on how librarians are perceived as educational workers. Being in the same union as clerical personnel or IT professionals will inevitably move librarians in the direction of staff concerns and away from faculty areas of interest.

All issues concerned with faculty status are significantly affected by whether a campus is unionized. Library directors need to understand union agreements and the history of bargaining over particular issues. When a campus is unionized, things are carefully spelled out, and the ways directors manage faculty librarians is specifically defined, as well as more rigid.

Administrative Staff

Colleges employ a relatively large number of administrative and professional staff. Some are classic "managers," people whose jobs are to supervise departments: human resources, financial affairs, development, and facilities maintenance. Others are professionals who may supervise no one but perform tasks consistent with an advanced level of education or expertise and employ significant independent judgment. Two offices on campus have professionals in positions particularly similar to the library, counseling and information technology, although their levels of education may differ. Counseling on a campus can cover academic or personal issues. Those who do counseling often have advanced credentials in psychology or in academic areas, while information-technology people often have extensive job-related skills reflected in certificates or demonstrated competence rather than advanced degrees.

When understanding where librarians can fit and the status they can have on a campus, it is important to notice other areas on campus where people with master's-level degrees have administrative positions. Does the comptroller have an MBA? Is the CFO a CPA? Librarians saying that because they have master's degrees they are properly considered faculty may run into resistance from administrative staff, who will say, "I have just as much education (or more) as those librarians and I am not faculty?"

Decisions about faculty status for librarians are most powerfully influenced by what the classroom faculty think. That is a necessary condition. If the classroom faculty are not in favor, if they do not consider librarians like them, it is impossible to engineer faculty status for librarians. By itself it is not sufficient, the college administration must agree. What administrators think will be influenced by their ideas about administrative staff, about librarians, and about how making a decision in favor of faculty status for librarians may set a precedent for other non-instructional people on campus.

FACULTY STATUS AND ACADEMIC STATUS

The position of the Association of College and Research Libraries (ACRL) expressed by its board and membership and reaffirmed in June 2007, is that faculty status for librarians is connected to two essential contributions of librarians to the intellectual activities of campuses: collections, which support research, and curriculum and instruction. ("Librarians perform a teaching and research role inasmuch as they instruct students formally and informally and advise and assist faculty in their scholarly pursuits.")

The Academic Institution: The Faculty

The faculty has primary responsibility for such fundamental areas as curriculum, subject matter, and methods of instruction, research, faculty status, and those aspects of student life that relate to the educational process (providing advice to the governing board/president).

The faculty sets the requirements for the degrees offered in courses, determines when the requirements have been met, and authorizes the president and board to grant the degrees thus achieved.

Faculty status and related matters are primarily a faculty responsibility; this area includes appointments, reappointments, decisions not to reappoint, promotions, the granting of tenure, and dismissal. The primary responsibility of the faculty for such matters is based upon the fact that its judgment is central to general educational policy. Furthermore, scholars in a particular field or activity have the chief competence for judging the work of their colleagues; in such competence, it is implicit that responsibility exists for both adverse and favorable judgments. Likewise, there is the more general competence of experienced faculty personnel committees having a broader charge. Determinations in these matters should first be by faculty action through established procedures, reviewed by the chief academic officers with the concurrence of the board. The governing board and president should, on questions of faculty status, as in other matters where the faculty has primary responsibility, concur with the faculty judgment, except in rare instances and for compelling reasons that should be stated in detail.[2]

From the point of view of professors, expressed by the AAUP, control over faculty status derives from the faculty's responsibilities with respect to "general educational policy" and the ability of "scholars" to judge their peers.

The language of the ACRL-AAUP Joint Statement on Faculty Status grounds librarians' claim to faculty status on academic freedom and the centrality of libraries to teaching and research. "Because the scope and character of library resources should be taken into account in such important academic decisions as curricular planning and faculty appointments, librarians should have a voice in the development of the institution's educational policy"; moreover, "academic freedom" is considered as essential to librarians as it is to classroom faculty.[3]

The ACRL also has a parallel statement on "academic" status to be used as guidance for all librarians who do not have faculty status. The purpose of describing "academic status" is that when librarians are not recognized as faculty per se, they nevertheless should have a status that allows them to support the educational enterprise. The preamble to the faculty status standards points specifically to three areas: collections and access, interpretation of collections, and "contributing to the sum of knowledge" in librarianship. The academic status standards are more general, just mentioning that librarians play an "integral" role. (Numbering in the table follows that of each original Standard).

The standards for *academic status* call for no fewer rights than do those for *faculty status*. The clauses in the academic status statement provide more explicit justification on each point, while those in the faculty status statement simply lay out the essential elements; a theme is "equivalence" ("similar," "same," "comparable to") to faculty. Nevertheless, the academic status statement also mentions peer review, participation in (some) library and college governance, academic freedom, and even continued employment: after seven years, effective tenure. "Academic status" ends up being faculty status by stealth, or put another way, what is important is what faculty status means, not what it is called.

OTHER ARGUMENTS FOR AND AGAINST FACULTY STATUS

The three perspectives of bureaucracy, politics, and human resources are all important in weighing the pros and cons of faculty status for librarians. A bureaucratic model asks, what rationales are there for faculty status? The political model asks how different interest groups, particularly faculty, support librarians as peers. A human resources perspective asks how

Preamble (excluding procedural information)

Faculty Status[4]	Academic Status[5]
The academic librarian makes unique contributions to the academic community and to higher education itself. These contributions include **developing collections**, providing bibliographic access to all library materials, and interpreting these materials to members of the college and university community.	In 1971, the Association of College and Research Libraries (ACRL) adopted the ACRL Standards for Faculty Status of College and University Librarians (revised 2001). The ACRL supports faculty rank, status, and tenure for librarians and has developed the following documents in support of this concept:
Specific services include **instruction** in the use of print and online library resources and the creation of new tools to enhance access to information available locally, regionally, nationally, or internationally.	ACRL also has developed the following guidelines for academic librarians without faculty status to ensure that their rights, privileges, and responsibilities reflect their integral role in the mission of their institutions.
Librarians contribute to the sum of knowledge through **their research** into the information process and other areas of study. Service improvements and other advances in the field result from their participation in library and other scholarly organizations.	

Faculty Status	Academic Status
1. Professional responsibilities Librarians must be able to exercise independent judgment in the performance of professional duties. There must be a regular and rigorous review of their performance based on a stated set of institutional criteria. A necessary element of this review is appraisal by a committee of peers who have evidence pertaining to the performance, service, and scholarship of those being evaluated, subject to appropriate institutional policy.	**1. Professional responsibilities** Librarians should be assigned responsibilities matched to their educational competencies and the needs of the institution. They should have maximum latitude in fulfilling their responsibilities. Supervisory personnel and peers should regularly and vigorously review their performance. Review standards and procedures should be published and uniformly applied; reviewers should have access to all appropriate documentation.
2. Library governance College and university librarians should adopt an academic form of governance similar in manner and structure to other faculties on the campus.	**2. Governance** (2.b.) Librarians should participate in the development of policies and procedures for their library, including the hiring, review, retention, and continuing appointment of their peers.
3. College and university governance Librarians should be eligible for membership in the faculty senate or equivalent governing body. They should have the same degree of representation as other academic units on all college or university governing bodies.	(2.a) The library exists to support the teaching, research, and service functions of the institution. Thus, librarians should also participate in the development of the institution's mission, curriculum, and governance.
5. Tenure Librarians should be covered by a stated tenure policy.	**3. Contracts** A librarian should be appointed by a written contract of no less than one year. The contract

(Continued)

Faculty Status	Academic Status
See "Dismissal" below (8–9) for academic status	should state the terms and conditions of service and grant security of employment for the contractual period. After a period of no longer than seven years and through a process that includes peer review, librarians should be granted continuing employment if they have met the appropriate conditions and standards.
4. Compensation (and contracts) Salaries and fringe benefits should be comparable to and within the range of those paid to faculty of equivalent rank. Salary scales should be adjusted in an equitable manner to contract period. All librarians should have written contracts or agreements consistent with institutional policy.	**4. Compensation** The salary scale and benefits for librarians should be the same as for other academic categories with equivalent education, experience, or responsibility.
6. Promotion Librarians should be promoted in rank based on their professional proficiency and effectiveness (performance, service, and scholarship) consistent with stated campus standards. The peer review system should be an integral part of procedures for promotion.	**5. Promotion and salary increases** Librarians should be promoted through ranks on the basis of their professional proficiency and effectiveness. Procedures for promotion and salary increases should include a peer review. Librarians should have ranks equivalent to those of the faculty.
7. Leaves and research funds Sabbatical and other research leaves should be available to librarians consistent with campus standards. Librarians should have access to funding	**6. Leaves and research funds** Librarians should be eligible for internal and external research funds, leaves of absence, sabbaticals, and other means of administrative support to

Faculty Status	Academic Status
for research projects and professional development consistent with campus standards.	promote their active participation in research and other professional activities.

8. Academic freedom

Librarians must have the same protection of academic freedom as all other faculty. Censorship of any type is unacceptable whether individual or organizational. All librarians must be free to provide access to information regardless of content.

7. Academic freedom

Librarians are entitled to the protection of academic freedom as set forth in the American Association of University Professors 1940 Statement of Principles on Academic Freedom and Tenure.

8. Dismissal or non-reappointment

The institution may dismiss a librarian during the contractual period only for just cause and through academic due process. Non-reappointment should involve adequate notice, peer review, and access to a grievance procedure.

9. Grievance[5]

Librarians should have access to grievance procedures. These should include formal steps to be completed within specified time limits and effective safeguards against reprisal by the institution, or abuse of the procedures by the grievant. They must be consistent with applicable institutional regulations and contracts.

well a status will motivate existing librarians or attract high-quality applicants.

Faculty status affects several different areas:

- Personnel benefits: salaries and ranks; professional development/sabbaticals
- Internal (library) governance
- Campus governance

Personnel Benefits

Salaries and benefits are the most pragmatic elements. Because they affect the budget, they might seem to be the most important for central administration. However, in reality, their relevance appears to be much smaller than one might anticipate. That is, faculty status does not itself make librarians more or less expensive to employ. No systematic evidence shows that classifying librarians as faculty means they are more costly to the institution or that a faculty-status librarian commands a greater salary. It is possible that conferring a symbolic benefit ("faculty status") acts as a substitute for higher compensation. That is, all other things being equal, if being faculty is desirable, librarians will accept lower salaries in order to have this status, or demand higher wages to compensate for its lack. This symbolic versus tangible trade-off is often seen in non-profit and government agency employment, where there are tight budgets and non-merit-based pay systems. Even for private for-profit businesses, if they are under economic stress, human resources advice is to use titles or other symbols of respect as motivators when raises are not feasible.

Setting salaries is not always a rational or even symbolic activity. Overall, salaries for college employees depend on the perceived "market" for job applicants. Wages and benefits need to be attractive to available candidates and in competition with other job opportunities. In general, hourly and some salaried staff positions are compared against the local non-academic employment market. The comparison includes wages and also tangible and intangible perks such as working conditions and benefits.

In the case of faculty, salary setting can take two forms. In one, there will be an attempt to have some sort of cross-campus equalization. This is usually based on rank, degree level, and years of experience. In unionized colleges and for some denominational cultures, the goal of equality across disciplines is associated with a philosophy of impersonal merit and transparency that takes into account only objective and visible qualifications, such as years of service and rank. Faculty merit particular pay because of their position in existing structures, unaffected by the opinions of their supervisors.

The other approach is based primarily on disciplines. Inter-not intracampus comparisons are the touchstone. In this for-mat, historians are compared to historians, business educators to business educators, and faculty in health professions are compared not only to other faculty, but to health practitioners. Disciplinary data are readily available from the Chronicle of Higher Education and the College and University Professional Association for Human Resources (CUPA-HR).

For faculty, the two systems are often in conflict. This is a bigger problem when the campus culture is more concerned with equality. For administrators and for faculty leaders such as chairs and deans, the disciplinary focus has an inexorable power. They are trying to attract and retain qualified individuals who them-selves are comparing positions at other institutions, not other positions on the same campus. The economics professor cares what other economics positions pay, not what the history faculty on her own campus receives. This is particularly true for new hires. Administrators have to compete at some level on salaries, although they can also employ non-monetary features such as teaching loads and the whole atmosphere of the small college. A denominational affiliation will attract some people and deter others.

If librarians are faculty, and if there is a rigid and pervasive insistence on using only longevity and rank to set faculty sal-aries, librarians may indeed receive higher salaries than they otherwise might. This situation is really quite rare. However much equality may be an ideal, faculty supply and demand vary so greatly across disciplines that colleges cannot stick to cross-campus equalization. Not when average associate professors in history command $60,000, those in health professions $70,000, and those in business $89,000.[6]

A disciplinary approach puts librarians in their own group; in CUPA terms, they are a variety of "middle management." This is a very affordable category for colleges. Therefore, determining salaries based on discipline means that for *faculty status* the salary issue is not relevant. Faculty status librarians are not more expensive than non-faculty status librarians. The opposite may work. Some librarians may see faculty status as more prestigious and thus may make a position attractive even if it is lower paying.

Rank is also important. Even though it does not matter on a day-to-day basis in teaching and in research, faculty are subdivided by not only tenure but also rank. A promotion in this professional context is not like a promotion in the business world. It does not mean that someone now supervises more people. Ranks are not hierarchical or even organizational, but recognize increased competence and achievement within essentially the same job. For faculty, rank operates as a parallel reward system outside the structural bureaucratic hierarchy that runs from instructional employee through department chair, division chair, dean, vice president, and president.

Rank is not tied to hierarchies of power, but does have some relation to salaries. An increment of $1,000 for a "promotion" is a surprisingly widespread and durable custom. A promotion serves as a primarily symbolic reward. It provides a way to motivate people to improve and develop, and to recognize their achievements, without expecting them to abandon their current valuable roles by moving into management. It is very important in the academic setting. The college needs good faculty to keep being faculty: teaching, doing research, and serving. Therefore, ranks and other forms of recognition are indispensible ways to provide continuous motivation throughout a person's career as they continue to fill the same basic position.

Story: At one small institution, faculty salary guidelines had two factors: longevity in rank and the rank itself. A special grid was created for librarians that included only longevity. This ranged from new to completely experienced at six years. Six years was about how long any faculty member might remain at each rank (except for professor). Since there were no ranks for librarians, they topped out after only six years.

The small college library needs a motivating structure for librarians because it is small. There are few or no internal steps for advancement, except for the directorship itself. Yet, similar to teaching faculty, the "ordinary" librarian can grow and develop within his or her own position. Therefore, academic status librarians often have a system of ranks.

Other compensation-related benefits include money for professional development and for sabbaticals. Even for classroom faculty, the sabbatical is not guaranteed, especially at the small college. In contrast, professional development is even more important for the daily responsibilities of librarians than it is for classroom faculty. When it comes to teaching, faculty traditionally are given great latitude and offered teaching development on a voluntary basis—there's no certification system for university educators. However, the significant technological infrastructure of libraries means that formal professional development is needed. In this respect, librarians will appear more like information-technology staff than classroom faculty.

Considering all the pluses and minuses of these salaries and benefits elements, faculty status ends up being neutral. Librarians who have faculty status are not more expensive, because their salaries are compared to other librarians, without regard for status. They need the same professional development whether they are faculty or not, and sabbaticals for librarians are no more easy or difficult than they are for classroom faculty—that is, even if librarians have faculty status, they may not receive sabbaticals.

INTERNAL STATUS

Internal refers to how librarians and library staff relate to one an other. How does the concept and the specific reality of "faculty status" at a college affect the internal workings of the library? Does having faculty status mean that some library workers have more status than others?

Faculty status is a status issue. Problems of status among library workers are not new or concerned just with faculty status. The role of the master's of library science qualification is subject to just as much discussion and speculation about its future as the role of tenure is for classroom faculty. In each case, some believe that the existing traditional frameworks—the MLS or the tenure system—present an unnecessarily rigid set of rules that prevents flexibility in the present and innovation in the future. On the other side, managers at many levels prize the very consistency and clarity (such as it is) of the systems as they exist: they have a rough idea of what an MLS means, and faculty know the elements, for good or bad, of what tenure means and how to get it.

The MLS requirement is subject to debate or dispute on two different ends of the professional spectrum of education or qualification for library work. Each of these ends interacts with the question of faculty status, and differently at the small college compared to a research institution. The two ends are the MLS compared to another professional (someone with another master's degree) or paraprofessional (someone with a high skill level), and the MLS compared to a doctoral degree. The status of librarians as faculty or not-faculty impacts how dividing lines around the MLS itself are drawn.

An important issue at small colleges is the blurring or sharing of responsibilities in the library between MLS librarians and support staff. Due to the small size of the staff and a team-oriented culture, MLS librarians often "pitch in" when needed with whatever comes up: reshelving books during an end-of-term rush, checking out books when a student worker has to step away, or doing copy cataloging. It is very important for either the academic or faculty status of librarians that these tasks be seen as extraordinary and generous, true "pitching in," and not the normal duties of librarians. When people lump all librarians into one group, including the clerk who manages interlibrary loans, the supervisor of student circulation workers, the reference librarian pointing out where the bathrooms are, and the director helping carry a handful of books back to the library, it is in those circumstances that outsiders, classroom faculty, and administrators will believe that all librarians are in one group with distinctions among them not important enough to pay attention to, and not partners with or part of the same group as faculty.

It is much easier to segregate staff and librarian roles in a library that is large enough to have at least one and often several full-time people in positions that have well-defined and separate sets of duties. If books need shelving, shelvers do it. If materials have arrived from shipping, acquisitions clerks take care of it. If copy cataloging backs up, the supervisor rearranges workflows, engages temporary help, or expands the staff. Those solutions are positional and bureaucratic, not the fluid and temporary trading of tasks that happens in a small library.

> **Story**: When a search was announced for a dean of a library school, the respected dean of the university libraries was appointed its head. A faculty member from the business school leaned over to a library science professor and said, "Why is he the search chair? Doesn't the library school report to him?" Here, the separation of the two units was not at all understood, even by an intelligent and experienced observer. That campus had full faculty status for librarians, but the library was an independent unit, similar to but apart from the schools.

It is harsh to say that sometimes pitching in, helping out, and doing what's needed can be harmful if it makes people think that all librarians are alike and that all library workers have essentially the same status. Criticizing the idea of pitching in goes against two prominent cultural traits. First, librarians generally like to be helpful people. The profession is a helping profession, and librarians are not socialized to consider things "beneath" them or incompatible with their master's-level education. Second, on many small campuses, the entire population is expected to have a team or family atmosphere: nobody is supposed to be above others, and everyone is expected to be helpful.

In order for librarians to have the same status as faculty, for them to work as equal partners, they need to seem to be similar to faculty, and not similar to support staff. Thus, all librarians need to be aware of how they appear to others and to make visible and vocal the exact meaning of what they are doing. If they are helping out, they should say so, conversationally, "Glad to help out the circulation staff when things get super-busy." Or a better response might be, "I'm on my way back from talking to

> **Stories:** When arriving on a small college campus, a visitor got stuck in a cul-de-sac without knowing how to get to the library. A groundskeeper came over and offered help, pointing out in great detail and with friendliness how to get to a good parking spot and get to the library. The library director pointed out that there was an explicit hospitality goal for all employees at the college.
>
> Another small college had a convenient parking space labeled for the president's use. This aroused intense irritation, as parking was quite tight. Eventually, the visible spot was eliminated, although it was simply moved to an indoor garage. The ordinary faculty as well as staff did not agree that the president deserved a reserved spot; the culture of one campus was too strong.

Jerry's composition class and thought I'd help out Mary since things are super-busy at the moment." These simple sentences are an essential part of educating others about what librarians really are, and are not. They inform the listener that the librarian works with faculty in instruction, that carrying books is not the librarian's regular role, and that the librarian is nonetheless a helpful, team-oriented person. Librarians involved may be thinking all this, but unless they say it out loud, they are in danger of having the observer come to the exact wrong conclusions, that a librarian is mainly in charge of book control and noise suppression. Put simply, how MLS librarians approach the range of tasks that need doing in a library will affect their status on campus.

Tension exists among all those who work at the library. Some support staff may be more experienced than many of the MLS librarians. Some may have developed important complex roles requiring a lot of independent expert judgment, particularly in cataloging and acquisitions. Some may have performed public services of a nature that seems indistinguishable from MLS-level work, particularly in doing reference, giving tours, and even delivering some instruction. The issues involved in distinguishing between MLS and support staff roles and responsibilities are discussed elsewhere. For here, the point is that the closer librarians' status is to that of faculty, the farther it will be from non-MLS staff.

It is best to have this understood as clearly as possible, in the library and among classroom faculty. Classroom faculty have very visible role distinguishers. Librarians need to be explicit and vocal about what it is that MLS librarians do.

The role of any newly hired person needs to be clear from the beginning. It is confusing to everyone if someone is hired with a non-MLS degree but fills an MLS-type role. Some of this may not seem to be important, especially when it comes to faculty status. For example, someone with a master's degree in instructional technology may seem to other faculty to be just as much faculty as the person with a library master's degree. That would not affect faculty status, but hiring someone at the bachelor's level of education, no matter how skilled, almost certainly would affect it. Although many colleges have faculty with master's but not doctoral degrees, very few have faculty who have no formal graduate education.

MLS librarians may also have distinctions. Faculty status does not always apply to everyone with an MLS in a library. The three common exceptions are the person with a doctoral degree, the director, and the cataloger. The long history of people with "surplus" humanities doctorates going to work in libraries includes the current Librarian of Congress. Whether or not they also have a library science degree is a different question. Here, it is the fact that they have a doctoral degree that may separate them from the others who work in the library. Some colleges begin by saying that librarians can have faculty status, but then require that tenure-track faculty have doctorates. In that case, a librarian who has faculty status does not have it by virtue of being a librarian; it is more that someone who has faculty status happens to be working as a librarian. Archivists and other special scholars on small campuses are examples of this type of library-sited but not really librarian faculty members. They are simply faculty who happen not to teach classes.

The director may be the one librarian with a doctoral degree. In many cases, college administrators specifically want the director of the library to be equivalent to faculty and to do this they prefer a traditional doctoral degree. They may insist on that more than they insist on the master's in library science, making a cultural and political assumption. The library needs to relate to a core group on campus, the faculty; and the library director represents the library. In this case, nobody except the library director needs to have this status. A very limiting aspect of this way of thinking is that it rests on considering other librarians as people who only work in the library. It ignores non-director librarians working directly with faculty and with students outside the walls of the library.

> **Story:** When reading historical accounts of college librarianship, it is important to read very carefully about the concept of faculty status. The word "librarian" may only apply specifically to the director. For the director to be the only one called librarian to have faculty status does not mean that other library staff have any sort of share in faculty affairs.[7]

This kind of attitude also indicates that people view the director as something different and separate from librarianship. Even though in a small college, by definition, the library director does "regular" librarian duties as well as being the director, those outside the library can have a blind spot about the librarian aspect. They separate the director from the rest of the people at the library. This is especially easy when the director has a doctorate and the other librarians do not.

When this is the situation, directors can either accept the situation or work to change it. If they think faculty status is appropriate for other librarians, then they need to make visible the ways in which they are like the other librarians. They can point out how academic department chairs teach as do other faculty, a comfortable cultural argument on most campuses. If the director does not work at it, librarians will be seen as staff, losing the parallel to academic departments. This tends to reduce the library itself to just another administrative support unit.

Catalogers are different and in some ways present a more difficult case. As noted above, of all library roles, the professional responsibilities of librarian catalogers are the least like teaching faculty, the most like administrative staff or information-technology professionals, and the least visible to anyone on campus. Catalogers in a small college library often are those who are most like a director, a bureaucratic supervisor.

If student interaction and even direct instruction are the primarily rationales for librarians to be considered faculty, it gives catalogers only two alternatives, taking on teaching assignments or not having faculty status. Taking on teaching runs into a human resources problem. People generally self-select into technical services and away from public-services librarianship. Many who devote themselves to learning the advanced skills needed for cataloging and technical services don't also love public services. Expecting someone to be a good reference librarian as well as a good cataloger is asking a lot of people who have already selected themselves into more technical and less extroverted positions.

The other alternative is to move to a more complex justification that it is librarianship itself that is like the faculty role, the totality of library responsibilities and not just instruction. This argument requires believing and effectively conveying that people who have the MLS are essentially similar to one another even when their duties are specialized, the way the student-teaching supervisor and the clinical experience coordinator are just as much faculty as are teachers of basic subject courses. It requires communicating that collections, organization, and technology are just as essential to the library as are public services and instruction.

Considering the point of view of the library as a whole, can the cataloger be spared from faculty roles and responsibilities? Every librarian is part of the library's presence on campus, going to meetings, interacting with faculty, and participating in the campus as a whole. To exclude catalogers would be to lose the benefit of their participation in the campus library presence. Catalogers who do not share the same status as the rest of the librarians will be isolated and will not be able to contribute in the same way, and therefore at the four- or six- or

10-person library, 10 to 25 percent of the library's presence is lost.

Internally then, the status of each librarian affects the status and the internal relations among them all, director, cataloger, "teaching" librarians, and support staff. Personal preferences intersect with the need for the most beneficial situation for all library workers.

At three unionized community college libraries:

- Library A: Librarians taught one-credit information literacy courses and worked to make them required for students; without teaching for-credit courses, they would not be considered faculty.
- Library B: The cataloger could not be considered faculty, because she supervised support staff and thus was management.
- Library C: The two-person community college library could not have a director, because neither of the two was allowed to manage the other or manage the library.

Campus Governance

Campus governance is where faculty status really becomes most important for the effectiveness of the library. All of the above affects how librarians see themselves and how faculty and administrators see them. Having respected positions and relationships helps attract and retain good librarians and enhances positive working relations with classroom faculty on a one-to-one basis.

Formally, faculty or academic status goes beyond what librarians are to include as to how they work on campus. Academia is unusual among American organizations in how it incorporates a parallel governance structure alongside and in ways subversive of the normal bureaucratic hierarchy. Faculty governance, the collective oversight and control that faculty exercise, primarily over the curriculum, is an embedded feature of academia supported by tradition, charters, and even accrediting standards. Because faculty and only faculty are the experts on the core purpose of the organization, knowledge, and its transmission: they have an acknowledged role and one that is exercised on an individual, faculty-member basis, not primarily or solely in terms of hierarchy. Faculty may deeply respect their chairs, deans, and provosts, but it would be unusual for them to consider that deans, chairs, and provosts got those jobs primarily because they had the greatest scholastic reputations in their fields. Faculty members individually have voices; they are not represented solely by their chairs and deans.

Where do librarians fit? Many arguments both pro and con can be mustered for faculty status for librarians on an individual basis, that the status may attract or repel good or bad candidates, or it may reward or intimidate current librarians; it may protect controversial innovators or ossify tenured slackers. Also, on a one-to-one basis, skilled, effective, and even charismatic librarians need no title to earn respect and cooperation; but the role on campus that their status gives them affects how they can or cannot participate in this influential parallel organizational structure.

Thus, even the ACRL statement for "academic" status librarians says the library exists to support the teaching, research, and service functions of the institution. Thus, librarians should also participate in the development of the institution's mission, curriculum, and governance.

During most of their working hours, librarians are physically separated from others on campus. Even if the library is not a stand-alone building, it is primarily a controlled-access facility, and librarians mostly do not have their offices out among classroom faculty. If librarians are not part of functioning faculty organizations, they will miss out on a lot of the ground-level, brainstorming aspects of how faculty think about the future of a college and they will have no ability to influence policies and decisions that impact and also can be impacted by the library. For example, it would be very difficult to create an institutional repository without faculty buying in to the concept.

Librarians need to be at the table for those issues that are central to the college's mission. At teaching-oriented colleges, this means curriculum committees, program-assessment teams, and task forces for general education, writing across the curriculum, co-curricular learning, and other academic endeavors. If librarians are faculty, they need to volunteer for or be voted into those bodies. If they are administrative staff, they need to make a compelling argument for *ex officio* seating. In colleges that expect faculty to conduct research, librarians also have contributions to make on bodies reviewing research support and initiatives.

Libraries also contain materials and can provide services that reflect a college's unique mission and engagement with its community. In this area, they also can participate in service-oriented groups. Libraries are big organizations, and the librarians who work there have the weight of their accumulated past decisions, and they don't turn over every four years the way students do. Nevertheless, despite this huge "tail," libraries are really about the future. To effectively execute, library staff have to be part of planning. Libraries cannot be effective when they are constantly trying to catch up with announced and finalized initiatives. Librarians don't just react, they can lead. New ways of teaching, of doing research, and providing service can come from librarians, not just impact them.

SUMMARY

The small organization can escape from visible structures. When who you are and what people think about your personal effectiveness and innovation mean more than your title, there is a great deal of flexibility, and people can think individually and creatively about the future without being tied to traditional formats and concepts.

That means that if the library really has excellent librarians, the formal structures and status do not mean as much as at larger or more rigid institutions. Seen in that light, the director takes a personal not structural approach. What is the best way to get good people and encourage them to get better? Anything that achieves that is the best. This works for the library whose librarians are all great, all the time.

For everybody else, structure does matter. Some structures will enhance the library director's ability to attract, support,

Faculty Status for Librarians

	Pro	Con
Bureaucratic/ rational	Placing librarians as peers to classroom faculty gives them a position from which to advise on innovations in information creation and delivery.	People who have faculty status are more difficult to manage in a command-control managerial framework.
	Placing librarians in faculty governance structures, particularly those concerned with budgeting and curriculum development, helps the library anticipate, advise on, and effectively plan to meet changing academic needs.	Lifetime tenure removes an incentive for professional development, which is acutely important in people whose profession faces inexorable technological changes
		The more people have faculty status, the more difficult "faculty" will be to deal with.
Political	Librarians are like classroom faculty because they:	Librarians are not like classroom faculty because they:
	Do work that is more central to "academic affairs" than other areas on campus.	Do not design and deliver instruction.
	Are directly (even though anonymously) involved in student learning.	Do not assess students and have no direct student assessment of their work.
	Possess advanced degrees similar to (many) classroom tenure-track faculty.	Are supportive elements similar to staff, such as writing centers or counseling.
	If not considered faculty, this relegates them to	Do not have advanced degrees similar to (many) classroom tenure-track faculty.

(Continued)

	Pro	Con
	employee groups that have little influence on campus and may have lesser educational qualifications or fewer connections with the curriculum or faculty research.	Having librarians as faculty may complicate bargaining (informal or formal) because the "faculty" group is more heterogeneous. If faculty status is conferred upon librarians, it might dilute the meaning of faculty.
Human resources	Attracts people interested in "research" (publication), therefore those who are interested in creating and testing innovations. Often means a more flexible definition of the workday and work responsibilities, similar to classroom faculty. Provides librarians with campus governance participation opportunities as equals to faculty.	Discourages those who view research as difficult or as distracting in time or effort from real librarianship. Requires support for travel or research.

and encourage librarians, and to work effectively on campus. When beneficial structures exist, each new director and every new librarian does not have to start from scratch to establish a powerful personal relationship; they can build on positive assumptions and roles that are already in place.

Every small college has an existing situation for faculty, academic, or administrative status for librarians and library staff. Librarians as managers and leaders need to begin with that structure, but they always need to think about the future and work for what is best for their college and their library.

MANAGING LIBRARIANS AS FACULTY: TENURE AND REVIEW PROCESSES

When librarians have faculty status, they participate in faculty-type tenure and promotion-review processes. These are so distinctly different from administrative reviews for staff personnel that they affect not only long-term retention, but day-to-day professional development. The most common negative image of tenure is that it is a system that means once you're in, you can be the worst faculty person ever and no one can get rid of you. Directors need to consider the review process in the whole ecology of personnel management within a library and on campus, how it works, who is involved, and what happens post-tenure. In each case for librarians, significant nuances are at work, meaning that tenure does not work the way people frequently imagine it does.

In a traditional model of personnel development, every year supervisors determine the extent to which each of their employees is meeting expectations. A rating form is often available, broken down by common skills such as punctuality and responsiveness and specific job responsibilities. An annual review for many higher-level employees adds a component in which the worker and supervisor set development or achievement goals for the coming year. A key feature of this annual process is that it has a top-down dynamic. The supervisor provides evaluative supervision to the supervisee. Good supervisors, leaders, managers, and directors welcome and encourage employee participation in the setting of goals and selecting methods for remedying deficiencies, but they are in charge of the process.

The tenure-review process has an opposite dynamic. After five or six years, faculty members must prove to a committee that they deserve retention, a decision with a lasting impact not only on the institution as a whole, obligated for salary in perpetuity, but also on their own units. Every faculty member retained is a position that cannot be filled with somebody new. In the small college, the mix of subspecialties within a discipline depends upon the faculty members who are present. Retaining that Civil War expert means giving up the chance for developing a center for revolutionary-period studies.

Reading the informal literature of the tenure-track probationary period shows an overwhelming number of complaints about how opaque, baffling, and thoroughly non-systematic this system is. Faculty complain that they get no regular guidance, are given no clear expectations, and experience no consistency. They can be told on hiring that teaching is the life of the university and then near tenure review realize that tenure committee members really only look at the length of their list of publications. The informal literature is by its nature a reflection of anxiety, not a scientifically representative sample demonstrating the prevalence of any particular problem, but it is hard to avoid the impression that however glorified life is after tenure is attained, the period before it is full of tension and anxiety. Some colleges developed an extensive "preparing future faculty" specifically to address these concerns.

Considered as a review process, the tenure system for traditional faculty has a distinctly different structure compared to a personnel-development system for administrative staff. It has advantages because waiting six years is easier than being evaluated every year, and lifetime tenure is more secure than annual contracts. Since it is frequently thought to be so wonderful for faculty, it is worth pointing out that there are also negative features in each type of review.

Faculty Tenure Track	Administrative Staff (professional level)
After five to six years: the faculty member provides a complete justification for his or her own future at the institution, with descriptions and documentation.	Every year: the staff member responds to questions from superior, and in some cases will generate annual goals.
More work, less often	Less work
Criteria are stated in broad terms; the relative importance of criteria (teaching, research, and service) is frequently unclear.	Criteria are stated in both broad and sometimes very specific terms.
More flexible, more opaque	More restrictive

Performance is judged by those who work beside but not with the faculty member; performance is usually represented by written documents rather than observed.	Performance is judged by one person who (usually) has the best vantage point for observing work throughout the year.
Some responsibilities (such as teaching) are comparable to the responsibilities of those doing the judging and hence more consistently judged; some (such as types of acceptable research) may be foreign to the judges.	Managers do not do the same work as their employees and so may not understand their technical achievements or how feasible their goals are.
Limited consistency to judgments Potential for personal bias (no accountability of judges to their supervisors).	Potentially more arbitrary.
Performance must not be terrible within the first year and reasonably comparable to others within next four to five years.	Performance must be within an acceptable range every year.
Performance must be demonstrably, acceptably excellent at one specific point in time.	Acceptable in comparison to other employees.
Consequence of almost-acceptable performance (cumulative over five to six years): loss of job (with one year's notice).	Consequence of almost-acceptable performance (each year): retain job with ability to improve performance.

The "up" part of tenure's "up-or-out" system is understood by non-academics; the consequences of "out" are less well appreciated. For faculty in professional disciplines, losing an academic job may not be a serious blow. They can go practice their profession. The relative scarcity of academic positions and non-academic alternatives to the tenure track make the "out" prospect an extraordinarily powerful motivator to people in the humanities. That is a main reason why the dynamics of tenure review are very fierce on the faculty for the reviewee side, in contrast to the standard staff performance-evaluation system, where primary responsibility lies with the supervisor, with employee input.

While this may vary in some institutions, in most, another notable feature of the tenure-review system that distinguishes it very sharply from staff positions is the role of peers in review. As can be seen in the ACRL standards for both faculty and academic staff, and seen in the general norms for determining research quality, the prevailing evaluative culture in the faculty arena is based on peer review, not hierarchical control. "Peer" in tenure review is defined in terms of overall role and status, not by rank. Assistant professors are not in fact judged strictly by their rank-peers, fellow junior faculty members. They are judged by fellow faculty, people who have achieved tenure and are senior in rank.

This has an extremely important consequence for librarians at the small college. The numerical facts of small college and small library life mean that each librarian will have a very small number of close peers among librarians. The library is small and so the number of senior librarians is small, especially in cases where directors, equivalent to department chairs, do not participate in peer review because they are administrators.

Subject departments on the small college campus are also small, but they are generally combined in order to form a broader pool of reviewers. Faculty join together from several departments, usually from disciplines considered somewhat similar, such as the liberal arts, hard sciences, or health professions. Peer then means a faculty in a same or roughly similar subject area. However, when a librarian application for tenure goes beyond the library for review, it may be judged by peers who are not particularly close. Few to none of those judging it will be librarians. This means that the process of judging librarians' materials may seem very different from judging classroom faculty or they may seem similar enough that faculty can have confidence in their own judgments and librarians can trust their conclusions.

In this situation, three types of institutions have a distinct advantage with respect to handling librarian applications. First, public colleges that are part of a larger system can use established guidelines and examples from librarianship as practiced and defined across the system. As noted above, often small college librarianship differs less from the flagship campus librarians than the teaching-research-service mix differs for classroom faculty even when they are part of a single system. Second, in institutions where librarians have had faculty status for a long time, a body of history, examples, precedence, and familiarity is available to guide faculty reviewers. And finally, campuses with a very diverse range of educational formats and programs will find that dealing with that diversity (e.g., practitioners turned faculty, internship supervisors as faculty) has prepared everyone to accept more diverse expressions of academic effort than on more traditional campuses.

Nevertheless, translating librarian work into terms that faculty understand requires careful attention. Faculty are used to reviewing syllabi and reading student evaluations. They won't see either of those for most librarian faculty. On all campuses, it is necessary to educate or guide non-librarian reviewers in the ways that librarian work meets equivalent standards for excellence. Directors who want their librarians to succeed in achieving tenure have to find ways for them to describe, demonstrate, and document what library standards are and how they have met them. This is especially challenging in a profession in which many encounters are anonymous and formal evaluations or feedback are rare. If librarians are not proactive, they risk having faculty make mistaken assumptions.

Story: At a small college, a psychology faculty member simply refused to conduct a vote on a faculty member who primarily had managerial responsibilities. The professor insisted that nobody could be judged as faculty unless he or she had classroom student evaluations. This person simplified "faculty/peer" down to whether faculty have student evaluations and administrators (non-faculty) do not. Even though that individual supported faculty status for librarians, the specific point about student evaluations had to be negotiated.

The following table describes some ways of handling individual evaluation points that tend to show up in tenure reviews, providing ideas about potential comparisons. Details will vary from campus to campus, especially depending on faculty roles, but some areas give more trouble than others.

Teaching syllabi	Provide descriptions of in-class instruction sessions, including both content and learning outcomes. Describe achievements in other areas (such as collection management) in terms of explicit goals and plans.
Teaching load	Describe in general terms "desk" duty schedule, presentations, collection management, and other tasks. Emphasize the one-on-one nature of most public service while providing numbers for group presentations.
Student evaluations	Point out that public service necessarily is anonymous in order to best serve patrons and preserve their confidentiality. Provide evaluative feedback from faculty whose classes receive instruction.
Peer evaluations of teaching	Invite classroom faculty to be present during library instruction; invite faculty to sit and observe at the reference desk during high-volume times. Directors should emphasize that they extensively observe librarians performing public service.
Teaching innovation, new course design, etc.	Describe new library services, Web sites, or other research tools designed by the librarian. Team projects are valuable especially when colleagues document the librarian's individual contributions.
Contributing to program or college learning outcomes	The library director should develop a map between the library's public services and any information-literacy-related

	goals at the college or program level; librarians would describe their responsibilities in relation to them.
	Confirmation from subject faculty, especially department chairs, strengthens a claim that librarians' work advances learning outcomes.
Mentoring	Librarian assistance to students doing research or projects will generally be anonymous. The librarian should explain this directly. Some letters of thanks from students may be useful, although some campuses do not place any weight on solicited letters.
	Letters from faculty describing the assistance a librarian provided to their students will be valuable.
Research	Documentation of research should follow the norms of the particular campus in describing presentations, publications, creative products, or any other activities.
Service	Documentation of service should follow the norms of the particular campus in describing community, professional, or charitable work.

LIBRARIAN RESEARCH

Research expectations for academic librarians is an issue in which librarians themselves have the most divergent viewpoints. Research responsibilities, the "publish or perish" situation, can be frightening. PhDs are clearly research degrees, but for MLS librarians, research may not fit with their profession education. Fortunately, many library schools include research methods in their required courses. The American Library Association competencies for beginning master's-level librarians include an entire section on research, not just knowing key findings of librarianship itself or being a thoughtful consumer of research but understanding quantitative and qualitative methods.

Even though research is one of the three classic responsibilities of faculty, laboratory or empirical and discovery-based research is not always part of the life of small college faculty. This happens for several reasons. A college can put its emphasis on teaching; there may be a lack of facilities or colleagues needed for traditional "big science" projects; and the tradition leads to research primarily conducted more at large universities and less at smaller colleges. Faculty seeking positions should consider teaching loads and research expectations and select themselves into institutions that fit the research demands that they want in their academic lives.

Some librarians feel that a focus on publishing is a distraction from their real work. Instead of thinking about how to best serve the patrons in front of them, the "researcher" is looking for abstract issues that have little relevance to real life. This is research-as-diversion and it is the mirror of "we focus on teaching" for classroom faculty. Librarians who select non-faculty-status institutions to work at often point to the benefits of focusing on what they need to do and not taking time for these external pursuits.

On the other hand, research can be very feasible for small college librarians. As far as facilities go, research in library science generally does not require expensive equipment. This can be a particularly significant point for the small college librarian. A librarian at a large university may need a great deal of coordination, processes, and permissions to try something out, to conduct research on some new idea. The librarian at a small college often has personal connections and a great deal of flexibility. The small colleges can be the pilot program for ideas that then disseminate throughout academic librarianship.

The barriers to faculty research on the small college campus thus are really strengths of research in the library field. Much librarian research focuses on user studies or research that supports user needs, which is similar to the scholarship of teaching. Complex equipment is not often needed, and librarians can usually find compatible partners on their own campus or at others—good networking is a great idea for practicing as well as researching librarianship.

Not all librarians arrive on a campus ready to conduct research. Not all library schools have included research methodology in their curriculum. However, academic librarians go to work every day on a campus where somewhere, someone is teaching research or statistics or other tools needed. Acquiring the skills is very feasible. If librarians are on a campus where research is valued for all faculty, there will be groups and partnerships that help facilitate publication.

Librarianship can be practiced at several levels:
Tell me what to do: I will perform library tasks accurately, conscientiously, politely, and even enthusiastically.

This is the level for library support staff: people without the MLS degree.

I love what libraries and librarians do. I strive to do the best job possible; I continually seek out new ideas to implement into my daily activities. I use formal and information continuing education to keep myself up to date as a consumer of library innovation.

This characterizes good practitioners.

I take a long view and try to plan for the future, examining today's possibilities and needs; I take a second look at how we do things and ask "why" and "how else" and "whether."

This is the mark of a manager: someone who manages the needs of the library into the future.

Besides being a good practitioner and manager, I will myself develop and test new ideas and concepts to advance librarianship as a whole. Instead of just reading other's ideas, I will publish my own.

Here people move to be leaders and researchers, creating the future of librarianship.

How does librarianship advance? Informally, it advances all the time, but the field as a whole benefits systematically when librarians look at what they are doing and think, "What about this can be shared with others?" Research and evaluation are characterized by a systematic approach to discovering new knowledge or ways of doing things that is of such obvious quality (confirmed by peer review) that others will learn from it.

Research broadly speaking demands a certain level of care and extra work. It means not just redesigning a Web page but testing to see what the redesign means for users. It means not just doing something but also examining it, linking the effort to other published information in the field, and sharing it. This extra work is very important to the field because all academic librarians suffer if nobody bothers to find out, discuss, and disseminate. It is worth it to the librarian, because research is inherently about something new, finding out something new to say. That makes it inherently exciting and different.

Pragmatically, for faculty status and tenure review, it is absolutely crucial to know exactly what "research" means on a particular campus. At research universities, there are clear guidelines and expectations in each discipline revolving around original creative or scholarly work published in nationally known and peer-reviewed venues. The same is not true on all small campuses nor for all areas, including librarianship. Activities at a research university might be considered "service," if acknowledged at all, but may garner significant respect at the smaller college:

- Running local conferences or speaking at state workshops
- Editing professional newsletters or magazines
- Writing how-to rather than research-based articles
- Giving presentations to non-college groups

Even ARL deans respect publishing in *American Libraries*, definitely not a scholarly venue.[8] "Journals" in many institutions refer simply to periodicals that have specialized audiences, not to those that consist of peer-reviewed empirical studies. All of this makes the research component of faculty status something that is compatible with librarianship at a small college.

Does the college provide "support" specifically for librarian research? Support sometimes can be monetary, such as for travel to conferences. Student labor to gather data can be provided. Much of support involves time, or what a librarian does with his or her day. When directors consider research as part of what librarians should be doing, that is an important level of support. Making it something extra that should not take away any time from what a librarian should be doing, making it something librarians do on their own time, is a sure deterrent. Research supports and is part of regular library work, the way that faculty research enriches teaching.

One significant difference between librarians and classroom faculty is that faculty have much greater flexibility in their time than many librarians do. They need to show up for class, meetings, and office hours, but are generally free to arrange everything else. It looks as though they have much free time, though just because it is not scheduled does not mean it is free; it is flexible, but full.

Given the fact that they have set required hours, often including evening and weekend duty, librarians may conclude that faculty have more time available for research. This is a false assumption; there are many data showing that faculty even at teaching-oriented institutions work 50–60 hours per week. One study that included both faculty and librarians and asked directly about time for writing showed that they complained equally about the difficulty of finding time for research. What is important is for directors and librarians themselves to consciously give priority to research along with all the other tasks they already manage around, like responding to faculty, answering questions, and selecting materials and designing instruction. Faculty also complain that teaching loads, including advising, committee meetings, and supervision, crowd out any time for research. It is always the case that non-research tasks can and will take all of the time available for them and more. Nobody can say that they have undedicated time. If research is part of one's role, then it is as important to spend time on it as it is to give that presentation yet another layer of polish.

Directors reinforce this by asking about research, talking about its value, and not emphasizing other work so much that it gives the impression that data gathering, writing, and giving papers or presentations is "on your own time." In the end, research is as feasible for academic librarians as any of their other responsibilities. Time for research is considered a part of being a good librarian, and being successful in library research is feasible, and the successful librarian researcher will fit very easily into the faculty of a small college.

NOTES

1. Moriarty, Joan, and Michelle Savarese. *Directory of Faculty Contracts and Bargaining Agents in Institutions of Higher Education*. Ed. Richard Boris. New York: National Center for the Study of Collective Bargaining, Hunter College, 2006.

2. http://www.aaup.org/AAUP/pubsres/policydocs/contents/governan cestatement.htm.

3. http://www.ala.org/ala/mgrps/divs/acrl/standards/jointstatement faculty.cfm.

4. Association of College and Research Libraries, June 2007: http://www.ala.org/ala/mgrps/divs/acrl/standards/standardsfaculty.cfm.

5. Association of College and Research Libraries, January 2007: http://www.ala.org/ala/mgrps/divs/acrl/standards/guidelinesacademic.cfm.

6. 2007–2008 data for mid-level administrators and faculty at four-year institutions; CUPA-HR, reprinted by the Chronicle of Higher Education: http://chronicle.com/article/Average-Faculty-Salaries-By/ 47059/ and http://chronicle.com/article/Median-Salaries-of-Midlevel/ 47386/.

7. Lyle, Guy. *Administration of the College Library*. New York: Wilson, 1944.

8. Nisonger, Thomas E., and Charles H. Davis. "The Perception of Library and Information Science Journals by LIS Education Deans and ARL Library Directors: A Replication of the Kohl-Davis Study." *College & Research Libraries* 66, no. 4 (2005): 341–77.

III
CORE RESPONSIBILITIES
OF MANAGERS

7 PLANNING

The key: Think, consult, decide, communicate: planning

What do managers do? They make sure the right people are in the organization in the right places and work well together and independently; and they take care of the longer view, such as where are we going? What do we need to think about to get there? Any librarian can take care of the daily activities of the library. The library director places those day-to-day needs in the context of the past, the present, and the future.

In a small organization, when you are doing work, you know everybody, and where you help with everything, it is easy to think that formal planning is archaic, unneeded, and a waste of time. Only large libraries need formal structures because they are bureaucracies, while small libraries are innovative organisms more than they are organizations. Focusing on these concrete managerial responsibilities seems artificial and deadening.

Communication is not deadening. Communication is the essential oxygen of effective management, and planning means three things: thinking about an issue, coming to some decisions or consensus ideas about the issue, and communicating those conclusions. Even if there is thinking or consensus without formal planning, too often there is no communication. Therefore, planning is important even for the smallest library.

Many librarians are not natural planners. Insofar as they view themselves as practicing professionals, they concentrate on the conduct of their profession, serving constituents through present service and future collections. A campus strategic-planning process often fails to engage their imagination. It could be too business-like, formalized, and alien to an academic atmosphere. It could be too vague and indistinct: how many institutions claim to "have an impact" and "change lives" and "produce leaders"? The major themes it lays out very often simply overlook the library.

All types of planning have value, though, and strategic planning has a vital role, particularly in campus communication. The process itself has benefits far broader than the list of objectives with which it ends up. When the process functions well, it is a powerful venue for people on campus to talk to one another about what they are all about. The library is part of the campus, and librarians need to be part of campus planning. The library-specific plans they create, such as collection management, evaluation, and disaster planning, ultimately are bound to the campus mission and its planning.

DEFINING PLANNING

At its simplest, a plan is a systematic presentation of thinking about a particular issue. That does not mean that when there's no plan, there's no thinking and no action. Librarians and academics think, dream, and do all the time. A plan formulates thinking into a shared framework.

Formal planning has four main strengths:

- The process is a way to involve many constituents in thinking about the issue.
- The structured format requires that the thinking be broad, explicit, and consistent.
- The end plan serves as a valuable communication tool about the organization and what it is and does at its best.
- It raises participants' awareness from day-to-day needs to where they think creatively about the future.

Potentially, an academic library director has or is involved with several types of plans:

- Collection development
- Preservation
- Evaluation
- Disaster recovery
- Strategic
- Master

When put in this context, a *strategic* plan is only *one* type of planning that librarians experience. The whole idea of strategic planning sometimes can seem like overkill for a small library, an over-mighty immigrant from the business world. It is more useful to see that it is not an isolated endeavor but is part of the spectrum of planning at a library and across a campus.

The various types of plans range from more to less library-centric. Collection-development and preservation plans are focused on the library; they apply to library resources and call upon very library-specific tools and techniques, even though they are strengthened by involving non-library stakeholders. A disaster-recovery plan for a library is likely to be a chapter with particularly important library concerns within campus preparation for disasters. A library's strategic plan may stand alone, but it makes little sense to do long-term planning that is uncoordinated with broad campus planning.

> **Story**: A small college campus in a small, relatively isolated town experienced a tornado. The college's insurers identified the companies that could provide disaster and recovery services for the library's collection as well as other buildings on campus.

This chapter begins by describing elements that are common across plans (generic), then outlines the key areas of each particular plan, and culminates in a lengthy discussion of strategic planning. Master planning is an even longer-term form of planning. Taking a look at all of these plans in relation to one another allows librarians in the small library to address its current, future, and potential needs and to coordinate their own planning with that of the larger campus. On every campus, and in different sections of a campus, there may be a greater or lesser degree of formality about planning. The library director needs to ensure that even if other areas on campus do not practice formal planning, the library staff does so to the extent that planning can benefit them. It is true that excessive rigidity in planning has its own problems, especially when it is not customized to take into account important local issues, and more when it discourages innovative thinking in between planning dates. As long as people retain a sensible, practical attitude as they implement and modify plans, the process and product of formal planning are worth the effort.

The description does not include how to perform academic librarianship or subsets of library science, such as how to evaluate databases or how to identify methods to preserve materials. It stays on the level of management and keeps its particular focus on the small. That is, each section lays out the steps in the *process* that the library manager needs to consider, and reflects on how the fact that the library and college are small affects how the planning proceeds.

GENERIC PLAN ELEMENTS

It may be surprising to see a "preservation plan" in the same listing as "strategic planning." Nevertheless, different types of a plan really do deserve the common noun, "plan." Looking at this variety of plans also highlights the reality that people *do* these functions without always formally *planning* them. Books get bought, books get repaired, a collection gets enhanced, the cleaners are called, librarians dream of new service areas, and someone is thinking about a new library building all without any need for collection, preservation, evaluation, disaster, strategic, or master plans. Planning for these elements makes this normal flow of work and ideas easier, more consistent, and better.

The common elements found in all types of plans are:

- Leadership by (internal) experts
- Involvement of appropriate (external) stakeholders
- Brainstorming about possibilities
- Some level of research or evaluation about options
- Agreement upon a final result that is explicitly documented

If these are not present, it is not really planning, but just day-to-day doing, talking, and thinking. For each type of plan discussed, each of these elements is expanded: experts, stakeholders, brainstorming, research/evaluation, and the final documented plan.

Experts/Leaders

Leadership by experts means that a particular person or small team has a special interest and expertise in an area. These people should be internal to the particular issue or organizational unit. If a process or issue is important, then someone close to it should take ownership. In turn, one of the benefits of explicit planning is that these processes give a variety of individuals a chance to show leadership and initiative in areas where they are the particular experts. The library director does not need to be in charge of all types of planning. A new MLS graduate fresh from a seminar on collection preservation could easily lead an effort to develop (or update) a preservation plan. This is an application of the human resources approach to management: encouraging people to develop and use expertise generally raises their morale and personal commitment to an organization.

Stakeholders

Each plan has its own group of appropriate stakeholders. These are individuals or units that have a structural interest in the issue at hand. Structural interest means by virtue of their position or responsibilities. When a library director is considering a type of plan that seems to be very library-centric and in particular when it seems to involve very library-specific knowledge and professional judgment, it is easy to think that librarians are the only stakeholders who are important. Nevertheless, there are two reasons why thinking more broadly and creatively about stakeholders pays dividends when a wider range of people are identified and then are involved. These are good inputs and successful outputs. Looked at bureaucratically or rationally, most plans need a wide range of expertise, especially on a small college campus. Not all knowledge is available in-house, and there will be people with expertise elsewhere on campus who can strengthen the knowledge base of the planning process.

Thinking particularly in a political way in respect to outputs, each finalized plan will meet with a higher degree of acceptance if it is not perceived as just "librarians telling us what they think." The library exists to serve its constituents, either present or future. Those constituents, faculty, students, researchers, and community members have or *should* have an interest in what the librarians are planning.

Stakeholders who are involved in developing or revising a plan will be a political interest group with a specific stake in implementing the plan. A wide planning process, then, assists in the plan's ultimate success.

Brainstorming

What "brainstorming" means here is to think about the issue as thoroughly, as systematically, and as creatively as possible. Systematic, thorough, and creative are not contradictions. Having all three is something that distinguishes planning from day-to-day "doing" in the library. The planning process should ensure that for each plan, participants try to make certain that all important areas are covered (systematically), push the boundaries of each identified issue (thoroughly), and take the opportunity to think about a range of wild and innovative ideas (creatively). Too often in the day-to-day "doing" of library activities, people work within their comfort zones with the knowledge they have on that day and pick the issues they like the most. Good planning pushes outward and upward.

Different people have different attitudes about the word "brainstorming," just as some students groan or cheer when "group work" is mentioned in class. Introverts may dislike a free-for-all discussion; they have difficulty tossing out half-formed ideas for people to tear at and can end up being silenced by lively conversational flows not because they have no ideas or creativity but because they need time to come up with a thoughtful comment. Extroverts can spark a lot of ideas and provide plenty of food for thought, but sometimes don't listen well or focus on coming to conclusions. It is more common for librarians to be introverts, and sometimes they see group brainstorming more as a problem than as an opportunity.

Brainstorming does not have to be time-consuming. Time limits for comments and input can be set. Brainstorming does not have to favor the verbally fluent or those who are most comfortable tossing out fragments of thoughts. Several techniques may be used to elicit input from everybody, such as asking people to write down ideas or taking deliberate pauses. Brainstorming does not have to happen in person. When people are committed to the issue at hand, there are several technologies available to get and share ideas. But every plan needs at least some brainstorming. The creativity that comes from sharing ideas is a very necessary way to counteract what the plan will eventually be, formalized and formal but not formulaic.

Tip: The smallest brainstorming can occur with the expenditure of about two hours. For an identified issue, say a plan for the health-sciences collection, identify the planners. About a week ahead of a one-hour meeting, ask them to spend about an hour thinking about the issue and coming up with at least three ideas: (1) something they feel very strongly is needed or important; (2) something that is a wild idea; and (3) something they think some outsider might wonder about the issue. During the one-hour meeting, share the ideas. Have at least one five-minute period of silence midway through the conversation to allow introverts to process ideas. "Vote" with tokens on what ideas should be pursued. Specific uses of brainstorming will be covered throughout the remainder of the chapter with discussions about the planning process.

Research and Evaluate Options

Professional development, noted as essential in the personnel chapter, comes into play in the process of researching and evaluating options. While professional development helps people individually on a day-to-day basis, it also feeds into longer-term library planning. Through professional development, people learn about new ideas on each specific topic or area that will be involved in planning. Through planning, librarians systematically apply these ideas to library needs and opportunities.

When a plan is created or updated, librarians don't just remember those bits and pieces of individual ideas when they show up in brainstorming sessions but seriously examine and research what is known about them. As they are in an information profession, librarians should believe it is valuable to see what other librarians and researchers have experienced and shared about ideas. This research consists of journal articles and books, Web resources, and personal contacts with librarians at other institutions.

How extensive the research and evaluation phase is depends on the issue, but doing at least some ensures that a library director and staff do not just continue on with only those ideas that they know about. This mental "box" is an equal danger for both small and large libraries. Directors of large libraries may believe that their extensive staff and resources already encompass most or all needed expertise and input. Directors of small libraries are in danger of believing that their own situations are so unique, so special, or so conditioned by their own campus culture and attributes that no one else truly has a comparable situation. That's a false assumption. Other libraries may not be 100 percent comparable, but no campus is definitively unique. Larger academic libraries are still academic libraries and other libraries and other academic units have something to teach one another.

Final Documented Plan

A planning process results in a plan. The process itself is valuable, but at least some of that time and effort would be wasted if it does not result in an actual plan. This plan is both useful and tied into the campus's mission and overall planning processes.

Plans have three audiences: actors, library, and others. The actors are those who carry out the plan or are concerned directly with the issue. They should have easy access to the plan and incorporate it into both their daily decision-making and also into their annual personal-development goals and assessment. Some plans will be more acted upon than others. Other than updating contact names or details as a library's resources or facility changes, hopefully a disaster-recovery plan never gets used. A master plan for building has exceedingly slow-moving parts but should remain active and should not be shoved into a closet.

If a plan no longer seems relevant, staff should revise it rather than abandoning the attempt to plan. Poor plans are just that. Suppose someone says that a plan is awkward, does not address important issues, and doesn't seem to match day-to-day needs. Then someone, that person, the director, or someone else, needs to understand if it is the staff person's perception that needs changing or the plan. Throwing away the plan will treat a symptom, not a cause.

In some cultural environments, a formal plan will look like a useless layer of unnecessary verbiage or rigidity. People don't need plans because they know what they are doing. So far so good because it's heartening that they know what they are doing, and why, and what will come in the future. The process of formalizing it by writing it down may not seem to be immediately useful perhaps to one particular staff member, but spelling out a plan ensures that staff can explain what they do to others, can coordinate their effort with others, and can check to be sure that others understand what they do. Writing out a plan, like pilots following a checklist, helps to make sure that nothing important is overlooked.

SPECIFIC PLANS AND THEIR ELEMENTS

This section goes through the specific types of plans and discusses how the generic elements work in each. The longest section addresses the strategic plan, the plan type that is most closely tied to cross-campus planning procedures and cycles.

Collection Development

A collection-development plan lays out priorities for acquiring and maintaining the resources a library staff is responsible for providing for users. It should derive from and serve the specific mission of the institution, from its general characteristics such as degree level and programs, and from any special responsibilities (e.g., for denominational history).

Leadership/experts: Here a professional librarian is essential. While many acquisitions procedures are carried out by staff, it is librarians whose education and profession focuses on determining the appropriate policies about resources.

Stakeholders: The two most important stakeholder groups for a collection-development plan are faculty and campus mission-developers. Faculty members are the personal manifestation of the college's academic programs. A college collection exists primarily to serve academic programs and student learning, and, to a greater or lesser degree, faculty research. On some campuses, there are formal faculty library committees that would be natural conduits for faculty input on collection-management policy development. If there is no library committee, this input would then need to happen through other connections that librarians have with the faculty, on a personal basis or working with departments or schools or other bodies.

"Mission-developers" are those on a campus who work on visibly and consistently making connections among the college as an organization, its central mission or character, and its most important external constituencies. They are usually located somewhere in the president's office or in the development (fundraising) wing. Public institutions have the equivalent of "mission-developers," people who plan workforce training for local industry or communicate with trustees or legislators. They have a stake in a collection's development because the collection provides intellectual infrastructure for the mission of the institution. They have a wider perspective than faculty; the college itself, while centered on faculty, does extend beyond them.

Involving stakeholders can be tricky. One danger occurs when faculty members have a tendency to see and thus represent only what they experience, the students they teach, and their own academic area. Librarians are explicitly educated to take a broad view across campus while faculty often do not until and unless they involve themselves in across-campus issues. Sometimes a role on a library committee can be the first step a faculty member takes in this direction. "Involving" these stakeholders does not mean giving individual faculty or disciplines control over the collection. Everyone needs to realize, and at best, see it as an advantage that librarians are trained to take all of their input and incorporate it into a plan that balances multiple needs.

Mission-developers have the great advantage of reminding the library director when and the extent to which there are responsibilities outside the daily curriculum. Small libraries may have materials that their students will possibly never use unless they have a very locally oriented professor but that need to be acquired and preserved because no one else will. At the least, mission-developers may be pleased that the library is aware of the college's extramural ties. In the best situations, they will work with the library on fund-raising that will build upon and enhance ways in which the library advances the institution's mission to a broad audience.

True stories: Which collections should you accept?

Every work written by two popular authors, neither of whom write for an academic audience but who are beloved by a significant local philanthropist?

The contents of a retired professor's bookshelves as he cleared out his office, old journals you already own, old books superseded by more recent materials and which the professor had already attempted to donate to his own university library?

A beloved and recently deceased voice instructor's personal collection of opera records, none of which are particularly outstanding and together do not represent a systematic collection?

Brainstorming. Two main areas of brainstorming are most important for collection management: format and content. Format is something that currently is extremely fluid due to changes in the nature of information and scholarly communication. Given that particular content is desirable to meet teaching, learning, and research needs, what is the most effective format in which to deliver it? Brainstorming is an effective means to determine formats, and many people can provide useful inputs for collection-management brainstorming. The format issue is one that involves both cutting-edge technology and clerical issues like interlibrary loan processes.

Content is something that faculty are wrestling with themselves. This is an area where broad principles can remain as constant as the general mission and aims of the college and library, but specifics will need revisiting frequently. Content is also less static than may be imagined. In a small college, adding new majors, minors, or degree programs can happen frequently. They are a much larger issue for a small library than at a large university where the new demands aren't trivial but are much smaller in proportion to existing resources. A small college enjoys no economies of scale at the collection level.

Research and evaluation. Collection management is central to librarianship in general, and there is plenty of information including manuals, examples, articles, and workshops on how it is done. This is not a how-to guide to library techniques.

One area of collection management reaches up beyond the specifics of selection, deselection, and prioritization: evaluation. A collection-development plan implies that the collection and its individual parts are being managed toward particular ends, to support a particular program, and to avoid travel guides and car-repair manuals. Evaluation measures how the strength, usage, or composition of the collection matches those goals. Evaluation also feeds into campus-assessment endeavors, the "culture of assessment" signaled by the use of data to guide decision-making. Evaluation plans are covered below. Evaluation of the extent to which a collection matches the goals that have been set for it is part of revising or creating a collection-development plan.

Plan. The final collection-development plan will guide purchase, borrowing, and licensing decisions. New librarians can review it. Periodically, the library director (or chief collection developer, if there is one) should check to ensure that budget allocations to subjects or formats are consistent with the plan. For one or two main reasons, they might not be. In the first, librarians responsible for one area of the collection may be unaware of or simply not pay attention to the bigger picture. They need to be informally reconnected with the plan. In the second, events have overtaken the plan and it has not survived its contact with the "enemy," such as format expenses, new programs, or new campus initiatives. In that case, the plan needs to be revised.

Preservation

A preservation plan consists of the policies through which a library's desirable combination of content and physical manifestation of items can be preserved. Each library accumulates by design or accident a wide range of content and formats such as old yearbooks, 1980s how-to videotapes of medical procedures, laser discs, and even books from the 1900s and 1800s and before. Content deselection is part of the collection-management plan. If the content is no longer needed, it does not need to be preserved.

Preservation aims at preserving the content *or* physical manifestation/format or both. In some cases, the content is migrated to or replaced by new formats and the originals are discarded. In others, the formats need preserving in order to keep irreplaceable content. In still others, the library will create new formats as well as preserve the originals.

What a preservation plan lays out are the current decisions about categories of items and content to be retained, priorities for spending staff time, equipment, and materials. It outlines money for content migration or item preservation. Because preservation spending is something that adds no new content to a library, it is in danger of being neglected.

Preservation isn't always the answer. Knowing when you do *not* want to spend resources on a category is valuable, too. Replace old videotapes and laser discs with current content in current formats, and consider digitizing your own old yearbooks, thus allowing more possible use.

Leadership or experts: In contrast to the collection-management plan that involves the large core element of the library, in the case of preservation planning, the director can reasonably delegate leadership to whomever on staff possesses, technical expertise in formats and their aging and use and an appreciation of how content (and possibly original format) ties into the library's and institution's mission. A small college library may or may not have anybody with formal archives training. It is more likely it will if the library has unusually large archives with responsibility for non-college (such as denominational) materials. It is less likely at public colleges or newer institutions. If there are no librarians with expertise, current or retired faculty or staff might have both interest and expertise.

Stakeholders: Preservation involves two main stakeholders, the library itself and local mission-development. It may seem strange to label the library a "stakeholder." The reason to do so is because the library director may not head up this effort, and those in charge may be in danger of mistaking the single valuable oak they are caring for with the forest as a whole. Preservation can use huge amounts of money and cannot be the only thing the library spends its funds on. Money spent on preservation has to be balanced against the needs of the library as a whole, including all of its missions for current learning and research support as well as historical conservation. Sometimes the decision will have to be that preservation needs to be given to some other library to handle.

The local mission-development office has as great an interest in historical items as in the collection as a whole, perhaps more so. A key reason to involve them is to see just how much interest they do have. If preserving special collections turns out not to be related to the mission of the college as a whole, the library director should rethink the commitment.

Brainstorming, research, or evaluation: The number of individuals on a small college campus who have enough expertise to brainstorm about preservation techniques will be limited. A better idea for both brainstorming and research would be to contact institutions that have similar sizes or types of collections for their ideas. A good preservation plan developed somewhere else may need only minor adjustments to be suitable for your campus.

Brainstorming on a higher and wider level than specific current techniques could be fruitful. Where will the institution itself be in 20 or 50 years? Since preservation takes a longer view than either collection management or strategic planning, this sort of creative thinking could use anybody's ideas.

One really important area for brainstorming is to think about projects that would attract grant funding. Preservation is paradoxically one of the most technologically cutting-edge areas of the library. The library director could look for local and national, technology and historically minded partners. A preservation plan can specifically prepare for including specially funded projects as well as the limited amount of ongoing maintenance that the normal budget and staffing can cover. The point here is that preservation is a key area where its special needs might be very attractive for special resources, and planning should prepare for this. Even though funders do have their own ideas about priorities, the library director who is ready with a comprehensive understanding of where the library stands and what is needed is in a very strong place to make compelling arguments for support.

Plan: At a minimum, the preservation plan conveys roughly what is needed for the library staff to accomplish on a yearly basis in terms of preservation of content or format (such as changing from paper to digital or moving original letters to acid-free boxes). This indicates what is truly essential so that, in a reasonable period of time, materials do not deteriorate beyond recovery. It is especially important for the plan to lay out options for major projects that depend on special funding. That part of the plan needs to be shared with the campus-development office.

Evaluation

An evaluation plan is an impersonal framework that tracks, on a consistent basis, how the library is doing. Evaluation data help the library director prove the case for library resources and improve its functioning. It is a systematic tool for gathering data for managerial decision-making. For all of the functions and collections of the library, there should be some periodic evaluation of their quality or characteristics. The most intense and frequent evaluation will concern those areas most central to a library, such as instruction or key collection areas; the framework as a whole will serve internal management and external accreditation demands.

Accrediting agencies encourage academic campuses to develop and continually strengthen a "culture of assessment." The most central focus is on assessment of student learning, but all of the purposes and functions of a college are part of this culture. In real life, it seems as though some institutions follow a schedule that goes, "Oh, the accreditation team is coming year after next. We'd better assess stuff." It is better to have an ongoing process. This accomplishes three things: (1) directors have data to inform their decisions on a regular basis; (2) data exist to make writing accreditation reports easy; and (3) an accreditation team can see that not only is there one-time data, but that a system for evaluation and improvement exists. This gives them confidence in the institution's managerial capability. Evaluation should be done for internal purposes, but making accreditation run smoothly and successfully is a huge benefit.

Leadership/experts: Library evaluation involves both the library and evaluation. Because it involves the library, library-specific techniques will be needed, and appropriate librarians should be involved. Library assessment draws upon data from acquisition and circulation systems, vendor statistics, and local citation analysis. General evaluation/research techniques such as user surveys, interviews, and tests for instruction, will be used. For those methods, if the campus has an assessment office or officer, it is both technically wise and politically smart to involve them. Working closely with a campus institutional researcher or assessment expert accomplishes three things: (1) it demonstrates that the library staff is active in general assessment, (2) it takes advantage of the campus institutional officer's expertise, and (3) the library staff can then piggyback on other evaluative efforts, such as campus or alumni surveys.

Stakeholders: More than other types of plans, evaluation planning is very internal and practical. Its purpose is to guide library staff in performing evaluative activities. External stakeholders such as members of a library committee will likely be interested in the resulting data, but not so interested in the plan that frames how to gather it. It is wise to inform any stakeholders who are involved in strategic planning that the evaluation plan exists, so that it is part of their grasp of what the library staff is doing and how they can support their proposals.

Brainstorming: Brainstorming about evaluation can and should involve everybody in the library, both librarians and support staff. The main parts are to figure out what the library has and does (and hence needs evaluating), to figure out ways to evaluate it, and then to design a schedule for the evaluation, the plan itself. Involving as many library staff as possible has two benefits. First, it means areas are less likely to be overlooked. Some aspects of a library such as circulation or interlibrary loans are often primarily managed by staff, and they are the experts in what gets done and hence what needs to be evaluated, even when it is the librarians who design the techniques to gather the data. Second, the process of coming up with an *impersonal and general* evaluation plan educates staff that their personal performance is not being targeted. If everyone can see that everything is systematically put on the table for evaluation, it becomes routine and not personal.

Research/options: Some librarians should take the lead in either having or acquiring expertise in evaluation techniques. Numerous books and articles on assessment in higher education or libraries in general are available. It is particularly useful to consult with campus-assessment experts on general patron studies such as surveys, interviews, or focus groups and teaching-learning experts on evaluating library instruction. Beyond those areas, though, it is necessary to add library techniques suitable for its specialized needs, and librarians add these.

Plan: The evaluation plan lays out what services, collections, facilities, and features will be evaluated and when. Timing and coordination are very important. It is neither necessary nor desirable to evaluate everything all at once or all the time; a schedule ensures that over a period of years, everything is covered. Everyone in the library or on campus who is involved in data gathering needs to be aware of the framework of the evaluation plan. Any information needed from campus-wide constituents, particularly students, needs to be coordinated with whatever else the campus may be examining. Any information collected within the library should be shared so as to prevent duplication of effort. Evaluation takes time and effort, so it is important to share the plans and the results in order for everyone to get as much benefit out of those costs as possible.

Disaster Recovery

Fire, floods, tornados; earthquakes, landslides, roof leaks: libraries suffer all of them. Having a prepared disaster-recovery plan with at least a minimum of steps to be taken and useful contact information increases the amount of effective damage control that can be done and makes recovery far easier than if people are caught unprepared.

Leadership and expertise: In disaster recovery, it is probable that someone else on campus will be in a better position to lead than any librarian. People in facilities management, information technology, and human resources often have much of the expertise needed. A librarian might form only one part of the group paying particular attention to those issues that are unique to libraries, such as book preservation.

If there is as yet no campus-wide planning for disaster recovery, the library director should be proactive in covering this area of responsibility. At the least, information-technology people should welcome planning for IT problems. Library systems contracts should provide for backup mechanisms.

Stakeholders: Just as in the case of evaluation plans, the library's general stakeholders may care that there is a plan, but they seldom care about its details. It should function, but they may not care how. This is particularly relevant in the case of special collections or archives. If a library houses unique materials that are important to an external group, they will be relieved by the fact that a disaster-recovery plan exists. Because disaster recovery is not cheap, a college's development office, or insurers, or both, should be aware of special needs for special materials. Replacing the library's copies of basic nursing texts will be trivial compared to dealing with soaked eighteenth-century books.

Library services also affect a wide range of constituents. This can be especially important in the case of not-quite-disasters, such as weather or health emergencies that don't involve material destruction but disrupt how people work and study on campus, the more residential the campus the more acutely. Libraries need to be tied into campus procedures for cancellations, but they also have to make plans for how they cover their own unique responsibilities consistent with the needs of both users and staff.

> **Story:** At one campus, the person in charge of deciding about weather emergencies had been an Arctic researcher. Even with this bias, the campus sometimes needed to cancel classes. By using librarians who lived close to campus and on-campus student workers, the library doors were safely kept open, providing both study space and research assistance. This was also welcomed by the weather-bound, on-campus students.

Research and options: Besides general guides to disaster recovery, two vital sources of information are other local libraries and the college's insurance agency. For example, a disaster plan does not merely state that books should be frozen before being dried, it should give contact information for companies that are able to provide emergency freezing and for others that can handle drying. Insurance companies have contacts with companies able to do appropriate work, and other library directors, whatever the size or type, may already have identified vendors for library needs. In this case, it doesn't matter whether that other library is large or small, public or academic. It is worth checking with them to see what they know. It is also worth exploring whether a joint plan can be developed to handle cases of wide disaster: flooding as compared to a fire that strikes only one library. In this particular area of planning, location is much more important than size.

Plan: A disaster-recovery plan needs to be more widely disseminated than some of the other plans. The campus facilities and human resources offices should be provided a copy and briefed on elements that are particularly important. The facilities people need to know about special materials considerations, especially the value of and plans for any irreplaceable items. Human resources needs to review and in some cases to approve anticipated service adjustments. The library serves students and perhaps external users (for special collections), so in cases of weather and other situations, the library director may plan on taking staffing actions that differ from other areas such as class scheduling. If classes are canceled, does the library close? Internally, all library staff need to be aware of their roles for responding to any emergency, from following phone trees to showing up for salvage efforts.

Strategic Planning

Collection management, preservation, evaluation, and disaster-recovery plans center on the library's resources and services. Each can be developed somewhat independently from the campus as a whole. The library director should coordinate library plans with any existing all-campus plans, but if the campus does not have any, the library director can still proceed and create effective plans for the benefit of the library.

Strategic planning is most strongly tied to campus planning. It has an internal, library-specific component in that librarians are always thinking about opportunities in library services and resources that are created by technological and other developments in the information environment. However, at a small institution, the library does not exist independently. It has its own mission but that is primarily to advance and serve the institution. That means that for truly large-scale and longer-term planning, the library can lead, it can run with, and it can follow campus planning but it cannot simply proceed on its own.

> **Story:** At a small college in the late 1980s, a variety of forms of "distance" education were being contemplated. A special cross-campus task force came up with standards for how the education should be conducted to ensure quality, but it was stuck in proceeding any further because the administration had not decided on distance education as a deliberate strategy.
>
> The library thus was in the position of responding to each individual course or program or option for a variety of distance needs (from mailing videotapes of movies to providing copies of articles) without being able to balance its on- and off-campus efforts with a strategic decision by the campus.

All accredited academic institutions are expected to have an explicit planning process in place. This is part of the requirements of the regional agencies that accredit colleges as a whole. One of the strengths of the American system of higher education is its flexibility with individual institutions operating within general norms of what "higher education" means but with great freedom and variety. Institutional accreditation teams do not dictate what a college should be, but instead asks each one individually what they intend to be and do. Each institution chooses its own specific mission and then demonstrates that it has adequate planning processes in place to serve that mission and the goals that it has set. That is the conceptual and pragmatic rationale for having strategic planning. Conceptually, planning is necessary so that an institution can continue to meet its mission, respond to changes, and initiate changes. Pragmatically, an institution's staff and faculty need to prove that they can plan and do plan.

In addition to the reasons that the campus engages in planning, to remain accredited and to shepherd its resources toward its goals, the library director has reasons for being a part of the campus-planning process. First, the library staff needs to be a visible participant at the table during the campus-planning process. The library will not ever be the biggest issue the plan covers, but it can't be invisible. Second, library-specific planning needs to serve the overall goals and major directions set by central planning. The library staff can't be the one to change the college's focus from residential students to online master's programs. When the campus decides to do that, the library director then plans how the library will serve that need. Finally, library staff needs to be proactive, pro-library, and pro-leadership. Librarians, directors, and others need to be active in knowing about, thinking up, and also incorporating new library-specific capabilities into library and all-campus planning. The library is a part of the academic enterprise, and so library resources and services are properly part of the academic plan.

Organizations use a great deal of vocabulary and several techniques during strategic planning. Campus administrators may begin a strategic-planning process by explaining to academic managers the process and concepts of strategic planning that they will use. More likely, they will simply begin and expect unit managers to have some familiarity. A section at the end of this chapter covers three specific approaches to strategic planning, including definitions and examples. The most important part for a library director to understand is what a campus means by the terms mission, vision, values, goals, and objectives. Previous strategic plans are the best source for how these are used on a particular campus.

The following describes how the four elements common to all types of planning are applied to the case of strategic planning. It shows how the elements apply to the process within the library and also how the library fits into the campus-planning process. Strategic planning has an important timing and coordination component. Other plans such as for collection management or evaluation can be designed and then updated whenever desired. Strategic planning has three essential timing points, times when the library *must* write or review its strategic plan: (1) along with the college's mandated planning cycle, such as every five years; (2) when planning for a fund-raising capital campaign; and (3) while preparing the budget: for every annual budget request and when special budget needs arise, such as a position becoming vacant.

Experts

When it comes to strategic planning within the library, "experts" means the librarians, all of them. Good librarians, not just the director, should be aware of and enthusiastic about developments in their areas of academic librarianship. While support staff have their own expertise and certainly can be excellent sources for good ideas, a director should encourage librarians to understand that thinking about the future is part of their professional responsibilities, something that distinguishes them from technicians who carry out directions and perform routine tasks.

Because planning is about things that have not yet happened, it is hard to anticipate just what might or might not be useful. For the director of a small library, planning is best tackled as a committee of the whole involving all librarians. Library resources, technologies, and services are inherently interconnected, and in the small library, everybody is affected by what everyone else does.

> **True story:** At a medium-sized library, a technical services/cataloging team carefully oversaw a redesign of the library's Web site, even performing extensive usability testing. They did not, however, involve librarians involved in instruction. Those librarians were in a different department, on different "teams." The technical-services librarians did not take into account the significant overlap between what people can do on a Web site on their own (with intuitive design), what they can do once educated or informed (such as being told in class about pathfinders), and what they can do with information-literacy instruction (such as using specialized databases).

Experts from outside the library should be engaged as well, especially about user group needs. It is particularly necessary to involve faculty to describe how their disciplines are changing and developing in terms of information use. Not all faculty members would be interested in or useful for this part of planning. The best faculty will be especially those who are recent graduates from some other institution because they have different and also recent experiences of what can be done in libraries. Other good choices for faculty involvement are those who are active in disciplinary research and those who are active in pedagogical research and innovation. This means more than just having librarians relate what they learn from their regular work with faculty. Explicitly involving faculty in the formal strategic-planning process is very useful for library relations. They will feel listened to, they will feel that their perspectives and expertise are respected, they can help the library see new possibilities or avoid dead ends, and they will develop a commitment to the library and its future. Rationally they add information, politically they represent valuable partners, and in human terms it enhances relationships.

People from other areas are also useful. Student-affairs personnel are aware of both general trends and what the particular college's student population is likely to have and need in terms of study resources. Information-technology staff will be essential partners in evaluating automation and application options.

Expertise goes two ways, from outside the library inside for planning, and then expertise goes from the library out to campus-wide planning. Librarians should be seen and involved as expert resources in two ways. First, they should provide input and expertise in areas of information needs and trends: for example, they can educate people about emerging trends in scholarly communication (publishing). Too often librarians seem like wallpaper; they are on campus but not part of the conversation. When librarians talk about how developments in their field are part of the future of higher education, then they are visibly part of managing that future.

On the other hand, input should not be too detailed. Institutional repositories are a growing phenomenon; our subscriptions just went up 10 percent; our carpet needs replacing. Librarians make the library look out of touch and self-centered if they try to insert details into the campus plan that look very minor and ephemeral compared to those of other areas. Much depends on how specific campus-planning documents are. In the campus plan, what levels are included? Do they include broad themes or detailed yearly items for each subarea? As a rough guide, if the campus-planning document mentions the state of the recreational facilities, then the state of the library, either a strength or a weakness, should be mentioned too.

The other involvement of the library is, well, as a library, an information source. Strength, weaknesses, opportunities, and threats (SWOT) analysis includes a great deal of empirical data such as local and national student-population estimates. Especially for external items (opportunities and threats), the library should be seen as the go-to place on campus for providing and verifying that kind of information. Reference services need to be real resources for administrators as well as for faculty and students. At the least, providing data for planning will show off the library's role as an information resource, and at best, it will further engage the library in the minds of campus decision-makers. Consider the alterative, where people in admissions and development pull data only from their own personal knowledge or studies by their professional associations, and people think that the library is only for "books." For the best effect, provide data that are better than non-librarians can achieve by googling. The only effective counter to "Isn't everything on the Internet; why do we need libraries?" is to beat that small box for quality, specificity, and usefulness of information.

Stakeholders

Stakeholders can be treated in two ways when it comes to library planning. If the library is a chapter within a larger campus-planning effort, then whatever processes are used for that should be used for the library. The campus administration may organize groups of alumni, residential students, and commuters; other units on campus may set up cross-campus advisory boards. A library advisory team needs to include faculty, students, and information-technology people, even if other support areas do not.

If librarians are doing planning on their own, or at least relatively independently, then the question of stakeholders means: who cares about the library, and who has the power to help make what the library needs come to pass? In terms of interests, this means faculty, students, and external groups served by special features of the library.

Individual faculty or students or community members should be chosen who are exciting, energetic, and forward-thinking people. Strategic planning is concerned about the future, so it is wonderful to benefit from their creativity. On the other hand, these individuals are being picked not just because they are personally wonderful. They also represent their groups, their areas of interest and power on campus. For this reason, it is useful to invite those who not only have ideas, but also have power within their own groups. These are the people who enjoy the respect of their peers, who are generally listened to on campus, those who are good communicators. Given the choice between a very technically adept loner and someone the entire faculty listens to, it is usually best to involve the respected person. When that person is not particularly forward-thinking or is full of misperceptions about the library or information in general, it is even more important to pick them. It lets librarians address their misconceptions directly within the strategic-planning process itself and get it resolved before a library plan becomes public.

GENERAL POINT: THE BUSY PERSON AND LIBRARY PLANNING

The most respected people on campus are in demand all over campus. When thinking about who to involve in what aspect of the library, from strategic planning to an ongoing library advisory committee, it is important to think strategically with identification, cultivation, and prioritization.

First, identify those people who are respected. It is especially important to notice those who have respect outside of functional bureaucratic positions. Someone who has earned respect is often placed into positions of formal power, especially in vote-controlled offices. This is especially helpful for student leadership.

However, the nature of the faculty, especially the value placed on disciplinary knowledge, teaching skills, and college collegiality, and an almost equally common measure of dislike of bureaucracy, often means that people can be highly respected even when or even because they do not hold formal positions. Some argue that the higher the formal position of a faculty member, the more dean-like they are tasked to be, and the less natural respect remains because they no longer share the experience of "normal" faculty. This is where careful observation, social contacts, and involvement in activities across campus will yield important dividends. Identify leaders, even if they don't have titles.

Next, ensure that these leaders have a positive attitude toward the library. This does not mean targeting them personally with blatant flattery or preferential treatment. In fact, the more respected these individuals, the more likely it is that they will resist or see through such obvious preference. Instead, do two things. First, try to ensure that the library's normal services are at their best when dealing with respected people. Not multiple special library instruction sessions, but the best one can do for library instruction. Fortunately, this is usually the most pleasant and easiest thing to do. People who are respected are a pleasure to work with and for; that is why they are respected.

Second, aim to increase their awareness of the library. A blank perception of the library might be worse than a negative perception. The library needs "mind-share," a level of recognition and knowledge. The faculty member who cares enough to complain about the library is easier to win over than faculty members who have decided they can do without it. Mind-share comes from not just helping the respected leaders, but helping their friends and colleagues, helping everyone, so that librarians become thought of as helpful. This is of course something library staff should be doing anyway, but it is also a crucial part of developing the benign attention of leaders on campus.

Finally, be very selective and specific about how and when these leaders are involved. Whether formal or informal, leaders by definition are busy people. Their contributions are valuable, so everyone wants them to contribute. Do not involve a leader in make-work. Do not persuade someone to contribute to a collection-development planning process if you will soon need that leader for strategic planning. While involvement in lower-level activities can be part of cultivation and building mind-share, the more important point is to think long-term about the best use of the leader's limited time and attention.

Part of the political aspect of strategic planning is involving groups and representatives of groups as stakeholders. This work builds strong connections between the library and the important interest groups on campus. Because the strategic-planning process involves explicitly thinking about what the library offers, what it could offer, and what affects it, it is an excellent way to develop greater appreciation among those interest groups.

The bureaucracy is not to be ignored, however. Besides leaders from these stakeholder groups, there are people who need to be involved because of their positions, vertically, horizontally, and also at an angle, so to speak. That includes the library director's supervisor, parallel support units, and any important units that the formal organization chart does not connect to the library.

Vertically, the library director's supervisor should be involved specifically and personally. When the library director reports to a relatively important person, such as the dean of the faculty or chief academic officer (CAO) (which is indeed a good thing), that can mean that the CAO is too busy to devote much time to brainstorming sessions and certainly will have no assigned tasks to do during planning. These high-level supervisors can be involved effectively in several ways, however. They might participate in an opening session, and during that can communicate the campus's overall strategic goals and thinking. The library director can brief the CAO during planning as it proceeds during regular meetings. The CAO can be involved in a final decision-making session. In fact, it is essential to involve the CAO in that session. No academic library director can live an independent life because the library must serve the overall goals of the institution.

If the library director reports to an intermediate person such as the associate dean or assistant vice president, that person should be involved as thoroughly in planning sessions as possible. Colleges that have created such intermediate positions usually expect them to take care of gritty details and time-consuming processes. Generally, the overall "chief" (academic or other officer) closely depends on the assistant for formal and informal input as to how their part of the college is going.

On a practical note, the schedules of the CAO and assistant, if there is one, will be key determining factors for arranging strategic-planning work sessions. Whether the library director reports directly, indirectly, or not at all to the campus chief academic officer, that person really needs to be involved in a final presentation or final decision-making session. Inviting and even involving the college president would be best, although it is often not possible. Putting the library's future plans face-to-face with someone at the level right below the president is the next best option and correctly reflects the library's rightful place in the academic enterprise.

Several units at a roughly horizontal level are relevant and equal to the library. Information technology generally and specifically any technology supporting instruction would be the most important functional department to involve. Finding out who in this area is truly parallel to the library and the library's director might be a little tricky. On many campuses, the "chief information officer" may report directly to the president and thus rank higher than the library director; the head of "teaching and learning support" may report to an assistant to the chief academic officer, and thus rank lower. Library directors need to be thoughtful about what they say about the library's position in the college to have this or that person involved.

Finally, there is what was called a "sideways" or "at an angle" unit. This means offices that are not directly parallel or within the same reporting lines as the library yet have important insights and assistance to offer. The most important instance of this is the chief academic officer. If the library director does not report there, that office is really essential. Other areas on campus that do not have formal links to the library can be useful. Alumni or development people are especially important if the strategic plan includes ideas relevant for a capital campaign or for foundation or governmental grants. If faculty research support is an important element of the library's future, people involved in designing and supporting research are key.

When it comes to campus-wide strategic planning, the library as a unit is itself a stakeholder. Library staff should be part of the groups involved in planning, as broadly as possible, not just specifically when the topic of the library is considered. In this process, librarians must be included rather than left as an isolated section that can be ignored.

Many small colleges have a very broad and inclusive approach to strategic planning, as well as for capital-campaign planning. In order to be inclusive, while specific administrators lead the discussions, an effort is made to include a broad range of campus and external communities. This involves open town-hall meetings and groups with deliberately "mixed" memberships to discuss issues outside of the normal bureaucratic organization. Often these are organized around themes rather than functions, and avoid stratifying participants by rank.

This is quite common in small colleges for several reasons. Many denominational institutions have cultures that encourage equality and a sense of community outside of and crossing or overcoming standard unit or status divisions. Small colleges also inevitably are like small towns, where everybody does indeed know one another's business, and that is a strength when it comes to developing a shared sense of purpose. Finally, accrediting agencies emphasize documenting that knowledge of an institution's mission, goals, and planning is widely shared throughout an organization.

In this situation, librarians as a group should take a correspondingly broad and proactive approach. Someone from the library should be present at every open meeting and at as many thematic meetings as possible. A library cannot achieve "mind-share" unless librarians have a share of the seats in a room and a share of the conversations in the air.

In a small library, this coverage is a responsibility of all of the professional librarians and also will involve support staff when possible. Involving everyone has external benefits. Using all the staff makes the library that much more visible. When library support staff (clerical personnel) are knowledgeable about the institution and about library-related ideas, they will impress others. This involvement will also have internal benefits. Library staff at all levels will understand better what people outside the library think and are planning, and that will help them approach library issues with greater creativity and flexibility and also a realistic sense of the library's position and the college's situation.

Brainstorming

Much of the important points about this element are incorporated into previous discussions about how librarians should be up-to-date on trends and ideas in academic librarianship. Also, the experts and stakeholders are selected specifically because they will have their own creative perspectives they can bring to the process.

> **True story**: In a small college's start-of-year staff-faculty orientation, cross-campus groups were encouraged to think boldly and creatively about possible futures. What could the college achieve in a bright, ambitious future? One member of the athletics staff became extremely focused on an admittedly bold idea: creating a rocket-launch facility. On the one hand, this was certainly "out-of-the-box" thinking, which had been specifically urged. Nobody wanted to be accused of not being open and innovative, so that group let it stand.
>
> But this college did not even have an engineering program nor a pre-engineering track.

A few procedural techniques can be useful in this context for in-library strategic planning. First, many librarians happen to have introverted personalities. Therefore, among typical library staff, many individuals will wince when the word "brainstorming" is used, or, worse, become silent in sessions where theoretically ideas are supposed to flow wildly and freely. To get the best from all potential contributors, the wise leader will allow for a variety of forms of input and discussion. Some of these can help promote thinking and talking after individual concentration, such as in a meeting asking people to be quiet for a few minutes and write down ideas, or coming up with ideas to be shared in an asynchronous venue such as a blog, wiki, or even a physical black- or whiteboard. Because some participants will also be extroverts who generally do best when thinking aloud, some open discussions will be useful as well.

Having a fairly large number of identified experts and stake-holders involved in strategic planning has advantages. Other types of planning are focused; this is about the library's whole future. Moreover, full-blown strategic planning doesn't take place every year, so when it does take place, it is an extra effort and justifies extra participation. However, to handle the larger numbers, even on a small campus, multiple brainstorming sessions may need to be held to avoid scheduling issues or having a group that is too large for free discussion among all participants. Ten people is about at the upper limit of usefulness, similar to a focus group.

Research About and Evaluation of Options

In the context of strategic planning, research has three different meanings. First, it can be research into ideas. That sort of research is not something that happens only every five or so years in conjunction with formal strategic planning. Instead, it is part of the normal professional development by which librarians keep themselves informed about what is new in their field. Librarians should not wait until they reach the "Let's plan" date and then say, "Now let's find out what academic librarianship is doing."

The next type is to research more fully specific plan options. If people have ideas about institutional repositories, or Web guides, or archival digitization, they will need to provide enough details so that everyone can see how feasible and useful the ideas are within that college's context. This isn't research to find out ideas, but to find out more about ideas.

Finally, research includes internal and external data that will help make decisions and choices. First, the library will use all of the planning information the college has gathered at the campus level, as well as general environmental and institutional information. Second, there are library operational data that have been generated for the purposes of institutional and specialized accreditation. Finally, librarians can perform some user or needs analysis specifically for the purpose of the strategic plan, including surveys, focus groups, or interviews with users.

As with evaluation plans, when considering surveying on-campus users, faculty, staff, and students, the first step is to consult with the institutional researcher if the college has one. This person is responsible for ongoing data collection and analysis, from reporting student characteristics to analyzing faculty workloads. They will have expertise in survey design and should be able to coordinate library surveys or library survey questions with whatever other campus data collection may be occurring.

Not all colleges have institutional researchers. If the institution is in the middle of preparation for accreditation, the self-study coordinator is the next-best choice. If not, the most important people to talk with are probably the dean of student affairs, the head of human resources, the dean of faculty, and the head of the faculty organization, senate, or assembly. The library director can work with them to select ways of surveying users that at the least do not interfere with anything else and at best coordinate with other surveys so as to get the most information, for the most purposes, with the highest response rate.

Final Strategic Plan

The final product, a library strategic plan, will primarily be written, edited, and overseen if not produced by the library director. Especially in the small library, it is difficult to think of any other activity or responsibility that is more central to the role of director than the thorough, thoughtful, and future-oriented content of and process toward arriving at a strategic plan.

Similarly, the director should be aware of and have as much input as possible into how the library appears, directly and indirectly, in the institution's overall plan. A direct appearance would be a special section devoted to the library, similar to sections devoted to information technology, to facilities, and to the faculty. Indirect appearances are where the library is mentioned in presentations of the strategic plan's outline of institution-wide initiatives or objectives.

Examples are two common initiatives, one more focused and one more general. A college may decide to become focused on undergraduate-level research. Library instruction, work with faculty, and appropriate resources should be understood as providing necessary support for that initiative. Or, a strategic plan that is very broadly worded may highlight "student-centered learning." Student-centeredness for learning often includes student exploration and construction of knowledge, the type of learning that involves doing and investigation, rather than simply receiving textbook information. Faculty and administrators should be made aware of how the library will be enhancing those types of independent experiences.

A final library-specific strategic plan needs approval and agreement by important institutional actors, the library's direct supervisor and the head of academic affairs if different, and any other person with a formal role in planning. It needs to be obviously consistent with campus mission, values, and any existing initiatives or goals. It should show creativity and innovation. Librarians always have to work against stereotypes of the library as a warehouse or museum. In a forward-looking plan, it is especially important to convey the message that librarians are ready to lead into the future.

A strategic plan is a powerful communication tool. The whole process of coming up with one, brainstorming, involving stakeholders, and identifying experts is an effective way of involving people in the library's future and hence strengthening support in the present. Showing decision-makers that you understand, appreciate, and can support campus-wide planning says "We are part of this team." And having a spelled-out plan gives all library personnel easy answers to the most mundane questions of, "What's going on with the library?," "Aren't libraries obsolete?," and "Do students really use libraries anymore?"

The preceding description of the steps and participants involved in strategic planning may seem daunting, complex, and even cumbersome for the small academic library. Certainly, there are numerous examples of vast and vastly ignored strategic plans created with great labor and ignored with equal ease. A cumbersome process can't be changed much if the campus itself is committed to a particular format for strategic planning. Library directors are mediators between individuals in the library and the whole campus process: they make clear to librarians and support staff where their thoughts and ideas fit, where there contributions count, and what happens when and why.

Short, Simple Strategic Planning

What follows is a suggestion for a way of doing planning that is very practical: it uses the least effort possible that is still truly strategic; it is thoughtful but not exhausting. It avoids the pitfalls of rigidity and business-speak while incorporating the minimum necessary amount of the valuable aspects of strategic planning. This minimal framework may be most useful when a library staff has not done formal planning for its own purposes before.

With library staff: Dynamic planning	With others: Focused brainstorming
Have ready a comprehensive list of the library's collections and services: what the library currently owns and does.	
Ensure that all professional staff understand the normal necessary functions of the library (and where they fit in them).	Prior to inviting others, share with them an outline of what the library is already doing.
Annually, **in conjunction with personnel review**, individually, ask each person to: • Link professional-development goals or proposed activities for the year to the campus mission/themes. • Come up with at least one idea for that year and one idea for something at least five years away that the library might consider doing.	Once per year, **in the middle of either fall or spring semesters**, invite at least one but preferably three groups: one with two to three faculty and one to two IT or other staff; two more with faculty only; talk about ideas for the future. The director can run this, with one or two other librarians, taking care not to outnumber the guests. Different people can be invited each year. Organize one or two groups of students to discuss ideas about libraries.
	(Continued)

MANAGING THE SMALL COLLEGE LIBRARY

Before the annual budget request is due:

- Meet with librarians and discuss ideas: short term and long term, definite and speculative.
- Coordinate phrasing and themes with any campus mission, vision, values, goals, or objectives statements.
- Incorporate at least a few sentences about these ideas in the budget request for that year's needs and also as alerts for future plans.

Publicly distribute a brief statement:

Current projects

Potential future ideas

Highlights from accreditation studies

Use phrasing consistent with campus themes

Acknowledge ongoing normal services and resources

Via: direct e-mail to *all* campus administrators and faculty; placement on Web page; update annually

Make appointments and formally discuss the ideas with direct supervisor and with faculty leadership.

This framework is a way to generate creative, thoughtful, and focused ideas for the future while taking care of, and deliberately publicizing, the normal, constantly evolving ways in which the library continually adapts to meet needs. It avoids the problem of the too-focused strategic plan, which ignores the need to get the carpets replaced, and the not-strategic/focused-enough plan, which describes nothing new or different.

Master Plan (Also Capital Campaign)

One of the most important all-campus processes that is or should be tied to strategic planning is the campus master plan, more properly, the master facilities plan. This is generally a design for how the campus's physical facilities such as area, buildings, and rented space are organized and will develop over a relatively lengthy time period. Planning periods of five years would be short; 10- or 25-year horizons are more common. Some master plans are primarily focused on new construction, but some include details of expected maintenance and renovation, such as when roofs need to be replaced and brickwork tuck-pointed.

Master plans are intimately connected to capital campaigns. Capital campaigns are about raising serious money, beyond annual donations, for endowment and also specific purposes. Some of those purposes are "soft," such as student support or faculty chairs. They often include "hard" objectives: physical facilities. While donors often have their own ideas, the master plan shows opportunities and also reveals how each potential physical addition fits into the campus both physically and with respect to its mission.

A master plan can be impressive and expressive. It displays current and anticipated buildings, functional for the college's many activities, and all the more beautiful when they are as-yet imaginary. It shows how the college expects to use its existing land footprint and any additions or changes that are anticipated. This is a key reason for the length of its time frame: thoughtful land acquisition is a very slow process.

Beyond the practicalities such as planning for boundary changes, the plan also expresses future thoughts about two different and necessary unknowns: funding and function. They are interrelated. Function means what the college intends to do with and within its buildings and other physical features and facilities; funding means where the money to do it will come from.

The library has four areas to focus on with respect to master planning, and only one of them is the idea of a new library building. The other three are minor library renovations and maintenance, changes in space usage due to new construction particularly of administrative or faculty office space, and what master plan themes say about the nature of the institution.

Minor library renovations and maintenance will occur nearly constantly at both old and new institutions. Colleges with older buildings need to deal with ADA compliance, with hazardous materials such as asbestos and mold, problems with roofs, and stone and brick maintenance. All of this external work will be handled on an annual cycle, which the library director needs to be aware of. Even new buildings often don't keep their initial configurations very long. Internal renovation and change is not only possible, it is bound to be necessary every five to 10 years or so. In the library, this can mean things like rearrangement of technical services space and service point relocation. Plans for or dreams of these kinds of change need to be communicated with campus decision-makers, the library's supervisor, the head of facilities, and, for larger issues, the head of finance. They will appear in the library's strategic plan, in a capital budget or donation request, and also be incorporated into the campus master facilities or master maintenance plan.

Academic and administrative functions and the space they need keep changing across campus. All of these changes potentially may affect the library. The library is space, and space usage sways all across campus, with one move leading to another. Some common examples include locating a teaching support center in the library, closing or opening a departmental or other specialized library, or developing 24-hour study space in or outside of the library. These will all affect the library. They may use library space, or they may draw library users elsewhere. The library is one of the largest providers of study space on a physical campus outside of residences, and any change in how student study needs are met will affect library usage.

Is it good or bad to move a particular office or service to the library's physical facility? That depends on how the library is viewed. It is a very bad perception if the library is seen simply as a source of space because libraries don't need space now that everything is digitized. If the library and librarians are as seen as part of a network of faculty or student co-curricular academic supports, it can be a good thing. The more alien to a library's mission the proposed office is (e.g., "let's put the bursar in the library's basement"), the more the relocation is a reflection not of the library's use but of its dispensability. The reverse is when the library is seen as a vital supportive center. In that scenario, what gets located there, like a writing center, becomes part of the library's identity.

Even entirely new buildings do not develop in isolation. The completion of a new building for any purpose tends to start a migration of offices, departments, and functions all over campus. Therefore, even if the library is not formally a part of a particular new building's planning, librarians should monitor the situation and be active participants in any campus-planning process.

The final reason to pay attention to master planning is to try to discern what the master plan says about what college leadership thinks the future of the college will be with respect to two particularly important issues: residential culture and size. That is, will the college increase, decrease, or change anything about its overall character as being mainly residential or not? A master plan may portray the same rough amount of housing, with some plans for keeping amenities competitive. It can also show either necessary limitation or planned expansion of student housing. Especially at the small college, how a library director designs or delivers library services is greatly affected by how residential and isolated the campus is.

College-size ambitions are also generally reflected in a master plan. Some institutions deliberately limit themselves in size. Size is considered an essential element in their culture and atmosphere, something that attracts students and in a way defines its market niche. Phrasing it that way sounds as though a college can deliberately choose its size, and the wealthier and more selective a college, the more it can do this. Others are small primarily because their market niche is small in a less-populated part of the country, and they then make a virtue of that necessity.

Other colleges become interested in not remaining small. They may have immediate, opportunistic plans for growing certain programs as much as possible. College administrators may also have deliberate plans to change the character of the institution and hence its perceived strengths and then reach an appropriate market. Since the 1960s, this phenomenon has been a factor in why the baccalaureate sector is so heavily private and also denominational. Public colleges had no inherent reason to restrict their sizes, so many once-small institutions grew into medium-sized or larger universities. Especially for public institutions, a master plan will encompass that kind of longer-range planning and ambitions.

The key point with anticipated growth is to plan for library services and resources to match the ambitions. Again, planners often proceed with the assumption that libraries are primarily about resources that are increasingly digital; they may understand some services. What must be considered is that for a campus to become larger physically, not digitally, planning for any anticipated growth of students *on campus* means the library, as space, may need to grow.

What about a new library? At least three reasons support building a new or substantially renovated library: negative, positive, and opportunistic. That is, there could be something or many things wrong with the current library building, there could be new and exciting things one wishes to do in and with a new library building, and there could be a donor or other funding source that wants a new library building. In the happy circumstance that someone wants to create a new library, the answer is easy. Yes! Seldom is there anything any small college library has or does that couldn't be done better in a new building.

That wonderful situation seldom pops up on its own. New buildings need new funding, and that is massive new funding. A slow process of cultivating funding sources, including donors, multiple donors, and ranges of donors, and coming to a mutually acceptable agreement on a new library's function, purposes, and possibilities is complex and far less dictated than organically grown. Strategic planning will nurture this as much in the brainstorming and input part of the process as in what goals any particular strategic plan came up with. A list of positives or the potentials of services and resources in a new building will be easy to compose if the librarians have been active in working with people across campus and also keeping themselves up to date on library developments. Strategic planning when it seems it is only the same old grind with the same old budget can be tedious, but strategic planning when a new building is in the future is exciting.

What about negative reasons? Here, a comprehensive and honest evaluation plan should be able to provide data to support the idea that changes are needed. While some evaluations are used only to provide fodder for boasting, scientific and systematic evaluation instead should gather information on everything and reliably identify library weaknesses as well as strengths. The evaluation plan provides valuable baseline data for planning for new buildings and then in turn documenting their effect. You can't point to an increase in library usage unless you knew what it was before renovation or construction.

All types of planning involve thoughtful and systematic attention to a particular issue, from what materials to own to what to dream about the library's future.

- Bureaucratically, plans give data and processes that can be analyzed rationally and coordinated with the established goals of the parent organization.
- Politically, the process of involving stakeholders in the process and communicating the results will increase support for the library across many important groups and influential individuals.
- In human resources terms, involving all librarians and library staff in appropriate parts of the plan, especially in brainstorming, draws from each of their strengths, encourages their creativity, and increases effective communication within the library.

Plans also connect to one another. An evaluation plan can give basic data for a strategic plan that should inform the library's part of master planning. Collection management is affected by preservation. Effort spent on one type of plan does double-duty in other plans.

Crucially, planning is part of budgeting. The campus attitude toward planning and budgeting is often related, although sometimes not obviously. At some campuses, annual or ongoing budget decisions are opaque or minimalistic: "Here's last year's line items with X increment." On those campuses, it would be rare to find an open and systematic strategic-planning framework. At other campuses, lines of communication flow easily up and down and sideways; people may complain that planning takes too much time and is too involved, rather than the latter; unit leaders may have to provide extensive explanations for all budget issues.

Nevertheless, every campus has a budget cycle. Even if the culture seems to ignore or give lip service to systematic planning, the library that does robust and realistic planning on its own is prepared to compete effectively in budgeting. When that capital campaign gets going, almost all the library staff's work is done, dreaming and data, ideas and effective support for them.

SWOT AND DYNAMIC PLANNING

Two approaches to planning are presented here, SWOT and dynamic planning. The latter is not really a defined form of strategic planning, but it describes what really happens on many campuses, particularly when applying the full formal structure of planning to a small unit seems too rigid, time-consuming, or alien to a particular campus culture. SWOT, on the other hand, is not precisely planning itself, but is a very commonly used preliminary step within planning.

SWOT

Before strategic planning gets started, planners gather data. One of the most commonly used frameworks for gathering data to support decisions about the future goes by the acronym SWOT: strengths, weaknesses, opportunities, and threats. This is a way of taking a systematic look at the present and possible future characteristics of the internal and external environments. These data and deliberation are intended to support plans that are feasibly creative: they seize opportunities but also are founded upon strengths.

Strengths and weaknesses are features of the institution itself. For example, a small endowment is a weakness; attractive physical facilities are a strength. For libraries, a unique collection with an important user group would be a strength; an aging infrastructure or several impending retirements would be weaknesses.

Opportunities and threats are features of the external environment. Changes in the population of 18-year-olds would be an opportunity or threat depending on what happens nationally and locally. New professions or professional developments are opportunities, such as physical therapy moving to require first-professional doctorates, or a growth in demand for pharmacists. Threats can be posed by the restructuring of some existing professions, such as the almost total disappearance of bachelor's-level library education, or local economic conditions, or local economic stagnation.

The SWOT framework can be very useful, a good way to think very broadly and not be either too internally or too externally focused. It can also get somewhat sidetracked by a lot of discussion and debate about where items fit, debates about how unchangeable an item is, whether it is good or bad, and whether it is internal or external. One example is small class sizes or small course loads for faculty. These are generally considered good things when thinking about campus climate, student learning, and external rankings. Student-faculty ratios are a facet of the *U.S. News & World Report* formula for ranking colleges. They are not a good thing when it comes to fiscal analysis. "Efficiency" in a service industry means economies of scale, and larger class size makes more economic sense. To what extent can an administration change class sizes or loads? In a unionized environment, this would be a key bargaining element in the category of working conditions and also pay. In non-unionized colleges, there are often general guidelines for course loads possibly appearing in individual faculty contracts; there might or might not be guidelines on class size. If these are changed, will important faculty leave or be discouraged if their working conditions change? Can a college recruit a faculty person if competitors are offering a lower load? On the other hand, at the small college, are there majors or classes that are just too small and can't be supported financially?

Another key example, one that really is strategic, requiring choice and decision-making, is online learning. What are the relevant strengths, weaknesses, opportunities, and threats? A college believes it has a talented faculty capable of delivering a quality education, a strength. A college's physical campus is geographically disadvantaged, remote, or located in a dangerous part of a city, a weakness, but moving online leaves behind the physical campus. The fact that more people accept that college education can be done online constitutes an opportunity. However, competing institutions also provide online learning, a threat. Meanwhile, some will wonder if the "talented faculty" and "quality education" the college started out with will persist if the delivery mode is changed. Faculty who came to a small institution to practice face-to-face teaching in an atmosphere valuing personal contact outside of the classroom (a strength) may dislike or fail to acquire the skills to teach successfully online (a weakness), while potential students have difficulty noticing the college in the barrage of multiple online institutions (a threat), all of which diminishes the opportunity for extra revenue.

True story: A program managed to subtract revenue with the addition of online opportunities. Numerous residential students chose to enroll in online classes, thus making face-to-face classes too small to be viable while not adding any additional tuition income.

The internal (strengths-weaknesses) versus external (opportunities-threats) distinction is often not entirely clear. External can be thought of as things the college itself cannot control, yet colleges affect their environments, as well as the other way around. Public institutions are often seen as drivers of regional economic development, rather than solely as affected by that development or lack thereof. Is a growing health care industry a cause or an effect of a college's health care programming?

The preceding examples are all at the campus level. How does the SWOT framework fit library issues? SWOTs affect the library staff's own planning and also library-specific SWOTs need to be brought to the attention of campus planners. Therefore, librarians need to do their own separate SWOT analysis. Some of it will be applied mainly internally, but important major points need to be brought to the attention of campus administrators.

True story: At one institution, faculty were asked whether the college provided a beneficial atmosphere for students from a particular minority group. The faculty replied that they guessed they did not, that they had a lot of improvement to do, a weakness. Not so, said the student-affairs staff. In fact, current students from that group felt that the college was a welcoming place, a good choice for their education, a strength. The college administration also noticed that that group's numbers were increasing in statewide demographics. An opportunity! But on the other hand, while the percentage increase was steep, the absolute numbers involved were small, and the college was not the only institution trying to attract students from that group, a threat.

The following is a list of some likely categories of strengths, weaknesses, opportunities, and threats. Real SWOT analysis focuses on current and future conditions, so these specific examples are just to show how to start thinking about the situation at a given college at a given time with an emphasis on items common to *small* libraries.

Internal *specific to that college and library*
Strengths:

- Collections that are unusual in topic or scope. In particular, collections acquired over a long period of time, which would be difficult for a competitor to duplicate, and collections with a vocal and grateful external user group.
- If something is unusually expensive and yet not identified as a strength, it is vulnerable.
- A physical library infrastructure that is sound, flexible, and with good visibility and usage among students.
- Physical library amenities of interest to and used by members of the community, whether local or tied to denominational and other affiliations, such as meeting

rooms, performance space, photogenic facades, or reception areas.

> **Story**: The music teacher's legacy: A local music teacher died, leaving a collection acquired over 60 years. The collection was gathered according to her own personal preferences and was strongest in some older and less used pedagogical techniques. The college it was donated to had very few students majoring in music with no faculty member interested in historical pedagogical research. Is the collection a strength or, given the space and staff needed simply to house it and to process it adequately, is it a weakness?

- Staff who are leaders in a particular area is better. The more specific it is, the better, more than just "excellent staff." In any organization, people are the prime resource. A polite and necessary acknowledgment of this is to always list them as a strength. It is very important, however, in planning and communicating with the rest of campus to not stop with the generic statement. Everyone will say they have high-quality staff. Library directors should be prepared with specific examples and details about how librarian knowledge currently advances research, teaching, and learning on campus and/or how they can do so going forward.
- Notably strong relations with faculty. Just saying "staff are our strength" is not enough; librarians need to be able to demonstrate that this strong relationship with faculty does exist, or the ways and the extent to which it exists. Consider the spectrum of library-faculty coordination. At the weak end of the line, the library director is told of new programs after they are approved; librarians work only in the library and do library instruction only with freshmen or only provide a few introductory and voluntary library tours, and talk with faculty only when they contact the library

with a specific question. At the opposite, the library staff is involved in new program planning, participates in orientation of new faculty with special attention to their research needs, and has a planned role in each academic program's degree goals with basic to advanced instruction. Faculty consult with librarians when new courses are planned and old ones are revised.

- The smallness and personal nature of the library and librarians' relations with students mean that they can be innovative and nimble and can take risks. They do not have cumbersome bureaucracies to assess needs or gather detailed feedback. With good personal relations, students and faculty can give quick and useful feedback about any library initiative. Ideas can be tried out, tested, and abandoned or adopted relatively rapidly, lessening the investment in any one idea and increasing the likelihood that something good will be thought up.

Story: A small college library became part of a network of libraries serving a particular health profession. It had some students located in rural communities, and worked out in the pre-broadband, pre-scanning era how to send copies of materials via postal mail upon phone, mail, or e-mail request. The university libraries involved struggled to set up special procedures and devote specific staff time to handling requests, while the small library simply did "whatever works" to erase the physical distance between the students and the information they needed.

Weaknesses:

- Library physical facilities that are smaller or less flexible than needed. Older buildings are especially prone to problems in using new technology; even more distressing, some expensive retrofits can become themselves obsolete, such as adding extensive wiring which in turn is replaced by wireless hubs.

It should be noted, however, that physical facilities are not static. Small-scale renovation is a constant process and can make huge differences in the usability of space within some features that are harder to change, like an overall footprint.

- Ugly facilities, especially buildings constructed in the boom in the 1960s. A library's physical appearance contributes to how viable, valuable, and attractive its space appears to a college applicant or student looking for study space. Just as outdated recreational facilities turn off applicants, a dismal library discourages use. Usage of most renovated or new libraries increases—is it because the space has different services or new resources, or just that it has more user-friendly and welcoming aesthetics?
- Awkward location of facilities and services, perhaps exacerbated over time as the campus develops (see the master-planning section). A library that starts out at the "heart" of a campus might not be near a new center of gravity as new buildings are added. Branch or specialized library units are also affected by changes in where student classrooms, faculty offices and laboratories, and residences are located.
- Limited parking. This is a weakness, although it is a good problem to have. Only campuses with declining enrollments have excess parking. Nevertheless, the library director needs to ensure that non-residential library users, both students and community members, are able to have reasonable access.
- A general absence of economies of scale for curricular/ program support. Small colleges start with a relatively comprehensive set of collections and services. At a minimum, they can adequately handle undergraduate general education needs. This is true even at community colleges that serve students preparing to transfer

to four-year institutions. Then, every area of advanced study, whether at the student or faculty level, individually comes with a need for a minimum basic level of expertise and information resources. It is very difficult for the small college; it is far more difficult to support 10 students in each of five new programs than 50 students in one new program. This is also affected by which particular new programs are involved and how they are implemented:

o Each new program has more or less overlap with existing resources. If environmental science is added, will it be concerned with political aspects of managing the environment or will it be biological or engineering?

o While new faculty for a new program often are hired specifically to teach mostly or solely in that program, in contrast at the small library, it will not be possible to hire a new librarian dedicated to that specific expertise. Every librarian must handle multiple curricular areas.

o Some colleges develop extensive research opportunities for students at the undergraduate level. This calls for a level of intensity and depth for the collection that is not present for general education or service courses.

The following are indeed weaknesses but they are not ones that will be formally stated in planning documents:

• Staff who are uninterested in or resistant to changes in their responsibilities or roles. The library needs to change with trends in information and in learning. It is not always the case that all librarians or support staff share a dynamic attitude about their work. Passive attitudes are weaknesses that should be addressed to the extent possible, but in reality, changing people's attitudes about change is difficult and slow—and might be impossible if it never rises to the level of a firing offense.

• Administrators who are uninterested in or ill informed about the role of and potential for the library. While there may be several causes of this, some are within the library director's control and others are not.

○ As noted throughout this book, it is important to be proactive about communicating with important campus actors in large and small, systematic and opportunistic ways. In a sense, strategic planning is where this kind of constant vigilance about ensuring the library is known and appreciated on campus and pays off: it makes non-library people naturally inclined to incorporate the library into their thinking and be receptive to library input. Not communicating means not being understood or appreciated.

○ Especially when they are new to campus, administrators will be affected by their own personal experiences with libraries either in their discipline (research and teaching) or in previous administrative positions. Those experiences could have been positive, or also passive or invisible or even negative. The remedy is to be particular about how libraries work at that college and keep in mind that when librarians work to enhance the perception of libraries at one college, it benefits librarians at all colleges.

External: *general*
  Opportunities:

- Library staff are well positioned to keep pace with changes in teaching technologies. Library technologies in fact are usually ahead of in-class developments and can usually be productively married to campus-wide technology initiatives. For example, research by undergraduates and other forms of hands-on learning involve independent thinking and background research that goes beyond textbook learning, precisely the kind of situation that the wide-open library is prepared to supply.

- Methods of supporting online learning have become very well developed. Initially, this was often done by very large universities with specialized staff, but their efforts have been well disseminated throughout academic librarianship to the point that supporting online learners is part of normal, not specialized, public services. Moreover, students themselves are now more accustomed to online methodologies. Some students in the pre-Internet era were ignorant of how to use an encyclopedia's index and cross-references. Now they are at least familiar with the concepts of links, site maps, and search engines.

- A vital, wildly energetic, and constantly changing landscape of library cooperation has emerged. State-wide library database licensing is only one example, though public funding means there is a distinct "threat" of cuts. Overall, however, huge gains in information access can be achieved with a variety of cooperative arrangements, far beyond the local physical lending networks of the past.

Threats:

This is a relatively limited section, not because there are no threats but because there are not many that are specific to libraries. Small colleges are subject to many environmental threats, such as local economic events (industry advancing or declining), the appearance of competitors, and demographic trends. An acute and very library-specific issue is often referred to as serials price inflation, but is more broadly stated as:

- Changes in publishing and scholarly communication can lead to high licensing or subscription costs, as well as expensive storage and access to databanks needed for faculty and student research.
  - Publishers may seek and gain additional control over resource sharing and charging.
  - Students, faculty, and administrators can have unrealistic expectations for information access. Is "everything" on the Internet? For free?

Threats can also be external to the library but internal to the campus. The library director needs to take into consideration campus-wide trends. One example is changes in the characteristics of the applicant pool and thus how well new students are prepared for college. Library instruction builds upon the skills and knowledge that incoming students already possess. If characteristics of admitted students change, they will have ripple effects on information-literacy instruction. This is something more on the monitoring than planning level, however. Compared to other issues, it can usually be adjusted to as it occurs, and with existing resources, librarians should be able to handle whatever students are admitted to their institution, even if that changes over the years.

Local SWOTs

Beyond these general library trends and issues, what are the internal and external factors influencing the library at a very local level? For example, where do you list the very smallness of a college and a library? Potential students may prefer an atmosphere where students have close contact with full-time faculty, an opportunity! It is a threat if they assume this happens everywhere, that all small colleges are like high schools with assigned full-time teachers, or if they simply don't value the smaller environment. Potential students may want a wide array of activities. Does that make the diverse offerings of Big University a threat, or can the small college creatively join with arts in the community to provide opportunities that are more personal, intimate, and diverse, an opportunity? When college faculty are the ones who provide leadership for arts in the community, is the arts situation internal or external?

Boundaries between strengths, weaknesses, opportunities, and threats can be difficult, vague, and even contentious. A SWOT analysis has the one internal major advantage of sitting at one point and consciously trying to find items that are S, W, O, and T. This is especially helpful when phenomena don't seem to fit. It is a good way to break out of one's normal daily activities. Here, the basic five-year framework for strategic planning is useful as it prods participants to think of trends and developments in addition to and even in preference to simply listing current conditions. So, systematically thinking more broadly is a good brain exercise.

Another reason is that it is one more way to develop externally oriented thinking, on the part of the director and also all of the staff. Academic libraries do not stand alone; their staff need to engage knowledgeably with their campus environments, and campuses need to engage knowledgeably with their economic and demographic environments.

Dynamic Planning

Looking at what many colleges often really do when they plan, a term seems to be needed to cover a particular middle ground in terms of types of plans: planning that is more than just a vague restatement of the mission statement yet is neither future-oriented nor focused enough to really be called strategic. This can be called "dynamic planning," a phrase that is a little more positive than episodic, or even after-the-fact planning. In dynamic planning, units are called upon once a year to lay out goals and objectives—sometimes these are for a year that is already partly under way. Often this is considered part of strategic planning because these goals are intended to tie either to longer-term strategic initiatives or to major campus themes or values. However, rather than being a creative projection into the future, this can devolve into a humble report on work already under way, and in the report, phrased in wording that ties it to ongoing campus-wide rhetoric and emphases.

Dynamic planning does have value. A retrospective "we are [already] doing X, which fits Y [vague and all-encompassing] theme" can be a mere evasion of the future perspective of true planning. Giving it its own name and identity acknowledges that what looks like rather backward *reporting* does legitimately reflect ongoing *thinking* and often considerable on-the-fly creativity. Just as people can select books without a formal collection-management plan, librarians on a day-to-day basis do go ahead and dream of what they want to do now and in the future, without heeding or needing a formal strategic-planning structure. A strategic-planning framework that is too rigid, too focused, and too selective runs a danger of leaving out important ongoing needs and the kind of incremental change that good librarians should practice on a daily basis. Deliberately engaging in explicit dynamic planning, tying one's ongoing creativity to campus priorities, is a way to bridge the tension between originality and freedom and the organization that the originality needs to serve.

8 BUDGETING

The keys: What obligations are ongoing? What control do you have over moving money from one category to another? Work within the campus's budget.

This chapter describes the most important elements of budgeting for a small college library in the categories that will make it easiest for a director to manage the budget. Budgeting proceeds on several levels, and understanding basic budget categories, both conceptually and in accounting terms, is the only solution for being fiscally competent. Budget categories determine what directors can do and what flexibility they have. After understanding the categories, library directors must keep an eye on the big picture. Directors must understand how the categories work within the library's needs and activities and how the library's budget relates to the rest of the campus. Finally, the process of constructing a budget request, including the general process, budget bases, and grants and gifts, is shown.

When considering all of this, some of what a library director manages is very library-specific, such as arranging as favorable as possible terms on database licensing by deciding whether to purchase only for the library or to buy with a library consortia.

Other aspects are specific to academia, such as the rules and fiscal implications of employing work-study students. Others seem more general and at first glance appear similar to common business practices, such as setting clerical salaries or arranging for copier maintenance.

This spectrum corresponds roughly to the director's scope of authority, which is strongest in very library-oriented matters and most constrained when it comes to practices common across campus, for example, the campus accounting and human resources software that eventually, if not constantly, library personnel will need to use. What is standard for the campus applies to accounting principles and rules that are audited. Nevertheless, some processes will be different for the library, and directors must make certain that the library's special needs are understood.

> **Story**: At a presentation about research into variations in budget allocations for colleges and universities of various sizes and types, a biology faculty member stood up in the question period and expressed genuine surprise that so little of a library's budget, 40–50 percent, went for personnel: "In our school, about 90 percent of our expenses are salaries." It's unclear where he thought the money for all the journals he used came from.

Personnel issues are a large part of management and a large part of this chapter because they are such a large part of budgeting. From 40 to 50 percent (most four-year colleges) to 70 percent (two-year colleges) of a library's overall budget is spent on personnel.[1] In this chapter, some decision points about staffing are reviewed. The human-relations perspective on management is still important. Decisions about the level, quantity, and combination or division of job responsibilities have to make fiscal sense but also need to ensure that some real person can and wants to fulfill each position, such as a consideration between hiring a reference librarian just for that midnight-to-2 A.M. slot or not.

While the director is responsible for the budget, the mechanics of spending the budget on library materials, supplies, and some services are the province primarily of the acquisitions person or persons at the library as well as the purchasing, human resources, and financial aid departments of the college. A library's finances consist of paying people, buying services, buying things, and accepting donations. All of these fit into budget categories.

THINKING ABOUT THE BUDGET: BUDGET CATEGORIES

It is difficult to find one framework for budgeting that is really useful for all aspects of academic library budgeting. Many different approaches to constructing a budget are offered at different times, and some become fashionable and then go away, such as zero-based budgeting, activity-based costing, or the favorite in real life, last year plus up or down. Technical details about particular functions of the budget include what qualifies as a capital expense, a division between personnel and other costs, and accounting for deposit accounts.

This chapter therefore provides not one but three different ways of thinking about budgeting. First, there are the conceptual categories of how the library's money is spent. Then in each section the accounting categories that influence how the library allocates funds are discussed. Finally, there is the process of making budget requests and specialized advice for a variety of issues and approaches that occur at that stage.

When library directors think about the library's income and expenses, they have a certain perspective on the library's needs that comes out of professional education and experience. MLS programs, for example, spend a lot of time teaching about the selection, acquisition, preservation, and management of library materials and providing services to patrons, including reference, instruction, and Web instruction. True to that preparation, librarians go on to experience those conceptual *expense* categories in their professional lives. They buy, provide access to, and replace materials and provide services. All of this takes money. We begin here with the income that comes in to provide the funding for expenses.

After the discussion of funding, the traditional and general way of grouping things money is spent on will be explained. These traditional categories are convenient but also conventional, and the divisions between each are, if not completely rigid, often difficult to breach under normal circumstances, with much more flexibility within each category than between each category. First, directors need to start with the income the library receives. This budget category becomes the starting point for all that follows.

INCOME

Income has three main categories: institutional allocations, endowments, and project-specific funding (grants). The institutional allocation happens every year after directors submit a budget request and the institution decides how much money the library will get in each accounting category.

The timing of the allocation is tied to either or both of two cycles, planning and fiscal. Many institutions follow a deliberate planning cycle, setting goals in the fall, formalizing them in dollar amounts in the spring, and setting them as the guidelines for the next year's budget in the late spring before the fiscal year begins in July. At tuition-driven institutions, this can be affected by concerns over fall enrollments. Library directors need to understand the current enrollment climate and predictions and need to exercise flexibility in requesting, receiving, and spending income. Cutbacks after a fiscal year begins when enrollments or endowments drop are not unknown and hit libraries harder than some academic units. For an academic department that uses adjuncts, a smaller number of classes means fewer expenses along with less income, and both happen in the fall when enrollments are known. In the library by contrast, at least two months of spending have already taken place before fall numbers become final.

At some institutions, there are dedicated endowments for collections. These are usually the result of donor legacies. They are not free or extra monies, however. The funding that is provided by the endowment will not also be provided by the institution. Fiscal officers consider money from any source to be money freed to be moved elsewhere, called fungible. In addition, endowments are subject to investment market conditions. Those who prosper by fat stock gains will also lose.

The final category, grant income, tends to be the smallest for small academic libraries, although everyone would like it to be bigger. Even at large research universities, where substantial overall income is derived from grants and some of that grant income intended for indirect costs applies to the library, the library seldom shares directly in grants to research faculty. Both large and small academic libraries look for special projects that fit the mission of donors, agencies, and other grantors.

Sometimes libraries can secure grant funding, from foundations, government sources (e.g., LSTA and Title III), and even individuals. The positive aspect of this income source is that it encourages creativity and innovation. Close work with the development office is part of grant success, and grant dollars make the entire institution look successful. The main danger is when campus officials harbor unrealistic expectations. The amount of library-related funding is meager compared to that available for social services, education in general, and scientific research.

Library directors and other librarians can work with other departments in the development of grant proposals and add in resources for the library as a part of the grant. This means an extremely collegial relationship between librarians and other units of campus, with greater possibility of funded research.

Accounting and Library Income

The bulk of a library's income, money placed in accounts from which it can be spent, occurs once a year at the start of the fiscal year. This is when the library's institutional allocation is delivered. Grant funding and endowment funding may occur on their own schedules, at more or less frequent intervals throughout the year.

Library Non-Income

An unpleasant surprise greets some new library directors when they think that they have other sources of income, such as card fees from special borrowers, proceeds from used-book sales, and late fines and lost/replacement book fees. Some even more antique categories such as fees for online searches, charges for interlibrary loan materials, and copier coins may still exist. It is easy to imagine the conceptual matching of these bits of cash to library needs; the amount charged for a lost book generally represents that book's original or replacement cost and a processing expense amount.

However, as far as accounting goes, libraries may have no income. Only some campus units will be set up to handle true income: bookstores, athletics, and food service. These are, through necessity, profit-making enterprises. The library is not one of them and, especially in a small institution, there will not be a compelling reason to warp generic accounting database categories to cater to the relatively small sums that come into the library. In general, cash and checks received by a library go into the institution's income. Unless the institution sets up a special way to track this and add it back to the library budget, library directors will never see any corresponding credit in library accounts. Instead, library directors need to budget as a reality that if items need replacing, that constitutes a normal part of the library's collection-development spending.

For the library, then, fines and fees are behavioral tools, such as ensuring that time limits on reserves or recalls for checked out materials are honored so more students can benefit from shared materials. Library directors, while they might fail at an attempt to claim the money directly, need to ensure that library monetary policies reflect an overall approach to encouraging good behavior and discouraging harmful behavior on the part of patrons.

Timing

Accounting procedures may collide with library practices in the area of timing. The campus itself has a distinct financial rhythm. A university may be able to select a fiscal year or it may be a part of the state fiscal year because it is state supported. If the state's fiscal year is July to June, income reflects tuition payments and personnel salaries, the two biggest items of income and expense. A library's spending cycle is usually different. Within the common July-to-June framework, it begins earlier and ends later than the academic year. If a library does not shut down for the summer, it has personnel expenses that begin in July. Materials spending at the other end of the fiscal year often peaks in the spring and early summer, and several significant spikes occur when big bills come due, such as for periodicals or database vendors. If the fiscal year is January through December, another framework exists. The example continues with the July–June fiscal year.

Most of the time, this does not cause problems. Three small points need attention. The first is that at least some purchasing is needed in July. Accounting offices, particularly if the institution is waiting to see how fall enrollment goes, may not populate non-salary budget lines as soon as the library needs them. That is, they may not actually deliver the library allocation into an account from which a payment can be made.

At the end of the fiscal year, the library's acquisitions people need to work closely to get purchase orders processed in ways that make sense for accounting, budgeting, and management purposes. Suppose a major database-licensing fee of $10,000 is due in June. The worst-case scenario would be when the library director has worked that into Year A's budget and carefully not spent that $10,000. If payment is delayed until July (Year B), then the library has lost the money that could have been spent in Year A, and now has to devote $10,000 of Year B's money to pay the bill. If the big payment is on a continuing subscription, then continually moving the payment date to July can work out, but if it is for a one-time purchase, it means simply $10,000 is lost, and if it is continuing but will need to be paid in June, that will be two big hits to Year B's budget. This scenario assumes that the library is unable to carry cash or allocations from one year to the next, which is the most common situation at small colleges.

Finally, there is the difficult issue of managing mid-year budget decreases. Taking the whole year's budget as a given, any director can organize big and small purchases to get the library what it needs. If the campus is facing budget problems and a decrease is considered, the director needs to be aware, and make others aware, that some disproportionately large amounts of spending may have already occurred or may be coming up and unavoidable. Managing library spending is different from hiring contingent faculty or travel or purchasing supplies, the usual discretionary categories for academic units on campus.

EXPENSES

Library expenses fall into several categories, many of which are unique to the library among academic and administrative units on campus. Library directors need to understand not only how their own library budget spending categories are organized, but how they fit within the overall campus schema. Discussing spending issues with the campus comptroller, purchasing officer, or head of finance is more productive when directors can explain what is similar and what is different.

The top-most division is simple:

- Personnel/services
- Collections
- Other services and equipment

A service that consists solely of staff time is covered by personnel spending. Creating Web pages when that does not involve licensing software or purchasing servers is a personnel-only service.

Personnel spending is divided into three basic groups:

- Professional librarians
- Support staff
- Student workers

Collection spending is divided by commitment level and purpose:

- Continuous/one-time
- General/program/mission

The distinction between virtual and physical format is needed for reporting purposes but is something that will change according to availability and user needs. What is more important to consider is whether an acquisition is one-time (a purchase) or a continuing obligation (a license).

Other services and equipment is a catch-everything-else category. It includes:

- Bibliographic utility/ies (the integrated library system, OCLC, and/or consortium memberships)
- Computer equipment and networking, for students and staff
- Facilities maintenance, replacement, or acquisition of items not managed by the campus
- General supplies

The following provides more definition and more detail on each category. It is also important to note who on campus cares about each category. The library director does not have complete autonomy when it comes to resources.

PERSONNEL

Personnel appears twice in the conceptual category list: one time as a major category in expenses, and one time as a subdivision of a type of income. For most academic libraries, an institutional allocation for the library's overall budget generally arrives already divided in two sections, personnel and all other expenses. Connected to this, decisions about hiring or retaining staff other than student workers generally follow a much different path than decisions about any other aspect of library budgeting.

From the campus perspective, a personnel hire is like the traditional serial subscription for a library. It is a long-term commitment that must fulfill a purpose and that entails significant resources. Therefore, small college library directors don't merely move money over to cover each position but usually make specific requests accompanied by extensive justifications when outlining personnel positions. Campus administrators will care mainly about three things: initial hire justification, ongoing position level (and therefore salary expense), and greater efficiency (which equals reduced staffing) in times of financial difficulty. This covers what the job consists of and how much it is needed, but not who the person is.

For budget purposes, library directors need to have a keen grasp of two aspects of personnel. First, they must understand and be able to communicate the reasons why a particular personnel line is classified as staff or professional/MLS. Whenever turnover occurs, by resignation or retirement, directors need to be prepared for questions about why a position should remain at the professional level. Faculty status and unionization will affect these issues and are discussed in the planning and personnel-recruitment chapters.

Second, it is important for the director to understand campus norms for staff-level classifications and the compensations for those classifications. Every position on campus comes with a set of duties and responsibilities and an annual salary or hourly wage. Each position fits within someone's idea of what is appropriate for a person to do or to be compensated for. Those responsible always include the campus human resources (HR) department even if they are not the only word or the last word on the topic. It is vital that library directors understand what the HR departments think about what librarians and support staff do.

Job Classification

Job classification is an area in which small college library directors may encounter anything from a purely informal or customary understanding to a formal standards-based, consultant-interpreted schema. Some small campuses, particularly those with a very distinctive culture or in relatively isolated employment markets, may take a very person-specific approach. People hired are paid based on what they personally bring to the position. Others may go in the other direction and contract periodically with consultants to review and professionalize their standards for positions and compensation.

For colleges, the most important standardized staffing information is organized by CUPA-HR (College and University Professional Association for Human Resources). Its surveys and databanks incorporate brief descriptions of librarian and library staff positions, and institutions can obtain comparative salary information for standard and customized comparison groups. CUPA-HR's national data are republished annually in the *Chronicle of Higher Education*.

For classification at the staff level, the library director needs to talk informally with human resources people to learn about their thoughts concerning levels of responsibility and job classification. It is important that directors and HR come to a mutual understanding about what a job entails. Three issues become very important, especially in the small library: judgment, multitasking, and position creep.

Proper job classification and compensation rely heavily on determining the level of judgment involved. A position where you depend on the individual to follow routine procedures reliably is a lower-level position than one where you expect that the individual will often make on-the-spot decisions consistent with the library's policies and campus culture. Compare someone who processes interlibrary loan requests quickly and accurately to someone who deals with students complaining about overdue fines. Compare someone who orders books and ensures all bookkeeping is accurate to someone who evaluates which vendors provide the best value. This judgment level is a special concern for small staffs because support staff are not likely to spend all or even most of their time on high-judgment activities, yet it is important to have someone who can rise to that level whenever needed. Writing a job description for someone who spends most of his or her time on daily mundane tasks will lead HR people to misunderstand the true demands of the position.

Multitasking, or combining different roles into one job, is another particular issue for directors of small libraries. The library does not have enough volume in some typical library tasks to have people assigned to them full time. Thus, library tasks are either assigned to a number of part-time positions or to those whose positions cover more than one role. Assigning part-time personnel to specific roles makes financial sense. Part-time workers generate less expense because they do not receive most benefits and their hours can be adjusted as work increases or decreases. Managerially, it is often a terrible idea. If the college is in a rural area, it will be difficult to identify multiple people with the right skills; if it is in an urban area, the best part-time persons will prefer full-time work elsewhere, if they can get it. In addition, managing eight part-time staff is far more difficult than managing four full-time employees. It is easier, in other words, to help full-time employees adjust to having multiple roles than to train multiple part-time staff in very specific roles.

What is important is that the campus HR people understand the variety of needs within the library and that multiple responsibilities need to be incorporated into an understanding of the compensation for each position. Multitasking positions are more complex to classify, but they are more flexible for the future. Directors can adjust roles to respond to changing needs.

Position Creep

Position creep is similar to mission creep. Mission creep happens when a project starts out with one purpose and over time evolves into something quite different. Position creep happens when someone starts out in a job that has a specific purpose and set of responsibilities, and then over time what that person does moves away from the set job description and evolves into sometimes very different tasks and duties. In a bureaucratic mode, job descriptions always match the jobs that are being done; in real life, positions change in an informal way depending on the person who has the position and the supervisor. A supervisor who allows employees to adapt their jobs to their interests will often have happier employees who will work at the job with an entirely different attitude than those confined to a prescribed, unchanging job description.

Position creep has an impact on budgeting, and budgeting has an impact on position creep. Over the course of time, good employees will become better at what they do. Moreover, some employees take on additional or more complex responsibilities so that over time their jobs end up involving a higher level of judgment than originally intended. In a formal system, this would mean a higher level of compensation; yet can the library afford that, and does the library need that higher level?

This is a very tough issue for the small library director. On the one hand, support staff grow and develop when they are engaged in, enthusiastic about, and committed to their roles, and committed to even more than their assigned roles. The staff member whose job is satisfying is probably the person who likes learning new things and sees best how this job relates to the larger library or campus. These are all good things. It's even better when those creative staff people come up with new and exciting ways of doing library things. They don't just add quantity or produce more, they change the quality of the value that is produced.

Fiscal responsibility means that the library director must take a sober look at the needs of the organization and at compensation that is both realistic and equitable. It is unethical to keep relying on contributions from staff members who are at a level higher than they are being paid for. Some of this inevitably happens. Indeed, as in the classic example of members of religious organizations who contribute their services, it can be a deeply embedded part of the history of an institution. However, it is not a good modern HR practice for a circulation clerk to take on the role of office manager without any change in classification and hence compensation. Does the library need a position for an office manager? Does this require advertising for the position, accepting applications, and perhaps hiring someone not in-house?

The library director in the small library is literally face-to-face with these realities. Many employees expect that when they take on new responsibilities or achieve higher levels of education that this will become embedded in updated job descriptions and in salary levels. It is the director who has to fit this into the needs of the library and the realities of the library budget, and with less flexibility than in a larger library with more personnel lines.

Any one of three ways can be used to manage the fiscal realities of an employee's new qualifications for a different position. The first is political, a continuous awareness of how the position, as it changes, compares to the levels of other staff on campus. The second is bureaucratic: a complete, rational, and impersonal examination of the position if it becomes vacant. The third requires a talk with HR. From the "creeping" employee's perspective, what are attractive opportunities to use new skills elsewhere? These all are part of managing the library's personnel budget; they are discussed in more detail in the personnel development and planning chapters.

> **Story**: A campus HR director with experience in a large for-profit company was hired with a mandate to increase the professionalization of HR. This included reviewing job classifications and comparative compensation. The HR director disliked job descriptions that spanned several functions and levels. The best job description was one that fit neatly into one preexisting business-type category. If several responsibilities were listed for a position, those that were more routine were considered determinative for pay placement. This turned position descriptions into lists of duties, the more the merrier, with little actual review of importance or appropriate compensation.

Staff Size

The size of the library staff is primarily determined by two things: institutional benchmarking, or what is going on with the college's size and income generally, and competitive benchmarking, or what other libraries work with. In real life, absent a crisis of either finances or confidence, most libraries will continue with the same size of staff as in the previous year. Most changes are caused by general campus trends such as changes in campus enrollments and thus income. This will spark campus-wide changes in personnel. The library should share proportionally in cuts and in increases. Cuts and increases may be more obvious for administration in teaching units—an English department increases or decreases class sizes or hires faculty or adjuncts to match increased or decreased numbers of students, but administrators may not be aware of changes in demands on the library. Directors need to make the case for the library to maintain proportionate staffing in order to sustain its level of service to the campus.

Competitive benchmarking is when the number of the library's personnel is compared to staffing at peer institutions. Federally collected data exist about staffing levels, including professional librarians, staff, and student workers for nearly all U.S. academic libraries. The data are usually a little old, which means the actual salary figures are not relevant, but staffing ratios are relatively robust. That is, a campus with a 200-student to one-librarian ratio four years ago is probably a relatively well-staffed campus even four years later.

Library directors should use this benchmarking by creating two peer groups. First, their planning or institutional researchers can tell them what the campus as a whole considers to be their peer institutions. Different institutions take different approaches here. Some important factors are degree level and mix of programs, financial standing, and prospective student competitors.

The other peer group is more specific and less easily defined. It consists of those institutions the library competes with in hiring librarians. A small Catholic college may have defined its peer group on the institutional level to be other small Catholic colleges across the nation, but applicants for librarian positions may primarily be recruited by nearby public colleges and universities.

Given those two groups, library directors can determine if their staffing ratios are within the desired range. For example, suppose a college has a group of 10 peer institutions, colleges primarily seen as competitors in attracting students. At this location, college administrators consciously keep tuition at about the thirtieth percentile in the group, not the lowest, but not above the average or even at the average. In context it is reasonable for the library to advocate for a staffing level that is not the lowest but is at the thirtieth percentile mark in measures such as student-to-librarian, faculty-to-librarian, or spending-per-student ratios.

Benchmarking looks only at the quantity of staff, not at their roles or levels. That makes it simple and flexible. It is simple and powerful to make the case for a size of staff that conforms to *accepted* general expectations of your campus and peer group. It is flexible because directors can then adjust responsibilities among the staff as they and their library world change. They can eliminate periodical binding, add artifact digitization, hire an outreach librarian, and change to a webmaster.

Accounting Categories for Personnel

Personnel have a limited set of formal accounting categories. Every college campus will have HR and payroll systems that will be used for personnel costs. The basic categories and issues will be salaried workers based upon contract length, hourly workers including overtime, and student workers.

For salaried workers, one important difference between academia and most businesses is the existence of contracts with 9-, 10-, or 11-month contract periods rather than simple continuous employment. How these are determined for salaried library workers who are primarily the librarians will depend on the college's yearly cycle. This may include summer courses or special programming. The important part is to ensure that the administration knows that the library's rhythms and needs are closely but not entirely tied to academic activity. If librarians have faculty status, their contracts will probably differ in taking account of summer work. For classroom faculty other than administrators, this is traditionally handled solely by special summer teaching contracts. For librarians, it will be part of their normal annual contracts, which tend to be longer than those of classroom faculty.

For hourly workers, there are two important points. First, overtime needs to be explicitly managed. In most circumstances, this generally means it is forbidden for library staff. It is costly and since it has to be paid if legally incurred even if not budgeted in advance, library staff cannot simply decide to work extra hours. Very few library emergencies require additional staff hours and if there are, library directors need to communicate with their supervisor about added costs. Second, overtime rules can make scheduling full-time employees difficult for the small library that desires limited weekend hours. Having a full-time hourly employee work one day shorter than eight hours means longer hours elsewhere. Public-services employees need to match public-service needs, while technical-services employees have more flexibility. For short open periods, student workers or part-time workers are the most feasible.

COLLECTIONS

The category of "collections" is less complicated. In contrast to the personnel section, where campus administrators will have both an interest and in some respects relevant expertise, library collections are essentially library-specific expenditures.

Collection Spending Control

For budgeting purposes, library directors need first to establish and then maintain (or control) spending for collections and then take a flexible, purpose-driven approach to spending categories. It may seem obvious to both the director and to administration that the library staff is in charge of library collections. To a large extent and at most libraries, this will be the case. Some common exceptions require attention: departmental collections, database licensing, and gifts. In each case, creating bureaucratic rules to deal with them will help the library maintain control and consistency, but political consequences are involved.

Faculty in academic departments may have their own subscriptions to journals, may receive their own desk copies of textbooks, and may have substantial private or departmental libraries. If these are all from personal funds, they are not an issue, at least not until the gift stage. If, however, any or all of them are paid with institutional funds, then someone is expected to exercise control over authorization and spending and over the housing of physical materials. If an effort is being made to control costs, it is convenient for academic administrators to designate the library director to be the bad guy, the "no you can't" person. This puts the library director squarely in the face of faculty who have very personal and particular interests in these materials.

Good personal relations with individual faculty are valuable, but long term the best response comes directly out of classic collection-management practice, the development of a collection-development policy that states the purposes of the collection, major exclusions, and priority areas. A rule of thumb as to what is covered in the small college includes two criteria: (1) if the item requires college resources to purchase, process, or store, and (2) if the item is intended for communal or shared, not personal, use. On the other hand, a purchasing rule that says that all subscriptions or all books must be bought through the library is unnecessarily formal and will lead to inevitable exceptions that will undermine the rule itself. Subscriptions to the city magazine for the president's office, copies of the APA style manual for psychology faculty, and software manuals for the IT help desk would be exceptions to a collection-development rule.

Each academic department chair needs to have a working understanding with the library director about what needs to come out of what budget. Examples include:

Department	Library
Style manuals for staff/faculty use	Materials students will use upon occasion and that can be used semester after semester
Textbook copies	
Anything used on a daily basis	
Safety and equipment manuals	Materials faculty from different departments can use
	Reference materials used only occasionally

Department OR Library?

A school-wide medical thesaurus database

Multiple copies of reference manuals

Personal copies of new books for faculty

Professional newsletters

A final rule of thumb is that if an item should be placed in the library after a department no longer wants it, library staff should exert some ownership over it. If it isn't suitable for the library collection, it need not be placed there. Examples are denominational directories used in pastoral education program, obsolete textbooks, and outdated manuals.

Once library directors and staff understand what belongs in the library, the other divisions come into play, although in a very fluid way. It is a cliché to mention how information ownership and access are in a state of flux. The division between virtual and physical resources is a very well-known example of this. It is impossible in any one book to delineate an exact and enduring framework. The following issues are important to understand and will interact with the accounting categories reviewed later: level of commitment, updating/permanency, and uniqueness/mission.

Collection Types by Commitment Level

Different library materials constitute different levels of commitment. The following are four major types of acquisition categories:

- Monographs, in print (or permanent virtual) format

    This is a one-time purchase item that remains accessible until deliberately withdrawn, lost or stolen, and unreplaced, and tends to be relatively inexpensive regardless of the subject area. This category includes audiovisual (AV) resources in whatever format. The only distinction is that AV materials have format-obsolescence issues more pronounced than do books.

    The average cost difference between an English monograph and one in medicine is much smaller than that between an English periodical and a medical journal. That helps make this a relatively easy budget category to manage. That is, it is the easiest to increase or decrease. Because it is easiest to cut does not mean it is the best place for a cut.

- Updating serials, increasingly in virtual format

  In considering updating serials, obsolete editions or versions have little or no value because users need the latest information. Serials almost always involve an ongoing commitment of resources and are seldom inexpensive. For those serials worthy of updating, the cost of updating a serial can be zero for government publications or extremely high for commercial products, but it is usually very task-oriented. Managing these entails an explicit analysis of projected usage compared to the priorities of the library's budget as a whole.

- Continuing serials, individual, in print, and/or virtual

  This is the classic periodical, but it also includes a standing order (meaning it is automatically renewed by the publisher) for a particular serial publication, such as collected musical works. The distinguishing feature is that not only are new items being continually added, but the old items still retain value. In some cases (e.g., a multi-volume dictionary), the set loses meaning without earlier items. This is a double-ended commitment, a commitment to keep the entire set virtually or on the shelf and a commitment to continue to buy it as it is produced. A big decision point with this type of material is whether to go virtual. Annual costs need to take into consideration not only new materials, but a commitment to the availability of the entire item or set. In addition, technological accessibility has to be managed.

- Continuing serials, aggregated databases

  Continuing serials usually means aggregated databases, such as from H.W. Wilson or Ebsco. The word "database" is used so broadly that it is more useful to consider what kind of database is involved rather than to lump them all together. An aggregator database is one in which a library has access to groups of materials. Staff in a small library are usually not in a position to pick and choose individual items. This leads to some interesting dynamics wherein the collection itself creates needs rather than needs driving the collection. If in order to get essential items one has to accept an aggregator with previously undesired items, once they are purchased the library can promote the use of those items it happens to now have to get the best use of the package as a whole. As with updating serials and individual continuing serials, an aggregating serials resource usually entails a significant ongoing commitment of money. It is primarily in this area that cooperative purchasing or licensing is most often practiced by academic libraries.

- Materials free to the library

    Virtually all academic librarians can take advantage of a growing number of high-quality free resources. Some are available to everyone, such as the PubMed interface into the premier index of medical literature. Others are provided by state licensing of databases for either general public use or for use by academic or other types of libraries.

    It is well to keep in mind the political aspects of these resources. Each represents content or access that can be extremely valuable and often essential to serving library patron needs. Here, the word "political" is used in the most obvious sense. If the state government is funding database licensing, recipient libraries need to be diligent and proactive *political* advocates. Since politicians are sensitive to any group's self-interest, it is especially valuable to promote an appreciation for these "free" materials to the campus and the community in general. The amount of money an institution can save with these databases is so large that library directors must make the college president and fiscal officer aware of the savings and the usefulness of these resources to students. Faculty and students should be made aware so that any attempts to have legislators cut such funds can be stopped by user pressure.

Collection Types by Purpose

Another distinction is important, especially for small, rural, and religiously affiliated libraries. Each item acquired by a small academic library serves one or more purposes, to contribute to general college-level education, to serve particular academic programs at that institution, and to address particular local, institutional, or denominational needs.

The first purpose is relatively easy to meet. For better or worse, even quite small and underfunded libraries manage to provide enough basic materials to support basic student work in general education fields of study. An example is how community colleges with libraries with smaller collections support students in doing acceptable coursework for transfer to four-year institutions.

The second purpose poses serious challenges to the small academic library. The small library does not benefit from economies of scale. Minimum levels of intellectual materials are necessary for education in accounting, in nursing, in education, and in management. A medium-sized public institution can do this very efficiently. This is a primarily *budget-related* reason why the library director needs to be part of conversations about new programs. To college administrators, new programs are generally a very linearly scalable item: more students, more tuition, and more faculty. To a library director, there is a much more curvilinear relationship. The library must have a base of adequate resources, regardless of how many students there are. The base can serve a growing number of students without much additional per capita increase. Finally, a large enough program will have faculty with research demands.

The final purpose relates to each institution's particular stakeholders. It could be the small town or region where the college is located. It could be the denomination for which the college is a flagship. It could be an association or organization that created and maintains a relationship with the college. In each case, the library may have responsibilities to serve that mission and those constituencies by acquiring and preserving unique materials. This is where the small academic college library directors must be politically sensitive to the fact that the library does not just serve academic goals but also the needs of those underlying groups. Doing so successfully will enhance the college's entire mission and standing.

Accounting (and Reporting) Categories for Collections

A number of difficult issues arise when it comes to fitting the types of purchases or licensing agreements needed in the library budget to ensure appropriate materials are accessible in formal accounting categories. One of the most interesting issues library directors face is designation of certain spending as either capital or operating. Overall, an operating expense is one that occurs and sees its benefits within one fiscal year. For example, one buys and then uses copier paper. A company maintains the library's security system on an annual contract. Individuals are paid for their current services.

A capital expense is something that is considered to have durable worth. It is not "consumed" and is usually a larger expenditure. Most expenses have to meet a monetary threshold to be designated as "capital" expenses. For example, library shelving is obviously intended to last a number of years, but if a given purchase falls below guidelines such as purchasing a new newspaper rack for under $5,000, it will be considered an operating expense, not a capital one. The library's building as a whole is the classic example of a capital expense. The college's capital budget and capital campaigns are designed to raise and spend large sums of money on such enduring assets.

All of this is simple enough as far as much of the library's budget goes. Directors should become reasonably familiar with the guidelines for capital requests in the budgeting cycle (e.g., furniture). The capital versus operating distinction has become more of a problem in recent years with respect to the library materials budget.

Over the course of 20 years, general accounting standards have shifted. At one point, the existing book collection needed to be evaluated and recorded as a capital asset. Then materials spending was taken from the operating budget and moved to the capital budget. In a way this makes conceptual sense. The price of each individual book puts it well under normal capital-expense guidelines. In aggregate, materials are a major expense, and most printed books are intended to have lengthy service lives. The up-to-date librarian will notice that the conceptual materials budget categories described above include items that are not or cannot be durable in nature. A yearly subscription to a virtual resource vanishes when it is not paid; therefore, electronic subscriptions can be moved back to the operating budget.

The library director needs to handle this carefully in two areas. First, much budget planning takes a year-over-year approach; one's request for a coming year is measured against a previous year. If large sections of the library's conceptual budget are moving back and forth between capital and operating expenditures, then people taking a very quick look at the library's spending over time may not grasp what has changed and what has stayed the same. Has library spending gone up or down? It is impossible to track over time unless both capital and operating materials and collections expenses are combined, which an accounting system may not itself do. In that case, library directors need to produce their own charts or data displays that combine information from a variety of sources to produce true conceptual tracking of what the library has received and spent over the years.

Second, procurement and budget tracking within any college's accounting system usually differs between capital and operating expenses, and the library is different from academic departments. An academic department would rarely need to check the status of its capital budget spending. A library budget officer would need to make daily entries as items are received and generate at least monthly status reports. The library director and acquisitions personnel need more detailed access to capital accounting information than may be the case with other units on campus.

Major surveys by the Association of College and Research Libraries, the National Center for Education Statistics, and some consortiums ask libraries to report their spending in several materials budget categories. This is and will be a moving target. Library directors should ensure that their acquisitions or accounting categories can be mapped to the survey categories. They should also use national data with caution. Currently it is obvious from the zeros that appear in many categories that different colleges are interpreting survey questions differently, which makes comparing spending by category difficult.

SERVICES AND EQUIPMENT

The services and equipment category is quite broad and diverse. Conceptually, it includes items that are part of the library's operations but that may not appear in the library's budget at all, such as furniture or furnishings and housekeeping. For those, the library director needs to communicate with the administrators who manage those budgets to ensure that they know about any changes in library needs.

This category also includes very important library-controlled items. The biggest is often the integrated library system. Other items are hardware, including staff computers and computers for student and faculty use, copier and security equipment service contracts, and publicity or special event expenses.

The most expensive and least flexible item in this category is the bibliographic utility, or library catalog. Everything a library possesses is accessed via this catalog. This is the key difference between a library and a pile of books—its catalog.

> **Story:** A small college was taken over by a large university. As part of the merger, the holdings symbols in OCLC for the small college's collection were changed to those of the large university. Sometime later, the merger was reversed, but the college's collection, even though theoretically now part of the new independent small college, had no holding symbols, hence no electronic records, and hence no effective access for students or faculty.

Library directors need to ensure integrated library systems functions are available in the most user-friendly and cost-effective way, two ideals that are not always compatible. There are a number of open-source catalog/database options, but they generally require significant local expertise and support. It is also important to ensure they work with campus purchasing and accounting systems.

Cooperation in licensing commercial systems is particularly crucial for small college libraries. Small college libraries by their nature need to rely on interlibrary loans, particularly to meet the needs of faculty when the collection's emphasis is primarily on supporting teaching. A good integration of the library system with various interlibrary networks will be important for both patrons and staff. That is one reason to belong to a group using a common system; the other is the increased bargaining power of the group. Large universities with big budgets are important clients for the major commercial vendors; small colleges are not. Belonging to a consortium is a classic answer to this problem—and small colleges can even add bargaining power. If a consortium can tell vendors that its members are threatening to leave, that gives them more leverage.

For hardware, there are three major groups of computer or networking equipment needed: student computer labs, staff use, and catalog use. Student computer labs, laptop programs, and wired or wireless network access are generally managed as part of the entire campus's technology infrastructure. For staff who primarily use office productivity software, their computers are generally managed along with campus-wide staff needs. Catalogers or webmasters who manage servers or other advanced equipment need special attention so that campus information-technology planners incorporate their requirements. This is very similar to the specialized needs in public relations or in the information-technology department itself, so it will not be difficult to explain to campus budgeters.

The most important library responsibility is to ensure that there are sufficient and functional public-access terminals. A computer lab may be managed along with other labs, but people visiting the library need additional access points. Public colleges sometimes may have a state-mandated responsibility to provide access to citizens who will not have college log-ins.

Supplies are a real though small part of the library's budget. It's important to remind campus personnel that supplies for a library include not only common administrative or office supplies, envelopes, and toner ink, but supplies necessary for library material processing. Some institutions have seen freezes or elimination of supply budgets generally, but materials can't be processed with donated paper clips.

The library generates a number of other expenses but, as stated earlier in the chapter, these are not a part of the library budget for a small academic library. These include security and housekeeping and may include student computer labs that are commonly budgeted for on a campus-wide basis. Copier maintenance may be handled through the library or the central campus. If the latter, the college needs to understand any special needs for the library.

Capital expenses related to the library as a facility are not part of a library's operating budget, but a library director needs to be responsible for tracking, promoting, and understanding library facility needs. This can range from very small to very large items. The most concrete and direct example lies under your feet, the carpet. Carpeting has a life cycle, and the campus may have a master plan for carpet replacement—or it may not. The carpeting might be done for the entire library building or it might be done floor by floor; the director needs to keep track of these plans over several years.

What about the library building as a whole? Is there a master plan for renovation beyond new carpets, such as updating HVAC, tuckpointing on older buildings, and for new construction? Library directors should work closely with the master planners on campus so that they will have an understanding of and vision for future needs. More on this is discussed in the planning chapter in reference to master planning.

Accounting and Services, Equipment, and Facilities

Because of its diversity, this area requires special attention from library directors, especially three issues: intercampus agreements, intracampus services, and facilities maintenance. Virtually all academic libraries receive at least some services through cooperative agreements with or among other academic institutions. Most are members of OCLC and additional interlibrary loan networks through regional or other consortia. These types of cooperative arrangements may be very common on campus. This would be the case especially for public colleges that are parts of larger systems. However, private colleges and their accounting systems may not be set up to handle those types of items. Systems administrators generally dislike creating special accounting categories that are unique to one unit, so library spending may appear in such diverse or generic categories as "memberships" or "subscriptions." As with noting how electronic materials have moved around in accounting categories, directors need to ensure not only that there are sufficient funds, but that the administration realizes the true nature of spending that is made opaque by categorizing that does not match library purposes.

> **Story:** At one small college facing a mid-year budget problem, it seemed appropriate to decree that college-paid "memberships" would be cut in half. It was an easy way to demonstrate responsibility, but "memberships" was how the library paid its database license fees. The advantage of a small college is that such a problem may be easily explained in person. This is not automatic, and for others it may take far longer to reverse a centralized decree.

Facilities upkeep often is paid for from unspent money at the end of a fiscal year. For private, not-for-profit institutions, the goal is often to return profit, revenue in excess of expenses, back to the institution, sometimes in the very literal sense of renovations. "Deferred maintenance" is a term for upkeep that is not focused on daily use, such as cleaning or cutting grass, but on preserving the lifespan of facilities.

Put another way, there is a second budget that is not written down in the overall campus budget either in requests or allocations. It does not exist at all, until it appears magically about two months before the end of the fiscal year. This is excess money that will be spent on deferred maintenance, maintenance that was deferred out of the normal regular budget.

Campus facilities directors will have a more or less formal agenda for the use of this money. The library director's job is to ensure that the facility's director understands specific library needs. This will require personal contact, as the very nature of this special second budget is that it often is not specifically planned. In that situation, typically the issues most familiar to facilities directors are the ones speaking directly to them.

MAINTAINING THE BIG PICTURE

It is important for directors to be aware of and keep others apprised of the big picture of the library and campus situation with respect to budgeting. No budget bullets, no magical secrets, and no creative or tricky accounting can create more money or more spending power.

The discussion about conceptual and accounting categories shows how bureaucratic procedures legitimately attempt to regularize spending so that everybody knows what money is doing where and when. Consistency and transparency allow decisions grounded in the reality of the resources available.

Although managing a budget as compared to managing a budget request seems not to involve the political dimension, the essence of the "interest group" is indeed present. How this is manifested is that campus budget officials will have ideas about how budgets operate based on their experiences with the majority of fiscal units on campus. A library has a number of differences from other units, and a library director needs to effectively communicate how a library is similar to and different from other areas while maintaining credibility in respecting non-negotiable accounting structures.

Library Within the Campus

When relating its budget to that of the campus as a whole, the small college library director needs to respect the given accounting structure as described above, operate within the campus's overall fiscal climate, and communicate in a user-centered way the library's special situations. In other words, "We obey accounting rules," "We understand we are not special," and "We are special."

The library budget will not increase by claiming that the library is exempt from pressures that other areas on campus face. Library directors should have a sense of the overall campus fiscal framework composed of building needs, enrollment and financial aid trends, and new initiatives. While the academic library cliché is that it is the heart of the university, in reality it is seldom more than 2 percent of an institution's budget, and other areas, particularly the teaching faculty, will nearly always be considered the true core of an institution's existence.

Effective library directors of small academic libraries can phrase the library's needs in terms of equality with other units on campus and the goals the institution is pursuing. All budget spending truly does serve the campus mission and it is up to library directors to articulate that rather than talking about library needs. Some examples are: students need better study opportunities, not the library wants new furniture. Faculty need resources to conduct research and teach up-to-date content, not publisher inflation is killing the library budget.

At the same time, library directors need to educate others on campus about issues they truly don't understand. A combination of Google, Wikipedia, and desk-copy textbooks are really not a substitute for a library's collection. Just because library collections become more virtual does not mean they become less costly. More seriously, serials and database inflation is something many non-librarians cannot believe until they are told, but it does have an obvious parallel in the uncontrollable rise of health-care costs in 2010. If this comparison is spelled out, small college administrators may more readily understand the weakness of the library's bargaining position.

Campus Within the Library

Those working in the library also need to understand how "their" budget relates to the overall campus situation. How they understand budget and budgeting processes begins with the overall approach that directors take to decision-making and communication. At one extreme is a director who controls the entire materials budget, makes all big decisions, and is assisted primarily by a clerical-level acquisitions person, with no input from staff, just making and delivering decisions.

In libraries with more than one professional librarian, budgeting is almost always a more collaborative affair. All librarians with responsibility for any collection-development areas are partners at least to some extent. Staff who manage student workers, or organize supplies, can also participate meaningfully in discussions about options, and everybody has a keen interest in salary levels and staff size.

Librarians and staff are generally well informed about their own areas of expertise. Book buyers know what a typical book costs; the interlibrary loan person knows how often the library has to pay for requested materials. What is important in a big-picture sense is to make sure that everyone who thinks about the budget, what they want and what they might get, does so with an accurate sense of the context. A reference librarian who reports that X database just increased in price by $2,000 needs to reflect on that in light of the general campus outlook for income and expenses.

If the entire campus has a budget freeze, the library budget will not get a 10 percent raise. Library managers are campus managers and their role in campus management is to communicate the priorities and parameters under which the entire campus operates.

PREPARING A BUDGET

Most of what is important to think about before preparing a budget request is covered in the chapter on planning. Types of planning, evaluation, collection management, strategic, and master are ways of thinking about where the library is, how it is doing, and what it needs. Budgeting is a way of allocating resources to accomplish one's purposes. Planning is a way of deciding what one's purposes are. After planning and budgeting, accounting verifies that decisions have been followed.

The most common type of budget request format is last-year-next-year. That is, the budget request worksheet given to library directors lists standard budget categories and what was allocated to, and spent within, each category in the past year and usually for several years previously. New directors need to determine if money can move from one year to another and from one category to another. The majority of library budgets are one year only. Any money that is left unspent at the end of the fiscal year cannot be moved to the next year. Some libraries (about 10 percent in this author's experience) do have the ability to preserve money for the next fiscal year. This can be very useful in terms of flexibility and of not being caught by rigid accounting time frames when, for example, trying to finalize negotiations over pricing with a vendor. However, it should not be used on an ongoing basis to create an undifferentiated "reserve" funding line. If a library director seems to be sitting on a growing pile of money, someone sometime will inevitably ask why the library actually needs as much money as it has been getting. If library funding has a history of fluctuations, which can happen when it is tied to formulas, then a modest (3–10 percent) reserve is prudent. If library funding is relatively steady, then it does not matter that the library has the ability to preserve the funds; its continuing to do so just convinces people that it does not have uses for the money it is receiving.

If there is a reserve, then the library director needs to be able to be very specific and direct about plans for the money. Saving up for major one-time expenses would be a reasonable plan.

Library directors also may or may not be limited in what they can move from one category to another, or overspend in one and underspend in another. If postage expenses increase, can photocopying money be moved? This has to be examined not only for institutional rules, but for any grants, which often come with a budget that lays out spending in specific categories. A common situation is for the director to be able to end the year with an overall balance in non-personnel accounts. That is, if one account is under, another can be over as long as the total institutional cost remains within the given boundary.

It is very unusual for library directors to have independent authority to move money from personnel to non-personnel needs even when the total spending remains constant. Some exceptions are overtime pay, contingent services, and student employees. As noted above, overtime pay for hourly employees needs careful management. A library director might budget for it specifically to handle known busy times related to customer service.

Contingent services are for items such as consultants or Web design. On the small campus, these need to be carefully planned for with the approval of higher administration and also in accordance with campus practices for contracting for specific services.

Student employees are not normal employees. For a small college with limited resources, students are almost exclusively paid through federal work-study programs. In these programs, some of the costs of employment are paid through federal scholarship funding. The library is often seen as a desirable work place for students receiving financial aid. It is important for the library director to talk directly with student financial aid personnel to make sure that the positions at the library are structured to fit within federal and campus guidelines.

Last-Plus

The steps in preparing a budget request that is based on last year's spending are straightforward: review past spending, check for unusual items, predict future items, and allow for contingencies within unwritten campus practice.

First, review historical spending in each category. What percentage of the category is typically spent or overspent? Here it is very important to understand what campus practice is in regard to spending versus allocations. On some campuses, units routinely spend up to and a little over what they are allocated. On others, going over the allocated limit is forbidden and units will have some level beneath it as an unwritten "real" ceiling. The library director really needs to conform to campus practice. If the library is careful to adhere to a ceiling when no other unit does, it is leaving money on the table. If it breaks the limit while others do not, the library director will be seen as an incompetent manager.

Next, scan individual significant items in each category. This is very possible in the small college library budget. The director needs to access individual items-payable information. Most items do not change much from year to year. Look for large nonrecurring items and areas where a cut can be made by changing to some less-costly alternative. Even when the campus is not currently cutting budgets, being proactive every year about looking for efficiencies and new ways of accomplishing the same goals is part of managing a library.

Some changes for the coming year can be anticipated. Materials inflation can be predicted to a high though discouraging level of accuracy. Library consortia generally try to give their members information about upcoming costs before budgets need to be constructed. Raises in minimum wages, increases in postage rates, and other items can be plotted out.

Finally, the budget request will be prepared at least 18 months before the last dollar it designates is spent. It is impossible to anticipate everything, so it seems prudent to allow at least some leeway for unexpected expenses. This is where it is essential to understand campus practice and culture, the collision between bureaucracy and climate. Practices evolve so as to allow for unwritten rules. It is a mistake to go solely by written guidelines. If most unit managers overspend their budgets by 10 percent, it is likely that central administration knows this and deliberately keeps a small cushion. If it does not, then unit directors and managers who overspend put the institution in serious danger.

Information about real spending habits is available from the college comptroller who is the budget director or from other unit directors and managers. The college comptroller will be able to explain the budget in general, and depending on campus practices, may be able to give very detailed information about actual practices. If not, in public colleges, state transparency rules may require or encourage the posting of detailed financial information.

Another avenue available on any campus is to ask other unit directors and managers. This is another way in which political ties across campus prove their value. New directors should chat informally with other unit directors on this topic, including both academic and support units. As stated before, academic unit directors spend their budgets primarily on salaries, which does not include the collection needs that account for up to half of the library's budget. Academic units also have contingencies in the form of money for adjuncts if needed that don't exist for library staffing. The IT department is another useful non-academic unit to talk with, because besides staffing, they have equipment to manage.

In the budget request, a change in amount from the previous year needs to be explained. This can take one or more of these forms:

- Uncontrollable inflation: This would include phone charges, postage, and most importantly, fees for systems. Here, the argument is that the library is doing the same and needs to cover expected increases. And importantly, here "uncontrollable" is in the eyes of campus administration. Library technology systems in small colleges are generally priced at a consortium level, and administrators will understand that individual bargaining power is minimal at best.
- Other inflation: This category primarily means materials inflation. That is not uncontrollable because the library does have the ability, though not the desire, to cancel or change purchases. Not buying a book or dropping a database is not the same as dropping the library's automation system.
- Efficiencies: The library is always in a state of change in terms of technology, the production, distribution, and communication of information, and pedagogy. The library staff does new things and therefore always also needs to explain where it is no longer doing obsolete or inefficient old things.
- New initiatives. Every new initiative needs two things: a tie directly to a college goal or initiative and an explanation of how this affects existing work or resources. The library serves the institution and it makes its case for new-idea funding effectively only when it makes this very clear.

The language these are expressed in can be either positive or negative:

- Unless we get or maintain this money, we will not be able to do this or we will have to cease that.
- If we get or maintain this money, we will be able to do this.

A candid and informal conversation with one's supervisor and with other unit heads about how they formulate their budget requests is essential so that the language the library director talks, the direction from which the library director approaches spelling out needs, conforms to what higher decision-makers expect and desire. Conservative administrators may view a request to do something new as an admission that it is unneeded. That person's attitude would be, "Isn't the library already getting along fine without it?" Innovative administrators may dislike negative wording. The library director thinks about new ideas rather than dire consequences, possibilities rather than limitations.

Activity Based or Zero-Based Budgeting

In theory, an activity-based budgeting approach looks not at accounting categories but is organized in terms of what is accomplished with the money. For example, a trip to Spain for a language course doesn't consist of expenditures from the personnel category for faculty advisors, supplies (advertising), services (travel agency fees), and travel funds. Instead, sending X number of students to Spain costs Y amount (and often, with Z revenue).

Similarly, budgets can theoretically begin at zero: imagine you do nothing; what do you need to pay for in order to get your work done? It is hard to imagine the zero starting point, because a library has such a large fixed base from which it operates: collections grow each year and so represent past as well as current purchases.

Even personnel costs are difficult to account for in a zero-based budget in a small college. The easiest way to describe personnel costs in terms of activity or in accomplishment is to precisely allocate staff time to various purposes. That is feasible in some administrative units and at large universities. For example, in large institutions, one person and his or her salary can be devoted to a discrete X ("we have 10 admissions counselors; admissions counseling costs 10 times salaries"). In the small library, staff do so much multitasking that it is almost impossible to get accurate records at the detail that zero-based or ABC-cost approaches require.

ABC (activity-based costing) and zero-based budgeting are very difficult matches for the small college library. In the unlikely event that they are attempted, the library director needs to work for the broadest and therefore most flexible categories or definitions of activities possible, specific enough to get some sense of the amount of time (and money) that is spent on functions like reference, digitizing, or circulation, but not so specific that more time is spent recording costs than actually delivering services.

Activity-based costing and zero-based budgeting are very seldom used across a campus for all units on an ongoing basis. However, they are often involved when there are special initiatives or externally funded projects. Examples would be special summer institutes for professionals or college-preparation programs for local youth. Specific budgets are needed for these in order for administrators to determine whether they are net additions to the college's finances, or to account to funders for spending. Library expenses generally would be considered part of "indirect" or overhead costs, that is, not allocated specifically to these activities. Directors need to be alert to when these special programs have special needs, such as extended hours or unusual materials.

Grants and Gifts

The library may receive grants and gifts either as a regular part of the budget—discussed above—or as a special one-time donation. Library directors must understand whether gifts or grants are considered a substitute for institutional allocations. That is, if $10,000 comes in from a donor, will it increase the overall budget or will the same amount be withheld by administration?

Along with the benefits, are there costs that come along with the gifts or grants? Some cash grants specifically require that the receiving institution commit its own funds to match the spending. Virtually all non-cash gifts cause significant expenses. These are inevitable parts of the library budget; it does no good to wish for pure unrestricted and additional cash. If the library budget is reduced from university funds because a cash gift is given, the library budget remains the same. The effective library director will work carefully with the college-development staff to get the most out of gifts, also helping the college get the most out of the givers. The library itself has an all-campus, mission-serving role that is very attractive to donors.

More on how to think about library needs appears in the chapters on managing for teaching, research, and service support. These constitute the mission of the library; without money, there's not much that can be done to advance the mission.

NOTE

1. Data from the Academic Libraries Survey, National Center for Education Statistics.

IV

SUPPORTING TEACHING, RESEARCH, AND SERVICE

9 MANAGING FOR TEACHING SUPPORT

The key: Being there for students

This chapter reviews issues relevant to the management and organization of library services that support teaching. Although electronic and physical resources support teaching, discussion of these will take place in the research support chapter, as the library manager weighs both complementary and competing user needs. Another area separated out is consideration of special grant-funded activities. Grant possibilities and approaches are addressed in the service support chapter, where "service" means the service of a college to its multiple constituencies (as in the division of teaching, research, and service).

Because this is just one chapter of a general management book, and one that is intended to have shelf life longer than six months, there is no intent to provide tips on the latest tools and techniques, nor, indeed, to replicate core texts on reference services or information-literacy instruction. Throughout much of this book, including especially the personnel selection and development chapters, there has been an intense focus on the need to recognize and be continually prepared for the inevitability of change in this field. Good librarians should be responsible for keeping up in and thinking creatively about their areas.

Instead, the focus here is on discussing aspects of key issues about the ways that librarians are distinctive in the small college situation, with a special focus on those who have managerial rather than purely technical or how-to-do-it characteristics.

Some important characteristics of the small college campus that affect how teaching/learning support that can be managed include:

- Campus culture regarding personal attention
- Staff skill availability
- Working with faculty
- The student perspective on different kinds of small college campuses

CULTURE OF PERSONAL ATTENTION

Pointing to culture is a way of emphasizing that while libraries have their own norms and expectations about patron rights, librarian roles, and potential services, when any specific library director considers how to provide services to clientele and especially to students, this will be done within a general context consistent across campus. That is, the director's conceptual anchor for how to do "reference," a quintessential library function, is not simply or even primarily models about user information-seeking in general. People in aggregate may seek information in certain predictable ways, but individuals attend college not as aggregates but as individuals. More importantly, they do not select colleges as aggregates. This is especially significant for small colleges.

Small colleges have many disadvantages when they compete with other institutions as destinations for freshmen. Those in the private sector are definitely more expensive than public institutions. Small colleges in the public sector cannot offer the level of amenities, the wide range of extracurricular activities, truly competitive or comprehensive sports, or even the "buzz" of a state flagship university or even larger regional institutions. The small community college cannot even offer a four-year degree; all of its baccalaureate-bound students will consider it only a temporary start and then will transfer. So why do students choose a small college? Sometimes because it is small.

A major marketing premise is that on the small college campus, an individual student receives individual attention. More specifically, small colleges both public and private tend to mention features such as small student-faculty ratios, the direct connection to faculty inside and outside the classroom, and personal attention to academic and career advising.

At a large doctoral institution, a typical freshman in a non-honors curriculum will frequently have a class schedule made up of courses directly taught by graduate students, or large sections with lectures by faculty but then with discussion sections led by and specific assignment feedback provided by teaching assistants; their advisors often belong to a cadre of staff specialists, not the leading faculty in that discipline. In that culture, having a reference assistant, a non-MLS librarian, provide frontline reference is compatible with limited direct faculty contact. The university library has a good pool of well-educated (even if not in library science) graduate students or long-term paraprofessionals from which to select reference providers. Students are often used to extensive self-service or peer-provided options on the big campus: writing center tutors who are other students and IT tutorials online, among others. In this atmosphere, MLS librarians may focus more attention on creating systems (e.g., LibGuides) rather than providing direct walk-up service because that is perfectly compatible with the whole campus culture.

Therefore, when the library director wonders about how to provide reference services to students in this new era, where it seems that "real" librarians often do not answer questions, or students are thought not to ask questions, a useful comparison is not just to decades-ago reference to the 24/7 e-mail of the 1990s, or to research university library services. Library directors should incorporate an understanding of how faculty-student interaction happens and is expected to happen on *that* campus. If full-time teaching faculty at all ranks routinely teach the full range of courses from first-year level on up, if on a residential campus faculty are in their offices and available daily and by appointment, then the reference librarian who is also available fits. If this same campus provides online instruction or even online support for classes, then a different reference service is required.

Staff Skill Availability

In a small library, a library director and all library staff are very aware of each other's capabilities and are very dependent upon them. The chapter in this book on personnel development discusses at a conceptual level the issues involved in the relation of non-MLS library workers, support staff, to various levels of responsibilities. The day-to-day reality in a small library, particularly for staff who have long service, means that decisions about what various staff members can *and should* handle in terms of helping students through reference, referral, and instruction can be very personal, depending not on categories such as "support staff do this" but rather "this person can do that."

Broadly speaking, many small colleges have a culture in which it is expected that every worker provides positive assistance to students and visitors because everybody is part of student learning. What library directors must do is reinforce this, paying explicit attention to and acknowledging changing and growing staff skills and incorporating them into the whole picture of who will do what at the library. It can be particularly useful, perhaps mandatory in a changing technical environment, for support staff to acquire important technology competence, such as Web maintenance or design or integrated library system (ILS) data management. These are part of keeping their jobs current, not changing what their jobs are.

Working with Faculty

Librarians at the small college have an advantage and a disadvantage when it comes to working with faculty, and the faculty relationship is crucial to the success of any support for student learning. This is an advantage with full-time faculty, and a serious problem with part-time faculty. The advantage is that librarians, working with individual faculty members, can build personal and specific relationships. They are used to create an atmosphere that fosters close relationships with their students and creates a small-town feeling among academic staff.

These relationships will show how the library can serve immediate faculty-teaching needs with new tools, different resources, and instruction for various assignments. More than that, the librarians who provide those specific instances give faculty a sense of how library support in general supports overall student learning. Faculty are often very focused and can have very acute instant needs ("I need to show my students how to judge a Web page"). Instant specific responsiveness is good, but it is worth the effort to keep painting a bigger picture. Faculty barely realize what librarians can do currently and it is not reasonable to expect them, unaided, to think creatively and comprehensively about the library's contribution to independent learning. In that respect, every request for a simple in-class presentation or every referral to help an individual student becomes an opportunity to deepen the relationship and hence the level of knowledge between librarian and faculty member.

It may be a disadvantage with respect to adjunct or other part-time instructors. The smaller the college, the more likely it is that the non-tenure-track faculty will be teaching one course at a time with no assurance of continued employment. In more rural areas, these adjuncts often have other full-time positions; in cities, they may teach at more than one institution. In both cases, these instructors' attention often is not primarily on their college course; and in both cases, they can be very difficult to identify and track down in order to make effective contact to offer librarian support.

In order to work most efficiently and effectively with part-time faculty, it is essential to have good relations with the department chairs who hire adjuncts and the human resources people who process their paperwork and hence control a set of college privileges. Making the effort to systematically and proactively offer librarian assistance to these often-stressed individuals can be a powerful benefit for them and produce good results for their students while impressing their home departments, the department chair, and the rest of the faculty who want courses taught by adjuncts to be successful.

Student Expectations

What does a student expect from a library as far as help for their learning? A key issue with students and especially with undergraduates is that they have no conception of a college library other than the one at their own college. They represent a digital generation; they are the Millennials, the digital natives. However, their ideas about libraries, as with students in the past, are heavily conditioned by their own experiences in high school and with public libraries. If they have only had a limited high school curriculum that made few demands for information use outside of using textbooks, or they had limited high school or public library resources or services, they will have a very limited idea of what a college library can or should do with and for them.

> **Story**: Many students in a master's of education program reported, when asked by librarians, that they never did any research papers or made use of the college library during their undergraduate years. This seemed especially true of those who had received bachelor's degrees during the 1970s and early 1980s. Their college curriculum was not focused in a way that they had reason to conduct independent searches for library resources.

Students, the same as faculty, are influenced by campus culture. If the campus reputation is "Everybody here helps you" and "You'll get all the attention you need," they will expect attention. This can lead to a sense of expediency and entitlement, including immediate answers for the project due tomorrow. They may have very narrow views of what a librarian can do, and yet have high expectations for immediacy and personal assistance.

Library directors must understand and be a part of what is expected for the student learning environment on the entire campus: the preferred mix of personal assistance *and* individual responsibility. The most important practical step for this is to listen to campus tours, talk with faculty teaching freshmen courses, and meet with student-affairs personnel. That helps library directors understand what is needed to be effective in connecting library services and policies to student needs and expectations. Library directors cannot expect to set their own service expectations in a vacuum.

LIBRARY INSTRUCTION: PREPARING SELF-SERVING LEARNERS

Library instruction, bibliographic instruction, or information-literacy education all define the way that librarians prepare students to be self-sufficient in some but not all of their information needs. In connection with their academic work, students face a spectrum of needs: where to get textbooks, where to find reserved materials, how to seek out a small amount of additional information such as a single article, and how to use a library to meet personal information and enrichment needs. They must also learn how to research a topic in-depth so they may respond to assignments to write longer papers.

Library instruction has two goals. The first is to give students basic knowledge about information availability, classification, and retrieval so that they understand their options, have competence in basic self-serve methods, and appreciate what a librarian can help with for more complex needs. This is often done with a tour and brief lecture or even a course with a set of information skills taught. In the small college setting, librarians can step back and design a more holistic approach to students and their academic needs so that students develop their information-literacy skills in a coordinated way throughout their college careers. The most intensive plans coordinate with cross-campus academic initiatives, such as the general education curriculum. The contrast is between ad hoc, one-shot instruction and the older "Earlham" model of course-related bibliographic instruction or the more recent information-literacy learning outcomes initiatives.

Dividing responsibilities among librarians is relatively easy. Each academic program with majors or minors should have a librarian assigned to think about and work with the faculty in that program to insert library instruction in places that make it most effective within the curriculum as a whole. Information literacy or library instruction is much more effective when it is taught within a curricular need to find and use information.

One goal is not missing anybody in a program and not being repetitious. This is easiest in programs with clear sequenced classes, and most challenging in those where students have the greatest flexibility.

Besides program-specific instruction, a librarian needs to keep track of general student learning outcomes. Each college structures its general outcomes differently, but in most areas of the country, information literacy is specifically part of each college's expected learning outcomes.

Another goal is to design library or information-literacy instruction that meets the information-seeking needs of all students and also provides extra instruction to students with special or advanced needs. This instruction builds upon a student's basic skills and leads into more in-depth instruction. The library director is responsible for seeing that this instruction remains up-to-date and connected with both library resources and teaching methods. To manage this requires several data steps built upon a framework of library instruction opportunities that has been mapped to general education and academic programs. The library director and librarians should track:

- Who is and how many are being reached and in what format and with what content.
- Measurement of general education information-literacy outcomes.
- Measurement of information-literacy outcomes within individual disciplines.

Most accrediting bodies will look for library directors to document not only their processes or outputs (attendance) but also outcomes that can be measured in several ways, such as examining student work products, giving specific tests, or using standardized information-literacy tests. All of these will tie into campus initiatives for assessment of student learning. Because academic librarianship has a well-established set of educational goals, the library staff can be a campus leader in this effort.

REFERENCE SERVICES: INFORMATION ASSISTANCE ON DEMAND

The goal in reference service is to provide on-demand assistance at the point of need for students in a way that is available, effective, and efficient. Available means that students should not hesitate to contact a librarian. Effective means that they should get assistance that matches their needs. Efficient means that the endeavor should not be overwhelming to the library staff. The goal is the best use of staff time for the best reference services for students.

Students' need for reference service fluctuates between the many hours when nobody comes and the end of the semester when research papers are due. At the small college information or reference desk, there simply will not be a steady stream of traffic throughout every week of the year. Many librarians in small libraries report about 110 to 120 reference questions per *typical* week per 1,000 students.[1] This means that librarians on the reference desk are not constantly busy, every day and every week.

Obviously, the smaller the library, the more difficult it is to assign professional staff to a reference desk when few students are asking questions. This becomes even more difficult if one tries to assign librarians for evening hours or even weekends if the library is open then. If a library staff (including the director) numbers only five, and if the library is open every evening, each person would need to work one evening each week and two weekends each month. In the small library, providing reference balances availability, effectiveness, and efficiency.

Availability. The following points will enhance availability and reduce real or perceived barriers to reference assistance. Even though the problem of students not wanting to bother a staff member will never entirely go away, a proactive approach can have an impact.

- A physically open layout for the main public floor of the library allows a librarian to be available to many people or needs at the same time. Making a public area open with good sight lines to a librarian's station should have a high priority for the library director, because this provides both flexibility and accessibility.

- Technology can provide a range of both real-time and asynchronous contact points for both course-related and independent needs. Students spend large amounts of time texting, talking, and e-mailing. The library director can coordinate with campus IT to make contacting the library as easy as or easier than contacting either a friend or an instructor. How to do this? Constantly work with the IT department staff and faculty to see what forms of communication are most readily used. Busy students appreciate on-demand communication, text or phone, and a way to leave a message to be returned, a voicemail, or an e-mail.
- Coordination with classroom faculty is essential. Student information needs are substantially tied to the academic cycle. Close knowledge of faculty demands on students helps with adjusting assistance schedules to actual needs, rather than simply blindly scheduling a set of hours.
- Integration with library instruction takes special note of the intersection between self-help and the need for additional assistance. One of the worst outcomes of information-literacy instruction can be students who believe they know or others who think they are already expected to *know* how to look for information and how to use the library. Therefore, both types hesitate to ask for assistance. This problem is compounded in the small library because it is so much more likely that the information-literacy instructor will also be the librarian at the reference desk. They may not wish to ask the person who already showed them how to do something how to do it again or it might be that the librarian giving instruction did not appear to be helpful. It is important for library directors to ensure that all librarians understand that how students view reference assistance is affected by the tenor and content of library instruction. Teaching librarians need to explicitly join the two functions of instruction and reference. They can

give students potential phrases to help them over that initial barrier of articulating a reference question and confirm very specifically and deliberately that even basic questions are welcomed, and librarians expect their questions to be a normal part of the learning process, as normal as working through writing exercises or math problems, even when a professor has already explained something that they have forgotten or realize they did not understand.

True story, or true dilemma: Library instruction at a small college was integrated into an English course on research writing. Performance on library exercises and a test was part of the students' grades, as well as providing them information for their papers. This ensured students took the instruction seriously. One librarian argued that it placed librarians on the "critic" side of learning, rather than the "helper" side. Librarians were the ones who "failed" students who didn't complete worksheets or pass the test, rather than being the ones who solved students' problems in finding information.

Effectiveness. These are points that will affect the quality of library reference service. The challenge for the director of a small library comes from the need for non-librarians to handle questions and for all the staff to be familiar with the entire array of academic programs offered by the college.

- Student-worker orientation includes how to deal with referral of reference questions to a professional librarian, something that needs continuous reinforcement. Professional library education emphasizes how challenging it is even to identify an information need in all its complexity as people typically articulate it only partially. Students don't understand the parameters of their own questions, particularly in the "imposed need" situation[2] of a class assignment. They don't understand all the options available and even what the librarian can do for them. The contrast with information-technology questions where the range of possibilities is much narrower, for example, "Where is the 'temporary folder'?" or "I think my file just disappeared," adds to the confusion.

Student workers cannot be expected to grasp a sophisticated level of question classification. They should not make a decision between this one I can answer and that one a librarian is needed. Even directional questions are not always directional. A "Where is" question can really mean, "I need information on." Moreover, in the small college, students are often less faceless and more empowered than on larger campuses. Students stationed at the circulation desk may know a large proportion of students who approach personally and be moved to help them immediately rather than having them go to the reference desk and wait for assistance or bothering the librarian. All that tends to hinder the appropriate referral process.

These techniques will help avoid the problem of non-referrals:

○ Alert new student workers to the issues of hidden complexity in patrons' questions. Orientation needs to include specific examples where things are not as simple as they seem. Providing clear guidelines can help, as can having students from time to time record all of the questions they are asked, so they and the librarian can review them and determine which ones a student could and should answer.

○ Include "hearing" lines in "sight" lines. That is, can a librarian overhear a student worker at the circulation desk? If feasible, this allows for immediate intervention.

○ Make librarians readily and consistently available upon request. Student workers won't want to bother librarians unless these referrals really take place positively and quickly. It only takes one uncooperative librarian to make student workers shy away. Students are in no position to correct or even to complain about poor responsiveness by librarians.

Library support staff (LSS) involvement in reference. Librarians are not always available, so it is inevitable that support staff will handle many patron inquiries. Generally, support staff should be expected to be familiar with question complexity. The longer they work at a library and the more they see librarians practicing this well, the more they will understand it and correctly identify when patrons have more complex needs. They should also know the library general philosophy about who should be available when, for what reference services, and with what priority. If library directors have decided that MLS librarians are to concentrate on instruction and faculty liaison with student reference only on an on-call basis with staff handling frontline questions, then this needs to be clear and widely understood.

Support staff also need to be kept informed of the current status of ever-changing library instruction and library resources. The librarian preparing instruction on a particular new database in preparation for a professor's new assignment needs to educate and alert *every* staff member who might encounter those students afterward. Even in a library where support staff are not assigned initial-contact reference duties, they will in fact handle some questions, so they need to be kept informed about new resources and particularly about instruction.

- Coordination with proposed courses and the corresponding faculty members helps librarians and staff to be prepared. The more informed librarians are about developments and needs in the classroom, the more effectively they can design solutions.
- Designing information for teaching is a requirement. Satisfying patron information needs is not only done through answering questions but also by providing instruction and designing online guides and tools. All of these need to work together to be the most effective.

In the best of all possible worlds, librarians will know more about students' information needs before they ask than the students themselves do.

• Communication among librarians spreads expertise where it will be needed. It is common and useful to organize librarian expertise along subject lines. This helps librarians work more closely with faculty for instruction and enhances their collection-management skills. Nevertheless, it is really difficult to match each walk-up person asking a question with the librarian who has the greatest knowledge in that subject area. The inevitable delays are very discouraging to patrons. Therefore, just as librarians need to communicate with student workers about question complexity and support staff about instruction, assignments, and resources, they need to communicate with one another. A regular time and place to share observations and developments in their own subject areas will help all librarians be more effective.

If at all possible, it is really valuable to have librarians attend and assist with one another's library instruction sessions. It may seem inefficient to tie up two librarians in this way; however, only one librarian has to do the time-consuming preparation, and in the hour or so the session lasts, having an assistant makes the session go more smoothly, shows students the faces of more individual librarians, and very efficiently educates the helping librarian in the topics and tools being covered.

Efficiency. Libraries with few librarians face a reality of multiple demands, many hours, and few hands. This is in many ways quite different from what happens to demands on teaching faculty time who, when student numbers increase, often face increased advising loads and sometimes larger classes but not a higher teaching load. More faculty, part-time or adjuncts, can be hired to cover classes and, in the case of sustained higher numbers, new full-time faculty.

While adding more full-time librarians should be a response to significant sustained growth, in the library there is no equivalent to solving increased usage by hiring adjuncts. Except in emergencies, a classroom faculty member, in the face of growing enrollments, typically has more advisees but no greater teaching load. In contrast, every library faces 180 hours a week when the library *could* be open, a substantial number of hours when synchronous on-demand reference service makes sense, and only 10 or fewer librarians for staffing with relatively little match to fluctuations in student numbers. The following are points that library directors can arrange to enhance librarian productivity.

- Networked computers and computer-literate librarians are essential to make multitasking work for both librarians and the library. Spending time at a reference desk rather than in one's office does not have to interrupt productivity. If files are available from any campus computer, then all campus computers can be librarian workstations. This simultaneously provides the very important availability factor and eliminates the concern that the stream of questions at the service point isn't big enough to need professional staffing.

  Librarians who are computer literate themselves should be able to field basic computer technical questions from students doing normal, non-specialized work on the library's computers. Both of these mean that students get the help they need, quickly, and with the least disruption to the librarian's other duties.

- Managerial prioritization, development support, and communication of a set of appropriate expectations for what among multiple tasks needs attention. Library directors decide on a particular format for student learning support in reference and in instruction and support that by making it clear how librarians should spend their time. Which things do or do not get done needs to follow expected priorities clearly communicated between librarians and director. Among the different models for handling student learning support, both the library director and librarians need to understand their own situation as a deliberate choice that needs to be supported and its values communicated within the library staff and to the campus as a whole.

This means that if librarians are spending their time personally meeting with faculty, preparing for instruction, and delivering instruction, they are not at the reference desk all the time. That is understood and accepted. Library directors must know how librarians are spending their time and must be able to communicate to the campus what decisions about priorities have been made and why they are appropriate in terms of the institution's general mission, culture, and student-learning goals.

> **Story:** When asked for personnel to provide library instruction during an explosion of new programs and additional students, a provost wondered if there was any more efficient way to provide instruction. Yet it was instruction itself that made reference efficient. Group instruction is *much* more efficient than handling basic student questions on a one-by-one basis. Good instruction should divert a large percentage of student information needs into effective self-help.

- Cooperation in standardized materials or services creates cross-campus efficiencies. Librarians in a small college library may indeed be willing, able, and eager to provide library services and materials that are highly customized to that particular institution through personalization. However, librarians should also recognize areas where they cannot do it all themselves and where using standardized products will provide acceptable levels of service. Contracting for library automation systems, sharing standard library guides, and collection-purchasing plans can all take care of student needs and leave librarians more time for the truly on-site customization for faculty and students, who are the most important aspects of the position.

LIBRARY FACILITIES AND PASSIVE SERVICES

In the life of a student, actually seeking out and identifying information to fill a need is only one part of the learning process, and it may be a relatively small part of a student's life. The students who have a real or virtual stack of printouts, books, and photocopies have only started on their projects. Much more is involved, including learning from faculty in class, thinking about a problem, working with other students, and writing or producing a final product alone or in collaboration. The library staff has a role beyond matching user and information. For that whole experience, the library signage, Web presence, and facilities all make contributions.

Physical Facilities

The library's physical facilities are likely to be a major contributor to the out-of-classroom learning process. How important the physical library is is highly dependent on the campus ecology as a whole: whether it is residential or commuter, undergraduate or graduate, and the availability of space in residences, campus centers, and other areas. When considering what the library provides students, it is important to see it in this larger context.

Ample and accessible study space is an important part of what a library contributes to student learning. The usual phrase, "the library is the heart of the university," is a testament not simply or even primarily to resources but to space. It reflects a "scholar's workroom" idea that consists not only of the books piled on his desk but the desk itself, and time to sit and think.

The library director will need to manage space as well as services. With the exception of residence halls and also some student centers on some campuses, the library often is the biggest provider of space with some of the most extensive open hours on campus. Besides seeing to circulation, reference, and other library-specific needs, for it to be effective space, there has to be effective security and housekeeping.

A final consideration for facilities is to think about exceptions. It is relatively easy to understand and plan around the traditional flow of the two-semester college year. However, small colleges also are places where small innovative and untraditional programs can be started, programs that happen in January, over spring or quarter breaks, or in the summer. While a large library can fit those irregularities into its normal open hours, it is a challenge to stretch limited resources for these exceptions, especially since libraries seldom receive a direct diversion of program income to cover the additional expenses of adding additional hours. The library director needs to keep a close eye on special programs in order to serve current needs, to keep track of proposals, and to reflect them in general library budget requests.

The Virtual Library and Reference Services

Even small libraries can have significant distance-education responsibilities. For students who seldom visit campus, the library's Web site is a virtual library and must be easy to use so that students and faculty can access online resources and assistance. Just as with on-campus students, library information provided online is part of the set of activities that give students what they want: class instruction, personal assistance, and passive Web information.

Librarians who design the Web site need to place services and information for distance students within this context. What library instruction is available for distance students? What needs do they have? Some programs on campus may offer their entire curriculum online; others, only specific courses or graduate-level degrees. The more specific the program, the easier it is to plan the information found on the Web site.

An early perception was that online instruction was easier, more efficient, and less costly than in-person instruction. This has long since been dispelled by reality. While many campus administrators see the income from online courses as a good thing, faculty often find it more difficult to teach and prepare courses.

The library director in a small college library must have an appreciation for both the labor involved in preparing courses and the importance of personalization in online learning. It is important for the library director or a designated librarian to work closely with any formal office or committee devoted to non-traditional educational formats. This may include online, accelerated, or satellite and off-site programs. This person will work with schools or departments to incorporate library concerns into planning and execution. Close coordination in this program means the library staff can plan how librarian time is spent within the broad context of campus needs. Close coordination also helps and is necessary for the library staff to handle any non-traditional education that is organized completely separately from on-campus or residential instruction. Library staff serve both and should know what is needed. This must be made clear to all who are involved.

Everything on a college campus contributes to student learning, the central purpose of the small college. Library resources and services are particularly closely related to class instruction. Instruction and personal assistance from librarians, online tutorials, and effective study environments in the physical library all support students. Librarians, teaching faculty, and others on campus can all work effectively together to achieve student goals.

NOTES

1. Applegate, R. "Whose Decline? Which Academic Libraries are 'Deserted' in Terms of Reference Transactions." *Reference & User Services Quarterly* 48 (2) (2008): 176–89.

2. Gross, Melissa. *Studying Children's Questions: Imposed and Self-Generated Information-Seeking at School.* Lanham, MD: Scarecrow, 2006.

10 MANAGING FOR RESEARCH SUPPORT

The keys: Both disciplinary and pedagogical research at that college

The role and definition of research on each college or university campus is highly dependent upon that institution's mission, history, and specific priorities. A large number of smaller institutions are primarily focused on teaching, and full-time faculty are expected to devote themselves primarily to effective and innovative instruction. Because at two-year institutions the universal focus is on teaching, interest in discipline-based research is limited at best whereas teaching-centered research is more often encouraged.

Other small colleges, particularly four-year institutions, are more likely to subscribe to the traditional evaluative framework and academic philosophy that says that the responsibilities of full-time faculty consist of teaching *and* research *and* service. Academics generally believe that research informs teaching and strengthens service. Research is not philosophically in competition with teaching or service but cooperation.

For this chapter, disciplinary research is defined as the most classical version of scholarship of inquiry, producing articles or books in the discipline such as chemistry, biology, history, literature, and religion among others. Pedagogical research is defined as research on effective teaching and learning and the effect of different methods on student learning. A third, undergraduate-related content research, is defined as disciplinary research led by faculty and carried out by students.

CHALLENGES FOR CONDUCTING DISCIPLINARY RESEARCH

Pragmatically, faculty who wish to conduct discipline-based research at their small colleges have three challenges. The first is prioritizing research efforts within teaching and service time constraints. Another is the lack of a larger number of faculty colleagues in the specific discipline and the number of funded students who are available to work on projects. The other challenge is the lack of facilities to carry out research projects.

Prioritizing Research

Academic blogs and personal narratives are full of descriptions of new and experienced faculty wrestling with the problem of the best balance between teaching and research activity given that one assumes faculty members are devoting their major time commitment to planning for and teaching their classes. In addition, they have service commitments and work on department and college committees. Time is finite.

Newly hired faculty are regularly warned to ascertain the *real* as well as the stated priority of research and publication and teaching (good pedagogy) for promotion and tenure decision-making at a particular institution. Understanding general expectations is crucial, even though in the best of circumstances no untenured professor is really entirely sure what "good enough" is.

An institution truly committed to an emphasis on teaching has lower demands for disciplinary research, while pedagogical research is more valued or emphasized. Undergraduate-related content research may also be valued at the teaching-centered institution as it attracts intelligent and motivated students, enhances learning, and prepares graduates for graduate school or employment.

Pure disciplinary research is the area that tends to have the least demand across all small institutions. It usually has the least supply in faculty terms. However, some small institutions fall into an elite category. Administrators at these colleges consciously position themselves to offer the best of both worlds, small classes and intimate contact with full-time professors who are also examples of the model balance of teaching, research, and service. These professors conduct disciplinary research as well as teach and perform service. At such institutions, expectations for research will resemble those at the labeled, usually much larger research institutions.

Lack of Colleagues to Share Research

In many fields and for many areas, typical inquiry research proceeds with teams of researchers working together and in cooperation on aspects of one issue. These institutions attract graduate students who can study and research with a recognized expert in an area. These experts have paid assistants who are sometimes at the doctoral level, financing from funded research projects, and a steady stream of publications in prominent refereed publications. Large teams of researchers are not feasible at a small college. In order to staff courses effectively, small college departments cannot have multiple faculty who are devoted to a single subspecialty. A four-member chemistry department is likely to have four different areas of chemistry covered, not four members who all are inorganic specialists. Nor do they typically have graduate students to provide high-quality research assistance. Undergraduates may work as lab assistants but without significant grant support, while small colleges may not have doctoral programs at all, and if they have one, the number of doctoral students who are available to work with significant and important procedures in research is very limited.

Facilities

Most small colleges cannot afford extensive equipment and facilities. Their facilities are generally matched to teaching needs, and specialized equipment that cannot be justified by undergraduate use is likely to be a low priority. In the sciences, grant money is often the source of funding for equipment. Realistically, few small colleges receive significant grant funding. Therefore, faculty are generally confined to those research topics and projects that have equipment needs of a type that can also serve teaching activities.

All of these issues are recognized by administrators and department directors as well as by faculty at small colleges. What is needed from the library director's perspective is an equally clear understanding of the ability of the staff and collection to support faculty research.

PLANNING CONSIDERATIONS TO SUPPORT RESEARCH

In planning for the library staff and collection to support the level of faculty research activity that is desired by an institution, there are five key points that require a mutual understanding by the library director and staff, by faculty, and by faculty administrators and leaders, especially department chairs.

- Mission, purpose, and expectations
- Limits on access to information
- Cooperative agreements for electronic items
- Cooperative agreements for physical items
- New fields or topic support (especially interdisciplinary)

Ideally, careful management of these issues and effective communication with campus constituents, administrators, and department chairs will produce library priorities that are well understood by the campus and adequately supported.

Institutional Mission, Purpose, and Expectations

Just as the campus administration and the faculty need a shared understanding of the relative importance of and resources to be devoted to research, so too the library director should take this mission and considerations and incorporate them into planning. The most direct impact is on the collection-development policy. Many directors of small libraries make explicit that the primary focus of their collections will be on supporting under-graduate or general-student needs. On the other hand, there are many small college libraries with no explicit collection-development statements. Day-to-day throughout the year, librar-ians make collection decisions based on a combination of their professional judgment about particular items and their general sense of campus priorities. On a daily and yearly basis, this is likely to proceed smoothly and effectively. It is precisely when a faculty member is unhappy about research support that having an explicit policy, especially one derived from a broadly based planning process, will be invaluable.

As stated in an earlier chapter, the library's collection-development policy includes both the campus mission state-ment and any available documents on faculty priorities, such as faculty handbooks and promotion and tenure documents. This reminds patrons that the priorities in the collection are those of the campus as a whole.

It is useful to have available examples of what this means in specific selection terms. Faculty members may be amused by tales of the university-based super-specialists who insist on jour-nals in their own area and care little about broad-based periodi-cals more likely to be used by undergraduates. The relative expenses and coverage of specific databases may not be as obvious. In addition, faculty and library staff need to know about the costs of supporting departmental as well as library subscriptions or reference materials that will support only the esoteric research of one faculty member.

Limits on Access to Information

Faculty may not be aware of the real limitations that persist in access to high-quality information for small college libraries. Despite the development of the open-access movement for journals and repositories, the increasing availability of archival materials, and the growth of Wikipedia, there are significant and important information resources that are not free. Nor are their costs declining. Faculty in their daily lives see ever-cheaper computers, slashed prices for magazines, ever-more abundant Internet material, and ever-more quickly delivered library information requests. In fact, the more the library staff succeeds in providing swift and transparent virtual access, the more faculty can think that it is *free*, because it is *free to them*.

Story: The 2009 ACRL biennial conference took place at a time of extraordinary budget pressures for university libraries. At the vendor fair, a very few vendors suggested that they might consider a reduction in price increases. Others offered smaller price increases but price increases nevertheless. Still others were holding prices steady—not raising them and not cutting them.

This syndrome of people thinking "information is free so why can't you afford my requests" can be especially acute at small colleges that are branches or regional campuses of a statewide public university system. Faculty often have little understanding of the fiscal and legal separation of their local college's library from the system as a whole. Every combination of "flagship," state library system, and individual library is particular and individual as to what each of them can and will share with another and at what cost. Both faculty members who come from other institutions and those with long experience need to be continually made aware of the realities of what access they do and do not have with respect to materials available at larger universities and systems.

Cooperative Agreements for Electronic Items

Digital access is one of the most important issues for faculty research support. Directors of small college libraries should take advantage of any and all available cooperative associations and agreements. The first place to start is at the state level, as many states have leased access to key databases for state residents and all educational institutions within the state. The library directors then use those as a base collection.

From the base collection, library directors in small colleges should look for others who would like to share in the acquisition of other databases. This may be other small colleges, both private and public, or something other than another educational institution, such as a local hospital system.

The more institutions involved in database purchasing, usually the better financially—and the more complex, in time and effort. Library directors need to budget sufficient staff time for this type of coordinating. They need to keep faculty informed as to what the licensing situations are. Many faculty simply don't realize that licenses are involved and that the information found on a database does not come to the library without charge nor that is not freely available to all colleges.

On the other hand, there are significant free materials available. This is a real opportunity for excellent reference service for faculty in the form of guides to quality free materials on the Web. It is indeed true that more research materials are being made openly available. Faculty, especially those with heavy teaching loads, may not themselves be able to keep up with all of the developments and new resources that are useful for their disciplines. Reference librarians can be a real asset to them in alerting them to useful sites. This is not a cost-free issue, as it does involve noticeable staff time, but it is a visible way to make the library more useful to faculty.

Cooperative Agreements (Interlibrary Lending) for Physical Items

Librarians have long used agreements for exchanges of physical items, interlibrary lending. Only a tiny handful of the most elite research universities have truly comprehensive collections in-house. Small colleges have always been aware of the need for borrowing to supply patron needs, and this is seen most intensively and usefully with faculty. Not only do they need a wider range of materials than students do, but they can be less impatient than students, who tend to want their requests to be satisfied immediately. Faculty researchers have a longer time frame and can be satisfied even when there are a few days between a request and an item arriving. Interlibrary lending is an effective way of serving disciplinary researchers on a mainly teaching-oriented campus. Even purchasing-on-demand can be very cost-effective.

> **Story:** Some small libraries have a policy of purchasing some or all items requested through interlibrary loans. One library has such an effective arrangement with its book jobber that a faculty who requests a book can have it in hand in two days' time, bought, processed, and delivered. This particular example is from a specialized library where journals are the primary collection need. Books are so small a proportion of demand that it can be met fully and effectively. Having this on-demand service greatly enhances the library's image generally. This particular library is a showcase for a library organized to satisfy user needs.

Effective interlibrary lending networks will depend first of all upon what arrangements each state has provided for public support and cooperation of public institutions. This is an excellent arrangement to join. In Pennsylvania, interlibrary loan materials are sent by commercial vendor and the charges for the service come from state funding; in Minnesota, the flagship university houses a free statewide system with efficient couriers. Two other common approaches are appropriate in different circumstances, by control and by geography. In the control situation, institutions that share either some denominational affiliation or the fact that they are all private or some other commonality join in a cooperative agreement for reciprocal borrowing. By "geography," institutions near one another cooperate. Some states have regional centers within those states that share resources.

The main point to keep in mind with these agreements is that they need to be carefully managed with full documentation. Faculty need to understand current policies and opportunities. Accrediting agencies will also want to know what kind of formal agreements exist.

New Field/Topical Research Needs

An important advantage for small colleges is they often can be more nimble and more flexible than larger institutions.

While larger institutions may have more people interested in the same area, sometimes those faculty members do not leave their own departments to discuss the possibility of joint research. In the small college academic department, as noted for the small college library, the size means that more personal activities cross departmental lines. If there are only 100 full-time faculty, it is not that difficult to really *know* many of them. This makes it easier to come up with new ideas that are innovative combinations of disciplines.

Working within a smaller college provides rich opportunities for "niche" research. This is feasible at the small college. The researchers can be on the cutting edge of their fields, create a reputation for innovation, and compete with larger institutions with creative approaches to research. This benefit comes with challenges for the director of the small college library. In fact, it is the same general challenge the library director faces with respect to supporting academic programs. It is far more efficient to support 50 students in each of five majors than 10 students in each of 25 majors. The revenue in terms of tuition is the same but the information needs are vastly increased. Interdisciplinary research may need resources from each of the contributing disciplines as well as new publication venues. Sometimes the parent disciplines fit within what a library staff and collection is already doing, but the more innovative or new to the college, the bigger the problem of effective support.

One resource, the open-source movement, can help with new fields of research. These rely specifically on their newness and on the flexibility for research rewards at smaller institutions. In most established fields, there has been significant reluctance on the part of faculty to abandon the most prestigious and usually the most expensive publishing outlets in favor of open-source journals. Less well-known journals are not attractive to faculty who are expected to become nationally known in their fields. However, open-source journals are most active precisely in connection with new fields, in places where there is no established hierarchy of journals. Faculty who are new to an interdisciplinary field may also be new to the growing variety of publication outlets. The library staff can have a significant role in educating professors about open access. Simultaneously, supporting open-access venues helps the library control costs for access to needed information.

PEDAGOGICAL SCHOLARSHIP

The scholarship of teaching is a good fit for most small colleges. It suits the mission and their primary function, and it involves less equipment and creates fewer resource issues than disciplinary-based scholarship. Faculty at small colleges are often more collegial and willing to work on cross-campus teaching issues, such as writing or other communication skills. Some of the most important teaching research problems center around beginning levels of education, particularly introductory classes, taught at the small college by tenure-track faculty. Professors at a small college may also be more appreciative of the institution's overall mission and distinctive marketing messages and more keenly aware of the fiscal importance of attracting and retaining students through to graduation. All of this makes research into effective pedagogy very attractive.

Pedagogical research is not particularly easy for the new researcher to find and use. In this area, the librarian needs to develop a distinct competence in locating information on teaching techniques and research applicable to higher education. It is a challenging area. Teaching goes on all the time. Pedagogical research often starts with an individual teacher's trial and error and then proceeds to individual campus showcases, conference presentations, and other gray areas in a profusion of poorly disseminated or organized outlets, not in formal traditional journal literature. This makes it difficult for faculty to get a handle on. Librarians need to develop an understanding of research in post-secondary education that they might not have considered when developing a collection and services.

The library is well positioned to support pedagogical scholarship. Generally, resources about higher education and pedagogy are relatively inexpensive and also apply to many fields, making them very cost-effective. The library is a place where all disciplines are represented and where cross-field resources are made available, which makes it a natural hub for cross-campus pedagogical support. Students need a level of competence in a field to be able to seek and evaluate new information. Therefore, a strong connection to scholarship of pedagogy on a small college campus is not only relatively feasible and useful, politically it positions the library very well as a partner to the teaching faculty. By strengthening that relationship, it has additional benefits for more effectively connecting with students and also impressing administrators and the faculty-governance system.

Centers for Teaching and Learning

Many colleges both large and small have a center or office concerned with advancing teaching effectiveness. These centers can be physically located in the library. Doing so reinforces the idea of the library facility as a hub for learning-support services. Whether they share facilities or not, the library director has two aspects to consider in managing a relationship with such centers: services and collections.

Many different offices on a campus will have their own small collections of handbooks, manuals, and ready-reference materials ranging from a simple style guide on most faculty's desk to a row of *Diagnostic and Statistical Manuals* in the psychology department and a series of virtual safety and ordering manuals for the chemistry department. If a campus has a physical center for teaching and learning, part of its physical presence is likely to include a small collection of books and periodicals on teaching, providing ready resources and a relaxed atmosphere for faculty collaboration.

The collection of materials in the teaching and learning center may be purchased, cataloged through the library, and put on permanent loan in the center. If a center is newly proposed, the library director should describe the efficiencies of obtaining and cataloging materials through the library systems, preventing unneeded duplication and enhancing access. Some accounting of the funds spent needs to be made apparent to the administration because this is precisely the type of non-disciplinary spending that tends to get forgotten in collection budgeting.

Librarians should be involved in the ongoing maintenance and development of the collection. Librarians have the professional skills not only to select materials, taking suggestions from faculty experts, but also to evaluate usage and planning for options such as electronic formats.

Both library and center collections and services benefit from close coordination between the library and center administrators and staff. This allows the librarians and center staff to focus effectively on areas of primary strategic interest for the campus. It is important for librarians to be highly involved specifically in the planning process for any cross-campus teaching support mechanisms.

Individual Faculty Support

Even in the absence of a formal center or office on teaching, individual faculty members may be interested in pedagogical research. For new faculty, this may be the way they develop their own research track record for promotion and tenure. For more experienced faculty, this may be how they revitalize their energy in the classroom. As elsewhere in what the library staff does on the small college campus, librarians should have a good sense of the personalities and preferences of individual faculty members. As stated elsewhere in this book, those faculty may not know what the library staff can do for them if in their new faculty orientation, the library was perceived primarily as a support system for student learning or if they believe the library collection has limitations on support for faculty disciplinary research.

When librarians develop expertise in information sources around post-secondary pedagogy, they can provide valuable, time-saving assistance to faculty members who are seeking to start or enhance their own pedagogy. They may be looking for new teaching techniques and may be planning to do research to formally test their own methods.

Many opportunities exist for collaborative research. Each year, many innovative ideas about college teaching involve technology and changing patterns of information flow. These are areas where the library staff could help match two professors who have similar interests as well as perhaps partnering with one or more faculty to test innovative teaching ideas for information-literacy instruction.

All of this means that time spent developing an expertise in current research sources and methods in pedagogy is time well spent on the small college campus whatever the level of support or expertise exists in the general faculty. The library is a place where technological advances are understood. Librarians are involved in supporting student learning. Librarians work closely with faculty for the classroom and for their own needs. If all of these are true, then providing expertise and resources on pedagogical scholarship is a natural function.

The library director manages the priorities of the library's collection spending and staff time. Disciplinary and pedagogical research both can be accommodated carefully within the small college's resources, balanced in terms of the college's overall mission, culture, and expectations, but flexibly working with individual faculty members to meet their needs.

11 SPECIALIZED COLLECTIONS

The key: Understanding when a collection is really special, and why

Collections in small academic libraries are seldom considered "special collections," for these libraries do not have the staff or the facilities to house truly rare books. However, they have both specialized and unique collections. Any unique or specialized program collection of a library's resources can be considered part of its "service" function. Examples of unique collections for small colleges include:

- Local history in conjunction with or in the absence of a strong public library or historical-society collection.
- Local educational history, including previous institutes, normal schools, seminaries, and the like. The growth, development, renaming, and merging of institutions can be the source of strong feelings among alumni and in the community. If the library houses institutional archives, its records are an important way in which the college and its development and community outreach people connect with those constituencies, showing that their historical contributions are valued and appreciated, even when the original institutions have been absorbed educationally.

- Denominational records. Particularly in non-hierarchical churches without extensive central offices with archival responsibilities, colleges may be the primary record keepers for the denomination on a local level, and even as a record of the denomination across the United States and beyond in terms of missionary work.
- Donor-driven collections. Donors with significant collections and targeted interests may choose a small college as the place where their focus can receive individual attention; they may also be aware of the benefits to the community in placing a tourist attraction in the college and town.

Specialized program collections:

- Collections devoted to special academic, research, and community interests, such as centers for the study of peace and conflict, Appalachian arts, agricultural folklore, or musical instruments. The difference between this and the previous category of donor-driven collections is that these are more tied to educational programs originated on campus.
- Curriculum materials with sample textbooks and other teacher-training materials for use in teacher-credential programs.

Four aspects are important for the effective management of these collections in the small college: mission, support, marketing, and segregation. With respect to mission, there is the question, how does this collection support or advance the mission of either the library or the institution as a whole? This is easy to answer when it comes to special program collections. As a special program is developed, it should be developed in conjunction with and to serve the institutional mission; the library then collects in order to support this already-established decision.

Local and local institutional history or, in religious institutions, denominational collections are also relatively easy to categorize in terms of mission. They are organizationally tied to the history of the institution, though sometimes that needs to be remembered anew.

The most difficult case is that of a donor-driven collection. The overall problem is a very common one in development, matching a donor's desires to an institution's need. The significant donor who is waiting merely to be asked for unrestricted money is a mythical creature, seldom glimpsed and almost never captured. Virtually all donors have some initial desires, ideas about what they would like to support; with care, they can be educated about effective ways to support and develop those desires within the mission of the college.

One of the most difficult circumstances in this donor negotiation is a very specific library problem, the gift of materials, not money. Many donors have a limited or inaccurate perception of the value of donations of materials. In the worst case, people use libraries as dumping grounds for things they are clearing out, such as books that were never particularly valuable and are now outdated and journals long since shifted to electronic format. For basic items, they may feel that they are surely useful to the library. For more unusual materials, donors can believe that the materials they are donating are more rare or unique than they actually are, and that rarity in itself makes them valuable.

Stories: Problem collections

- A collection of "women's studies" materials that is neither unique, interesting, nor particularly well used.
- A donation of Montessori guidebooks and manuals dating across several decades: not complete, comprehensive, or systematic, and not the focus of any academic program on campus.
- The economics professor who clears out his office upon retiring.
- The community member with years, but not quite all issues, of *National Geographic* in her attic.

In all these cases, the donors genuinely believe that they are doing the library a favor with their donation.

Mission-connection should lead to support. The library director needs to make a connection between each specialized collection and the mission of the college, including prioritizing each with respect to institutional needs. In some cases, the library director creates a special mission and arranges funding through targeted endowments. Support also means marketing. If the library has a resource that serves the college's mission, it can and indeed should market that. If not, there is no point in putting resources into a special collection unless it is going to be used, at least in the sense that people know you own it and value that. Here, the library director should not only make this clear on the library's Web site but periodically work with the college's marketing and development offices to make the most use of what the library has. "Under a bushel" is not where any library's collections should be, if they are worthy of the name "special." Finally, is a specific collection really "special" when it comes to materials that are not in themselves rare or valuable? If they are special only because they are all about a particular program or topic, the question is whether resources for a topic area should be integrated or segregated. Consider these examples, stipulating that none of them contains rare or fragile materials:

- Quaker history
- Women's studies
- Sioux Indians
- Higher-education pedagogy

In what circumstances should these be shelved, labeled, and organized separately from the rest of the library's collections?

In considering resources, the users of these materials should be able to benefit from having a preselected, set-aside collection. This will vary by discipline and focus. Some topic areas are a good match to either Dewey or LC categories. For example, in Library of Congress classification, individual Indian tribes have their own numbers, and the social aspects of women's studies are relatively well defined. This means that these collections can be feasibly both integrated and segregated, contained within the usual call number order but set aside partially through signage and shelving gaps.

Some interdisciplinary or cross-discipline interests are not a good fit with classification schemes. Some of that is the inevitable conceptual mismatch between any classification system and people's changing ideas of their own interests. A more difficult problem arises with whether or not it is better for the users to see them in a separate area, next to other books on this special topic, or to see them in their more specific area. Should a book on women's biology be next to a book on women's social standing, or books on women's social standing be next to books on various groups' social standing?

Donors or supporters, on the other hand, primarily work from the supply rather than the demand side of the materials they are donating. They see X topic as important, as consisting of X collection of books or journals, and in many ways see a segregated, unique collection as a symbolic expression of the importance of that topic. This can be entirely separate from whether they themselves will be the users of the collection.

Even donors who are initially committed to an idea of separation can be persuaded that their true purpose, advancing support for that particular subject area, will be more effectively served with an integrated approach. If not, however, politically speaking, it may not be viable to completely ignore donor desires.

These issues really require a big-picture, long-term collection perspective or cumulative effect. A decision for any addition of a donation or purchase of a so-called specialized collection has an inevitable impact on *all* specialized collection decisions. This can be the single most powerful argument for integration. If the new addition is segregated, what others will need to be? If some collections are segregated, the list of those that might be will be long and troublesome. Users can get used to an integrated collection, and donors can understand a rule that applies equally to all.

All of these groups of materials require significant resources in terms of staff time for processing materials, especially free materials; staff knowledge to assist users and to develop the collection or supporting materials; preservation supplies and environment;

and space. The director needs to ensure that this expenditure of resources is matched as fully as possible by a match with institutional mission, funds from donors or the institution or denomination, and ties to educational or other programs. Not all of these aspects will be as strong for each added collection or in every case. Each situation needs weighing of them all. On the one side, it is key to know how many resources are needed; and on the other, how important the collection is and what resources are made available.

Potentially a collection can indeed be a net contribution to the library. It can bring with it more resources than it consumes. When it doesn't, the library director needs to weigh the cumulative costs of all specialized collections at the library. In fact, entire specialized collections may become less useful or used over time. When collections, specialized or not, are no longer important to the mission of the college, they may need to be offered to another institution with more resources to care for them.

The Library's Unique Materials

The final and most special collections of all are those materials that are unique to a particular library. Every college library is part of the entire community of libraries, and library directors have an obligation to make a long-term commitment to digitizing unique collections. The small college library may not have many unique collections, but what is unique may be very useful to other libraries. Many of the books it owns are also owned by larger and wealthier libraries. If they are no longer being used, even for interlibrary loans, they do not need to be preserved solely for posterity; such works might include the college edition of the collected works of Shakespeare, a copy of the latest presidential biography, or the popular novels that students or faculty might sometimes read.

Everything that is unique, though, should have unique handling. Resources are necessarily limited, and thus preservation and ultimately digitization will be arranged by the director on a priority level according to the campus mission and strategic goals. Materials are likely to fall into one of these categories in this order of precedence:

- Unique items vital to and valued by the libraries or organizations with which the small college library is affiliated;
- Unique items vital to the history and culture of the college itself;
- Unique items that have limited connections to current or future college identity or directions but are deemed important by libraries or organizations with which the college is affiliated. In this case, the library may serve as the resource not just for other libraries but perhaps for a local youth-services organization. This is part of serving external constituencies, and such constituencies are not all libraries.

The reason that affiliated organizational items are at the highest level of importance is because of their potential for both funding and use. Items that only the college finds important will likely be funded only by the college, but if items are of potential value to others, those organizations may be willing to participate in funding digitization activities. Locally important items present something of a challenge. In contrast to organizational affiliations, there may be no locally focused source of external funding.

The library director needs to think carefully about the last two groupings and consider moving the items elsewhere if he or she has no realistic plans for digitizing specific materials or preserving them effectively. It may better suit the scholarly and historical community to have them consolidated where they can be of better benefit. This need not be a negative for the library. Moving materials elsewhere frees up space, staff time, and attention. The institutional donation can create a good partnership with the recipient library or historical organization. The library director can then focus on other specific and important items.

Libraries of all sizes and types are part of a larger web of information. While this book is focused on local needs and environments and acknowledges the real limitations of the small college's situation, the library nevertheless always remains a library. However small, it is part of the entire library ecology. Its unique items add to the entire ecosystem.

THE SPECIAL COLLECTION

While it is less likely that a small college library will be given a donation of rare, valuable materials, it may be that a benefactor wishes to leave a collection of incunabula to the college or donate personal papers of a faculty member or resident prominent in the college's history or the local community. Another benefactor may have manuscripts collected at auctions from a smattering of European writers. Even good-quality materials require special handling. Unless the library already has a significant number of archives, staff may not have the expertise or time for processing. Someone at the library needs to know enough about special-collection preservation and processing to be able to provide a reasonable estimate of the time, supplies, and space needed. These may appear to be valuable for a special-collection archive when no appropriate space is available to house them. Different from specialized or unique collections, a truly special collection needs financial support to provide for the essential housing for these materials. If they include ongoing purchases (e.g., for program-specific or local-history publications), they need a line within the library budget devoted to them. If they consist primarily of boxes of miscellaneous materials, they need significant processing time. An unprocessed box takes up space and provides no value to anyone. These rare books and other materials will need proper storage facilities and security. They should also be cataloged at the rare-book level. Any rare book or other item that is not taken care of and that no one knows you own does no good.

12 MANAGING FOR SERVICE SUPPORT

The key: Understanding college constituencies besides faculty and students: administration, alumni, community, and donors

Library directors of small college libraries ensure that service is offered to the administrative staff on campus. They also lead their staff in participating with community outreach consistent with the mission of the college, partnering with people and organizations outside of the college. Library directors are responsible for encouraging and providing opportunities for their staff to volunteer. They provide services both within the college and the community that are more than library-related information activities. They also may serve on institutional and community committees.

SERVICE TO ADMINISTRATIVE STAFF

While it is true that the core function of a college is a place for teaching, learning, and the advancement of knowledge, many throughout the school support but do not directly perform teaching, learning, or the advancement of knowledge. In this respect, the library functions like a corporate or special library with a specialized clientele. Administrators who need information from time to time to do their work within the college's infrastructure are crucial. It is always important for the library director to make the president and other higher-level administrators understand that the staff can serve as personal information specialists. While there are limited resources and staff time to acknowledge that the whole purpose of the college is instruction, it is also true that those in charge of business functions and other areas of the campus also have information needs.

What does the library mean to non-teaching people on campus? It may be seen as a backdrop for photos, a place to have chic receptions, and a location to show parents who come to visit the college with their high school seniors, but it needs to have and be seen to have an information role for them. Academic librarians are serious about preparing their students with information-literacy skills and an appreciation of libraries as resources for "lifelong learning" for their lives after graduation, their lives as workers. Those who make up a college's staff are also engaged in lifelong learning, both for their jobs and their own personal needs. To do this, the library director and staff must highlight the value that library services and resources can provide for non-teaching personnel, how this can help them solve problems, and that this needs to be marketed throughout the college.

A library director who is well informed about administrative functions and cycles should be able to identify areas of research that a library can provide or, if not immediately available, can acquire. This makes the library very valuable to administrators. One of the most common opportunities would be in connection to strategic planning. Librarians can provide appropriate statistics about other colleges and find supporting information about new technologies being considered.

Another area that will be extremely valuable is development or fund-raising. Small colleges probably cannot afford dedicated prospect researchers, and the information that librarians can find will reduce the amount of research that the development staff or paid consultants must do.

Grant proposals also usually need significant information. When such proposals are research grant applications from faculty, they usually provide the information needed, although they may depend upon library staff for help. Grants that support teaching, student services, or community partnerships usually need some level of data for needs assessment and justification for their proposed designs, and non-teaching staff who are writing these will need information help from the library.

Finally, specific major initiatives such as adding new programs or services require extensive information in order to support design decisions or funding requests. With respect to these, the small college library staff has the opportunity to show how it is a vital hub for information that is real and useful. That directly enhances the value that administrators place on the library.

What works against the small college library is its inherently limited resource base. With respect to non-faculty information and research needs, the library staff handles this by being clear and honest in its collection priorities that student and faculty needs are the priority for its budget. This does not mean that no information will be available. A great quantity of valuable background information is generated by the government and hence is essentially free for skilled reference librarians at the price of their time. Also, if some specific tools or resources are not free, the library director is in a good position to make a clear and very targeted case for funding for those resources, doing the professional work of analyzing the pros and cons of each resource, and then leaving it to the administration to fund or not fund.

COMMUNITY OUTREACH

Most institutions have a mission that includes some constituencies in addition to its own faculty and students. For public institutions, this is usually based on location; for private institutions, in addition to locale, there may be denominational or other affiliations that may have a national or even international scope.

As a normal part of the director's and librarians' understanding of the entire enterprise of the campus, the library director and staff will know what sorts of constituencies are being served and their priorities. The library staff is in a position to provide both specific and generic services. Specific services include collections or programs like talks and perhaps search strategies and instruction that serve specific projects such as a "peace and justice summer camp" or "music for the holidays." Generic services are those that open all or some of the resources of the library to all members of a defined external constituency. This could be career research for alumni, book-charging privileges or database access for local citizens, working with public libraries, or providing book delivery/lending to congregations.

Providing library cards is often seen by college administration as a cheap or even free way to please local people. However useful this looks in concept, there are also some areas that can become problems, and the director needs to specifically manage the exact terms of this service.

At a public college, widespread use of library cards by local citizens potentially can crowd out college students for whom the collection is primarily provided, as when a high school student checks out all the books on Hamlet. It can even weaken local library resources if high school or public library administrators feel they do not need to build their own collections or services if those of the college are available.

> **True story:** A public community college with nursing assistant and licensed practical nursing programs was located within the same small town as a private university with a baccalaureate nursing program. The two-year college faculty regularly sent students to use the nursing resources at the private college as their own library did not provide them.

Cooperation is great, but parasitism is bad. The interaction and overlap of public and school libraries with college libraries is always something that requires specific managerial attention. There are important benefits, but also potential problems.

For public colleges, citizens have the argument that it is public and supported by taxpayers. The private university is in a stronger position when it comes to putting terms and conditions upon local users. However, private colleges sometimes do have people who feel they have a special relationship with and a natural claim on the resources of the college: alumni, significant contributors, and significant community members. When a wealthy elderly donor borrows all of the Jane Austen books and does not return them, the library director has a problem.

The most important thing in these cases is to keep track of the volume and demands. Significant benefits derive from providing services to important constituencies. Both the library director and the campus's managers of outreach can weigh the costs such as duplicating or replacing unavailable or stolen materials with the benefits.

These examples are framed in the context of unduplicated physical resources, the true zero-sum game in which what one patron is using is not available to another. Those sorts of situations are an important but diminishing area of concern.

Digital resources present their own set of issues. For commercial databases, administrators need to understand that licensing agreements usually require a library director to specifically identify a limited set of users and exercise password control. Campus administrators and external users may not realize that in no case will a commercial database vendor allow a library to provide open access to a database for any person who navigates to the library's Web site. If community or other special users have database-access privileges, that needs to be taken into account in vendor negotiations and worked into payment formulas.

Fortunately, when it comes to digital resources that the library itself generates and supports, the exact opposite happens. Everything the library owns that can be legally and financially feasible to digitize can be controlled and made available. In many cases, it will be the needs of external constituencies that provide the most important justification for digitization efforts. Some undergraduates might find the campus yearbook archives interesting, and alumni who wish to revisit their college years will be delighted by their availability. Widely scattered denominational historians will welcome virtual archive access. This is a very attractive, unique, and compelling service that the library staff can provide to advance the college's mission and should be worked into planning and budget proposals.

For all of these issues, husbanding physical resources, negotiating commercial digital resources, and extending homegrown digital projects, effective management will include documenting their role in providing service to external constituencies. The tracking mechanisms that a library naturally possesses, such as numbers of circulations and Web site hits, provide an important source of evidence. This will become very handy while analyzing mission performance for accreditation studies and can be used in conjunction with major fund-raising campaigns. Actual usage is a powerful thing to boast about.

VOLUNTEERISM

For individual employees of a small college, whatever their departments or level, service generally includes a wide variety of community outreach. In a large or more research-oriented university, service is sometimes defined as, confined to, or focused on disciplinary or professionally based activities or is oriented around student engagement. Small colleges often have very intimate ties to their communities that go beyond research or teaching activities. They serve their local geographic area, any denominational affiliation, any special programs or centers, and any special alumni focus. In the local geographic area, often any service is seen as valuable, including:

- A team of admissions counselors helping clean up a park
- A social work professor organizing religious education at her church
- A group of librarians running a Thanksgiving basket drive

Managing volunteerism as a component of the library staff's contribution to the campus service mission includes understanding just what is considered acceptable forms of extracurricular service, relating them to the library, and providing time release. These are part of thinking more broadly about how volunteerism helps librarians and the library's role in the college and community. One measure, discussed later, will be its place in a faculty member's service component of the research, teaching, and service requirements.

Most colleges value volunteerism that gets the campus name before the public and helps the perception of the college faculty and staff as being good citizens in the college's local community. Each individual doing any kind of work is seen as a small part of a marketing campaign to convey the college's brand to the community. This portrays the college as the opposite of the ivory tower stereotype.

Campuses value volunteerism even more when it is based on professional competence. When service is based on expertise, not only is the campus name synonymous with helper, but the help provided is skilled and therefore more valuable to the recipients. It also reinforces not only the mere presence of the college, but that the college is a place where professors have, and students can gain, expertise. Professionally based volunteerism creates connections that can be used in many ways, such as in teaching (finding guests for classes and sites for internships), research (partnerships), and grant proposals.

Therefore, the first and best use of a librarian's time in volunteering is in ways that are connected to librarianship and the college library. These experiences will be professionally rewarding as well: helping high school and public librarians can enhance knowledge of what current and future college students understand when they think of "libraries" as well as providing ideas about sharing resources.

After specifically library-related volunteer opportunities, the next priority for the library director is encouraging activities that would be most consistent with what the campus finds important and what the teaching faculty participate in. As noted in the chapters covering professional development and faculty status, librarians are more effective on campus when they are considered most like classroom faculty, and if the faculty are active in volunteerism, it is useful for librarians to join what they do rather than join in what administrative staff may be focused on.

None of this means that library staff do not have the right to personal choices for volunteering or any other form of charitable work. There are several additional considerations for everyone, staff and manager, to think about: diversity, release time, and public image.

Many campuses value diversity. When employees are involved in diverse activities, this demonstrates and strengthens this value. If staff members are hesitant to become involved in some different activity, they might need a little encouragement for them see that it is as just as valuable as a more mainstream activity.

What individuals legally do on their own time is generally up to them unless it is part of a campus code of conduct, applying to staff and faculty as well as students. (That will be made very clear by the institution.) Release time for volunteerism does involve institutional choices, however, and some choices may be more supported than others. The library director should be aware of what the human resources experts and his or her own superiors say about what types of activity qualify for release time. For public institutions, release for voluntarism is likely to be very neutrally phrased.

Whether they intend it or not, what someone who is known to be part of a particular campus community does in his or her private life inevitably reflects on the institution, and small college employees *are* known to be part of the campus. This is the unavoidable "small town" aspect of the small college. Staff at small colleges in big cities can sometimes avoid this, but for the small college in the small town, it is all a small world. Anonymity is not a realistic option. Library directors and librarians will be much more comfortable if everyone understands campus consequences of their decisions about volunteering and how they reflect on the college and library.

The phrase "reflecting on" does not need to mean conformity. It depends on the institution, the community, and their values. The act of allowing something as seemingly problematic as being a member of an unusual social organization, even one that might seem to outsiders to be in opposition to an institution's brand, can be a visible signal of the institution's commitment to intellectual diversity and an open marketplace of ideas.

Support for volunteerism therefore means several things. It can range from flexible scheduling to allow someone to devote her own time to a cause, it can mean release from other duties to do volunteer work on college time, or it could mean monetary contributions to cover expenses or even contributions matched or directed to other organizations. It can also mean including volunteer activities in personnel evaluations. Volunteerism can even shade into being a requirement, especially when librarians have faculty status and are expected to perform service.

Since it is the overall responsibility of library directors to set priorities for work, it is their responsibility to manage how time devoted to service fits within how the library operates. Staffing a small library is not easy, especially when it comes to providing on-demand public service with a small number of librarians and support staff. This is where the director and the librarians need to have a common understanding about library needs, campus priorities, and individuals' choices.

Support staff are also involved in volunteerism. Here, the library director should ensure that library support staff have the same opportunities or restrictions that other support staff on campus have. Support staff are part of the campus culture and expectations, and their contributions to campus and community service are as valuable as those of any other unit on campus. It will benefit the library when support staff serve on committees and tasks across campus units, such as clerical or professional organizations or cross-employee groups for wellness or charity organizations.

It is true that the library's own needs can be more demanding in scheduling than for some other units. In particular, ensuring the library is actually open and adequately staffed can be more challenging than for units that can simply proclaim a "service day" closed for regular business. It takes some creativity to make the library's commitment to service equal when it sometimes cannot be identical to what other units are doing.

It is in the area of managing for service that the ties to the broader community are the strongest. Colleges serve many constituencies, and college libraries are part of that service. As this book has demonstrated throughout, library directors are most effective on campus when they consider campus issues and the library's position within the campus's bureaucratic, political, and human resource systems, rather than focusing internally on only library matters. This area of service is a way to connect the library to the college's role within its larger community, and thus benefits the community, the college, and the library.

CONCLUSION

Managing means getting things done, doing what is needed to advance the mission of an organization. Leadership has many definitions, library directors have many different personal styles, and the future of small college libraries is full of many different challenges. The small college library director works within the ecosystem of the library, the academic campus, and the communities that the college serves. Directors will be more effective managers the more they understand how and why decisions are made. Some are made bureaucratically on rational and procedural grounds. Some are made because groups seek to advance their interests—a political system; and some are made for the purposes of individuals, the human development dimension of how people act in organizations.

This book began with organizational theory and organizational charts, and ends discussing when odd collections can be service to the small college's wider constituencies. Through all of this there are people and the organization. Library directors work through their staff and with the college as a whole to advance the teaching, research, and service missions of their colleges. They keep track of small things and also always think about how each small thing contributes to and affects the whole. This book's purpose is completed when library directors approach daily activities, thoughtful planning, and the inevitable sudden crises with greater understanding and effectiveness.

SELECTED BIBLIOGRAPHY

MANAGEMENT THEORIES

The following books and articles are excellent resources for learning more about management theory.

A truly outstanding guide is Gareth Morgan's *Images of Organization*. This book devotes different chapters to a wide variety of theories, from bureaucratic to "psychic prison." Morgan sees each theory as presenting a "metaphor" (machine, organism, and even a psychological disturbed brain) through which an organization can be understood. He does not include libraries in any of his examples. The executive edition is the more succinct, and there are some obsolete choices for examples, but it remains a very efficient way of learning a lot about management theory.

Morgan, Gareth. *Images of Organization*. Updated edition, 2007 ed.
   Beverly Hills: Sage, 1986; Executive Edition, 1998.

Within educational organizations, the work of Karl Weick is influential and important. This article is something of a rebellion against an overly mechanistic or power-oriented view of organizations as places where managers decide and what they decide is carried out. Instead, Weick points to how "loose" the "coupling" or connection is between an educational leader and those professionals he or she supervises. The setting is primarily K–12, but it applies as well, and even more so, to post-secondary education.

Weick, Karl. "Educational Organizations as Loosely Coupled Systems." *Administrative Science Quarterly* 21 (1979): 1–19.

For academic libraries, David Lewis succinctly reviews various management theories and approaches in a discussion of effective academic library leadership.

Lewis, David. "An Organizational Paradigm for Effective Academic Libraries." *College & Research Libraries* (1986): 337–53.

A rare example of truly collegial organization is described by librarians at three small colleges in:

Lesniaski, David, Kris MacPherson, Barbara Fister, and Steve McKenzie. "Collegial Leadership in Academic Libraries." In *Crossing the Divide: Proceedings of the Tenth National Conference of the Association of College and Research Libraries.* Denver, CO: Association of College and Research Libraries, 2001.

THE ACADEMIC ENTERPRISE

These resources give the reader perspectives on the lives of colleges—their strengths, opportunities, and challenges.

In this article, the president of Earlham College describes how the "ideal" size of a small college is arrived at—why they will not pursue greater growth, but also what the minimum is for a well-rounded independent college. The key is the minimum size of an academic department: three or four professors.

Fain, Paul. "Is Less More at Small Colleges?" *Chronicle of Higher Education*, September 9, 2005.

This book is published by the professional organization of business officers who work in small colleges. It is found more often on the shelves of business officers than in libraries. The ratios and discussions of fiscal implications of various organizational decisions in both editions are relevant.

Townsley, Michael L. *The Small College Guide to Financial Health: Beating the Odds.* Washington, DC: National Association of College and University Business Officers, 2002.

Townsley, Michael L. *The Small College Guide to Financial Health: Weathering Turbulent Times*. 2nd ed. Washington, DC: National Association of College and University Business Officers, 2009.

Some college employees assume that because colleges have existed, they will always exist. They can feel free to rebel against requests for frugality or layoff proposals because they don't really feel threatened. This article provides a very detailed and devastating portrait of a small college that mismanaged itself into extinction. Maybe nobody would consider cutting the library the way they would consider cutting an academic program; but if the college flounders, the library will, too.

Van Der Werf, Martin. "Mount Senario's Final Act." *Chronicle of Higher Education*, June 14, 2002.

This last item is the personal memoir and description of the life of a very large university president. It is useful nevertheless, for two reasons. First, many small college administrators get their start on larger campuses; faculty, after all, receive their doctorates primarily from research universities. Therefore, the experiences described herein form part of what even small college people think of when they think of academia. Second, this book has very interesting sections on how departmental libraries come to birth and on faculty status for librarians.

Flawn, Peter T. *A Primer for University Presidents: Managing the Modern University*. Austin: University of Texas Press, 1990.

THE LIFE OF THE FACULTY MEMBER

The teaching faculty member is the most important person with whom a librarian will interact. Just because, or when, both the classroom instructor and the librarian have "faculty status" does not mean that they both face the same daily responsibilities or longer-term pressures. Having a feeling for what faculty members are going through is vital for productive relationships.

The immense variety of academic experience can be viewed in the Careers section of the *Chronicle of Higher Education*. An amusing, alarming, candid, and thorough cross-section of this can be found in the collection of Ms. Mentor, an advice columnist for academics. However tough the life of a librarian, it pales beside the quest for a humanities PhD graduate to find a good job. These are real questions with reasonable answers on job-hunting, work life, working with colleagues, dealing with students, and succeeding (or not) in small and large colleges.

Toth, Emily. *Ms. Mentor's New and Ever More Impeccable Advice for Women and Men in Academia*. Philadelphia: University of Pennsylvania, 2008.

This novel takes the perspective of the chair of an English department at a small college. While there is a lot of humor, it has a clear and real perspective on the lives of adjunct professors. Even small colleges have many of these "contingent" and thus perpetually anxious faculty.

Russo, Richard. *Straight Man*. New York: Vintage, 1998.

The stresses of academic leadership are ably reflected in this pair of articles. They are about the role and contradictions of "deanship." Although they mainly take the perspective of a larger university and apply to "school" deans, many of the issues are seen in the small college for the overall academic officer and other higher administrators.

Bedeian, Arthur G. "The Dean's Disease: How the Darker Side of Power Manifests Itself in the Office of Dean." *Academy of Management Learning and Education* 1, no. 2 (2002): 164–73.

Gallos, Joan L. "The Dean's Squeeze: The Myths and Realities of Academic Leadership in the Middle." *Academy of Management Learning and Education* 1, no. 2 (2002): 174–84.

SMALLER ISSUES

What really is strategy? The following article describes strategy as a deliberate choice, not simply a description of a generic mission or prediction of a foreseeable future.

Porter, Michael E. "What Is Strategy?" *Harvard Business Review* (November–December 1996): 60–78.

How do people work? Working alone, and working with others? Even if one does not subscribe to every aspect of "typing" people by psychological traits, an appreciation of how different people can think and that different ways of doing things are each "normal" is very useful. This book is very practical in that it is focused specifically on habits and assumptions that make appearances in important work contexts, such as group work, deadlines, and attitudes toward authority.

Kroeger, Otto, and Janet Thuesen. *Type Talk at Work.* New York: Delacorte, 1992.

The process of strategic planning can often go awry—this article describes a strategic plan that ends up in a closet. It is set at a large research library but probably is close to the truth at a number of smaller colleges.

Ladwig, J. Parker. "Assess the State of Your Strategic Plan." *Library Administration and Management* 19, no. 2 (2005): 90–93.

Finally, the most important overall view of academia for each college will be the accrediting standards for the organization that accredits the institution as a whole.

Most institutions are accredited by *regional* accreditation organizations:

Middle States: Middle States Association of Colleges and Schools: New York, New Jersey, Pennsylvania, Delaware, Maryland, the District of Columbia, Puerto Rico, and the U.S. Virgin Islands.

NEASC: New England Association of Schools and Colleges: Connecticut, Maine, Massachusetts, New Hampshire, Rhode Island, and Vermont.

HLC: Higher Learning Commission/North Central Association of Colleges and Schools: Arkansas, Arizona, Colorado, Iowa, Illinois, Indiana, Kansas, Michigan, Minnesota, Missouri, North Dakota, Nebraska, Ohio, Oklahoma, New Mexico, South Dakota, Wisconsin, West Virginia, and Wyoming.

Northwest Commission: Northwest Commission on Colleges and Universities: Alaska, Idaho, Montana, Nevada, Oregon, Utah, and Washington.

WASC: Western Association of Schools and Colleges: California, Hawaii, Guam, American Samoa, Micronesia, Palau, and the Northern Marianas Islands.

SACS: Southern Association of Colleges and Schools: Virginia, Florida, Georgia, Kentucky, Louisiana, Mississippi, North Carolina, South Carolina, Alabama, Tennessee, and Texas.

Some institutions have national accreditation organizations. These are primarily for-profit, or very specialized, or very small institutions. Two examples are the Accrediting Council for Independent Schools and Colleges, which accredits primarily for-profit trade schools, and the Association for Biblical Higher Education, which accredits Christian colleges.

INDEX

ABC. *See* Activity-based costing

Academic affairs, as a college unit, 47

Academic freedom, in relation to faculty status, 138–139

Academic status for librarians, compared to faculty status, 153–160

Access services, in the organizational structure, 39–40

Accreditation and strategic planning, 209–210 and student information skills, 290 list of organizations, 339–340

Acquisitions, in relation to budgeting, 245

Activity-based costing, 245, 278–279

Adjunct faculty, 287

Administrative staff and faculty status for librarians, 153

providing library services for, 325–327

Advertising, for library positions, 69–71

ALA library support staff certification, 100

ALA-accredited MLS, 67

Alternative degrees for librarians, 67–68

Alumni/ae, providing services for, 328

American Library Association. See ALA

American Association of University Professors (AAUP) and probationary period for faculty, 147–148 joint statement on librarians, 155 statement on faculty importance, 154–155

Annual performance evaluations, 117–120

Assembly, faculty, 51

About the Author

RACHEL APPLEGATE is associate professor of library and information science and teaches evaluation of libraries and library management at Indiana University, Bloomington, IN. Her published works include a contribution to Library Unlimited's *Our New Public, A Changing Clientele: Bewildering Issues or New Challenges for Managing Libraries?* as well as articles in *Public Library Quarterly*, *Journal of Academic Librarianship*, and *College & Research Libraries*. Applegate served as library director and academic administrator for many years at the College of St. Scholastica in Duluth, MN.